# ON TRANQUIL LAND OF STORM

Gravestone Inscriptions and Interments
Islandmagee New Cemetery
Co. Antrim
1925 – 2002

•

Compiled by
Heather Baird and Edna Orr

•

Edited by
Heather Baird and Jim McKinty

Published by
Larne Branch
of
The North of Ireland Family History Society

Published 2003
by the Larne Branch
of
The North of Ireland Family History Society

ISBN 0-9544813-0-5

Printed by Styletype Printing Ltd.
Glengormley Park, Newtownabbey

Photographic cover by Robin McIlwain

The printing of this book was funded by
"AWARDS FOR ALL"

# CONTENTS

# INTRODUCTION

Islandmagee must have been among the first places in Ireland to be occupied by humans because worked flints from the Mesolithic period are to be found in the raised beaches. Excavations during the 1990s have added to the evidence that people have made their homes in Islandmagee in all the archaeological periods known to Ireland.

The ancient name for the peninsula was Rinn Seimhne and it probably means "the headland of a tribe of people called Seimhne". In the early annals Seimhne is mentioned a number of times in connection with kings, forts, and battles.

Saint Patrick is credited with founding a church in Kilcoan dedicated to Saint Coemhan, and several more churches were erected in the Early Christian or Medieval periods.

John de Courcy invaded Ulster in 1177 and soon after Islandmagee must have been incorporated in his earldom. In 1213 the Justiciary of Ireland was directed by King John to consign to Robert FitzSerlon his lands of *Ransanem* provided the Castle of *Cragfergus* could spare them. Michael of Kylkenan (Kilcoan) was summoned to a parliament at Kilkenny in 1310. The ecclesiastical taxation of 1306 had six entries for the parish: the rector and vicarage of Portmuck, the rector and vicarage of Ransevyn, the church of Kilkenan, and the church of Saint John of Ransevyn.

As the Anglo-Norman Earldom of Ulster crumbled during the fourteenth and fifteenth centuries the O'Neills expanded from their heartland in Tyrone across Lough Neagh and eastward until they reached Larne Lough. Meanwhile the McDonnells of western Scotland had acquired the Glynns by marriage and especially in the mid-sixteenth century were actively consolidating and expanding their Irish territory.

There is no known use of the modern name for the peninsula until about 1570, after which time it appears in various forms such as *Iland Maghies* and *MacGuy's Island*. No direct evidence tells us when and from where the Magees came. The name means the son of Aodh (Hugh) and may have originated anywhere in the Celtic speaking areas of Ireland or Scotland. Akenson believed they came from the Island of Islay after 1550 with Sorley Boy McDonnell, although Sir Henry Bagenal, writing in 1586, reported that the Magees paid tribute to the (O'Neill) Lords of Clandeboy.

Walter Devereux, Earl of Essex, obtained Islandmagee by royal grant in 1576, but it returned to the crown on his son's execution in 1601. James I granted "the island" to Sir Arthur Chichester, who leased it to Moses Hill. Sir Moses built a tower house at the southern tip and named it Castle Chichester (alias Castle Chester). For the next few centuries the Chichester and Hill families remained as landlords with the respective titles of Lords Donegall and Dungannon.

The Rebellion which broke out in October 1641 did not have an immediate impact on Islandmagee, but in January a number of Scots in Ballycarry decided to vent their anger on a soft target: the peaceable Roman Catholics of neighbouring Islandmagee. About sixty may have been slain in their homes or on their way to Carrickfergus as they sought the protection of the landlord, Colonel Arthur Hill.

Writing in 1840 James Boyle repeated an accepted truism: "… the present inhabitants being almost to a man the descendants of the Scottish settlers of the 17th century and still retaining in their habits, manners, dialect and religion the striking characteristics of the country of their forefathers." Yet a consideration of their surnames throws doubt on the absolute verity of the statement. Some are undeniably Irish.

Kane is the anglised form of *Ó Catháin,* the family that dominated the Roe Valley. Brennen could be either *Ó Branáin* from Fermanagh or *Mac Branáin* from north Connacht. Ferey or Fairy is the Donegal sept of *Ó Fearadhaigh.* After 1800 this name became Faires, then Ferris. Nelson could be English or Scottish, or it could be another form of O'Neill. Crossan was *Mac an Chrosáin* from west Ulster. McClenaghan is also from Tyrone. Could these represent the pre-Plantation inhabitants?

Hill was the most common of all surnames in Islandmagee. Donaldson conjectured that Moses Hill brought his relations over from Devon to populate his land. Another possibility is that after 1642, under the duress of knowing that a name marks a person as a target, the surviving Magees changed their surname to fit into the new social reality. What better name to choose than that of the protecting landlord? In other places at other times the same stratagem was employed.

Farming was long the most important industry on "the island", but fishing became a significant second source of income in the early nineteenth century and for brief periods in the same century the export of quicklime or limestone was important. Islandmagee men were prominent in the British merchant fleet during much of the nineteenth and twentieth centuries. To reduce the risk of wartime bombing on electricity production, a power station was built at Ballylumford in the 1940s. It was a large employer for many years, but now, more efficient plant requires only a small fraction of the former work force.

The earliest census in 1669 gave the number of inhabitants as 990. In 1813 it had grown to 1,931. It rose to a peak of 2,786 in 1861, then dropped to 2,085 in 1911, and to 1,835 in 1991. Some of the old surnames have died out but new ones have appeared, especially in recent generations. The great majority now find employment outside "the island".

Today there are four burial grounds with substantial collections of memorials. Ballypriormore and Ballykeel were both medieval ecclesiastic sites, which continued in use as graveyards for the parish, and in which no new grave plots are now opened. They are in the care of Larne Borough Council. Saint John's or New Church in Ballyharry is a post-reformation site and is maintained by the Church of Ireland, but all denominations bury there. Islandmagee New Cemetery, also in the townland of Ballyharry, is a twentieth-century creation of local government and is now used for the majority of interments in "the island".

In 1977 the Ulster Historical Foundation published *Gravestone Inscriptions of County Antrim, Volume I: Islandmagee*. The transcription of gravestones was limited to those containing a date of death before 1901 and so only the three older sites were included.

The present book greatly augments the information available to the researcher of local families. Members of the Larne Branch of the North of Ireland Family History Society deserve our thanks, not only for the work of copying all the inscriptions, but also for combining additional data from the interment book in the form of bullet points.

George Rutherford

# ACKNOWLEDGEMENTS

Larne Family History Society thanks everyone who helped in any way with the production of this publication and acknowledge especially the help and assistance of the following individuals and groups.

We are indebted to "Awards for All" for granting the funding to print this book.

Our grateful thanks to Mr. George Rutherford for his help and advice, for supplying the Bibliography of Publications on Islandmagee and writing the Introduction.

Thanks also to Mr. J. Ian Duffin for giving of his time to research and write the article on Islandmagee Seafaring.

We are also indebted to the Commonwealth War Graves Commission for permission to use the Memorials in their Debt of Honour Register.

We also appreciate the encouragement and interest of Mr. Robin McIlwain and thank him for his photographic input.

A special thanks to Mrs. Janet Long, Registrar, for her helpfulness and patience while we worked through the "Register of Interment" books.

Thanks also to the staff of cemeteries division of Larne Borough Council for their assistance.

We also wish to record the invaluable assistance of the staff of Styletype Printers.

Thanks are due to those members of Larne Family History Society who assisted with various aspects of this project. Especial thanks to Heather Baird Edna Orr and Jim McKinty for transcribing inscriptions and compiling this publication.

# BIBLIOGRAPHY OF PUBLICATIONS ON ISLANDMAGEE

Akenson, Donald H., *Between Two Revolutions: Islandmagee Co. Antrim 1798 – 1920*, PD Meany Co. Inc., 1979, ISBN 0 88835 004 X, 221 pp. + plates.

Day, Angelique, & Patrick McWilliams, *Ordnance Survey Memoirs of Ireland, Volume Ten, Parishes of County Antrim III (Carncastle, Killyglen, Islandmagee, Kilwaughter, and Larne) 1833, 1835, 1839-40*, Belfast, Institute of Irish Studies, 1991, Hbk. ISBN 0 85389 396 9, Pbk. ISBN 0 85389 389 6, xii + 132 pp.

Deane, John D., *Islandmagee Methodist Church – Historical Souvenir 1829 - 1979*, Methodist Church in Ireland, 1979, 16 pp.

Donaldson, Dixon, *History of Islandmagee: Historical, Traditional, and Descriptive Account of Islandmagee*, The Whitehead News and Ballycarry and Islandmagee Reporter, 1927, 154 pp. Facsimile reprint by Islandmagee Community Development Association, 2002.

Donaldson, Dixon, *History of Islandmagee*, revised and adapted by Victor Glenn, 1968, 96 pp.

Islandmagee Community Development Association, *Islandmagee Community Web*, http://www.Islandmagee.co.uk.

Niblock, Alexander, *A Short History of North Islandmagee*, 1991, 36 pp.

Ó Direáin, Dr. RS, The Townlands and some Placenames of Islandmagee, 2001, http://www.Islandmagee.co.uk/names.htm.

O'Donnell, PJ, *Whitehead: the Town with No Streets*, Belfast, n.d. [1997], ISBN 0-9531883-0-2, 300 pp.

Porter, Emmet Classon, *Witches, Warlocks and Ghosts*, Belfast, Northern Whig, 1885, 31 pp.

Rutherford, George, *Gravestone Inscriptions of County Antrim, Volume I: Islandmagee*, 1977, Belfast, Ulster Historical Foundation, 101 + xv pp.

Tisdall, William, *The Islandmagee Witches: a Narrative of the sufferings of a young girl*, 1711.

Waring, Joseph, *St. John's Church, Islandmagee, 1595 – 1985: A Short History*, 1985, 5 pp. Second edition, 1986, 12 pp.

Williamson, Noel, and Ernest Crawford, and Arnold Dick, *Second Islandmagee Presbyterian Church*, 1978, 36 pp.

# SELECT BIBLIOGRAPHY
# WITH REFERENCES TO ISLANDMAGEE

Bailie, W Desmond, *et al*, *A History of Congregations in the Presbyterian Church in Ireland 1610 – 1982*, Belfast, The Presbyterian Historical Society of Ireland, ISBN 0 950 1446 6 5, 1982, vi + 808 pp.

Brett, CEB, and Michael O'Connell, *Buildings of County Antrim*, UAHS & UHF, 1996, ISBN 0 900457 47 3, xiv + 306 pp.

Carleton, ST, *Heads & Hearths: the Hearth Money Rolls and Poll Tax Returns for County Antrim 1660-69*, *Public Record Office of Northern Ireland*, 1990, ISBN 0 905691 27 X, xvi + 191 pp.

Corcoran, Doreen, *A Tour of East Antrim: Historic photographs from the WA Green Collection in the Ulster Folk and Transport Museum*, Belfast, Friar's Bush Press, 1990, ISBN 0 946872 38 4, 92 pp.

Hickson, Mary, *Ireland in the Seventeenth Century or Massacres of 1641-2, their Causes and Results*, London, Longmans, Green, and Co., 1884.

M'Skimin, Samuel, "A Statistical Account of Island Magee" in the *Newry Magazine* III, 1817. Reprinted in *Carrickfergus & District Historical Journal* V, 1990, pp. 6 – 20.

O'Laverty, James, *Historical Account of the Diocese of Down and Connor, Ancient and Modern*, volume III, Dublin, 1884, 492 + iv pp. Facsimile reprint, Davidson Books, Ballynahinch, 1981.

Reeves, William, *Ecclesiastical Antiquities of Down, Connor, and Dromore*, Dublin, 1847, xxiv + 436 pp. Reprint with new introduction, Braid & Moyola Books, 1992.

Young, RM, *Ulster in '98: Episodes and Anecdotes*, Belfast, Marcus Ward & Co., 1893. Facsimile reprint, Davidson Books, 1983.

# NAMES FROM EARLIER TIMES

## ~ *13 February 1770* ~
## *Viscount Lord Dungannon Estate*
## ~ *IslandMagee tenants* ~

Adams, James
Aikin, William
Alfinder, Robert
Allen, John
Anderson
Auld, James
Auld, John

Bole, John late
Bole.
Boyd, James
Brakenrig, Widow.
Brannon, Alexander
Brannon, Robert
Brannon, Widow
Brison, Widow

Cameron, Nathaniel
Colvill, Robert
Colvill, Thomas
Culloh, Widow

Daff, Samuel
Daff, William
Daff, James
Davies, John
Donnan, James
Donnan, John
Donnan, Susan
Downey, Brice

English, John
English, Samuel
Esner, William

Feer, Samuel
Flack, James
Flack, John

Galy, Thomas
Giffen, Joseph
Gilliland, Widow
Girvan, John
Guillis

Harvey, Robert
Hill, John partner
Hill, Samuel
Hill, Arthur
Hill, Hugh
Hill, James
Hill, Janet
Hill, John
Hill, Thomas
Hudson, Edward
Hunter, Edward

Johnston, Widow

Kaine, John

Loggan, Widow

Mc Alexander, George
Mc Calmont, Widow
Mc Camont, Andrew
Mc Camont, John
Mc Clelland, William
Mc Craye, James
Mc Crery, Thomas
Mc Ilhago, Nathaniel
Mc Kergon, William
Mc Maken, Widow
Mc Murtry, Matthew
Mc Murtry, Thomas

Makisok, Robert
Mann, Widow
Mann, William
Miller, Jane
Mitchell, Robert
Moore, James
Mulligan, James

Nilson, John
Niper, Joseph
Niper, Samuel
Niper, William

Rea, Ab.
Rea, David
Ross, John

Seller, John
Smith, John
Stinson, John

Templeton, Samuel
Tosh, John

Vocock, Widow

White, James
Willson, David
Willson, Hugh
Willson, James
Willson, John
Willson, Robert
Woodside, Widow
Wright, William

Young, Alexander

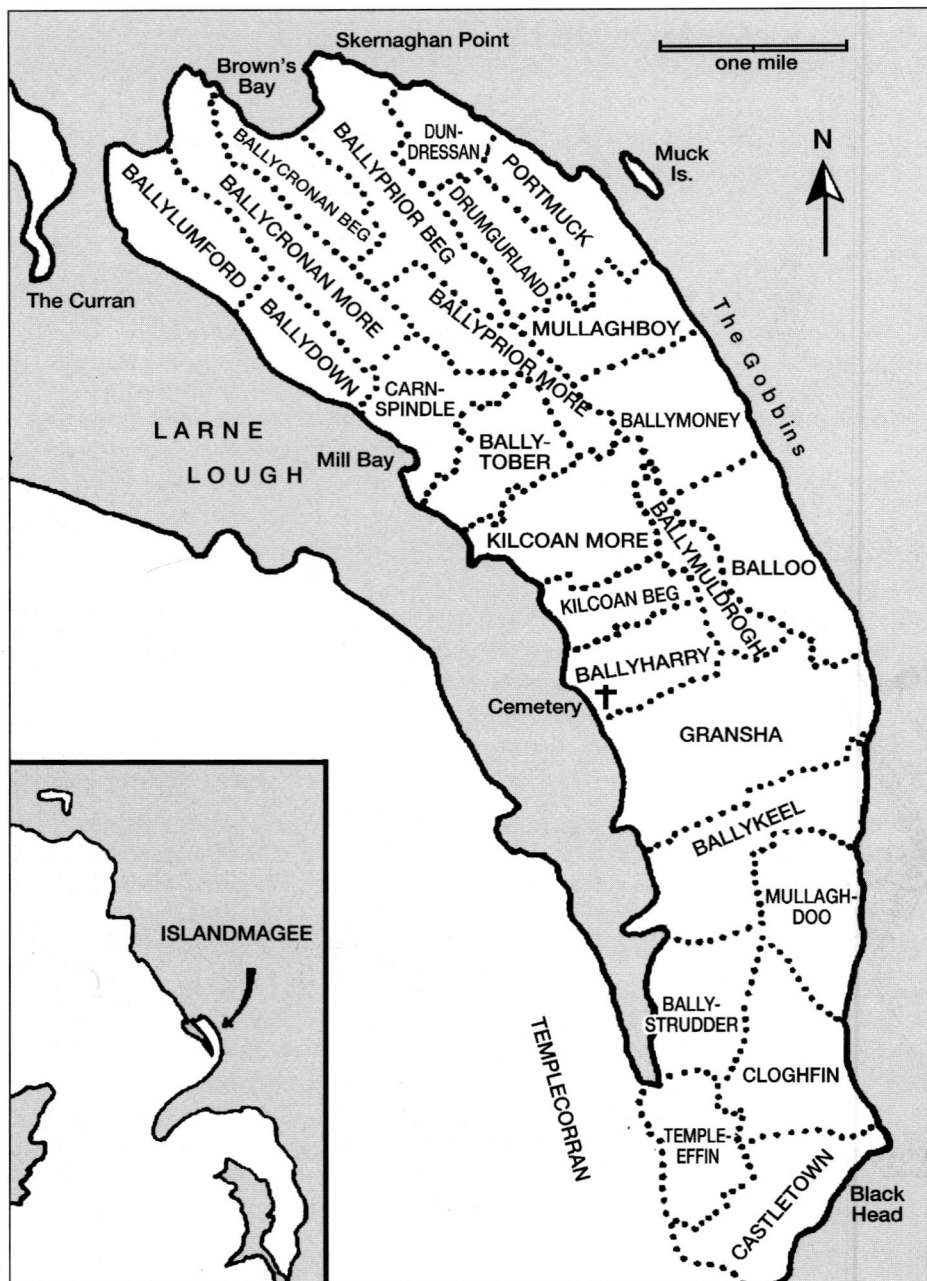

*Townlands of Islandmagee.*

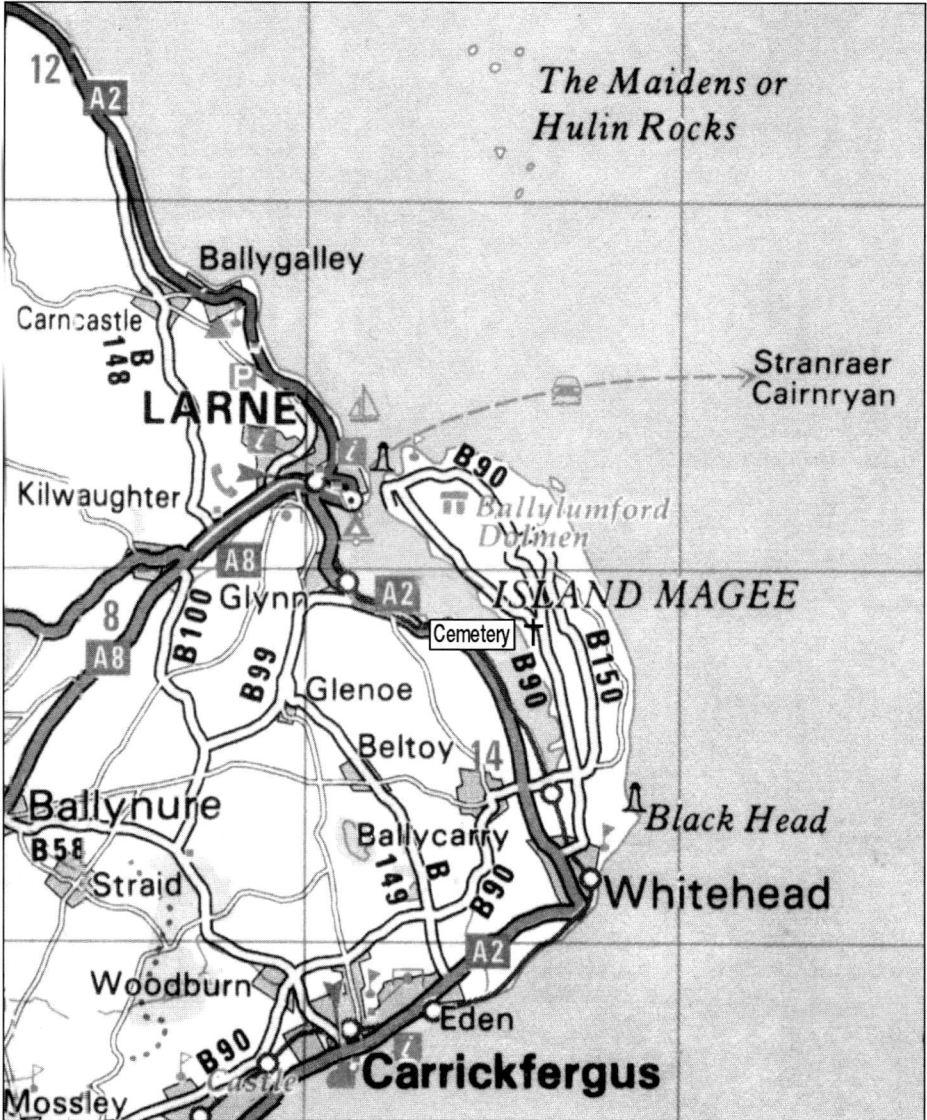

*Location Map.*

**Grave Block Plan**

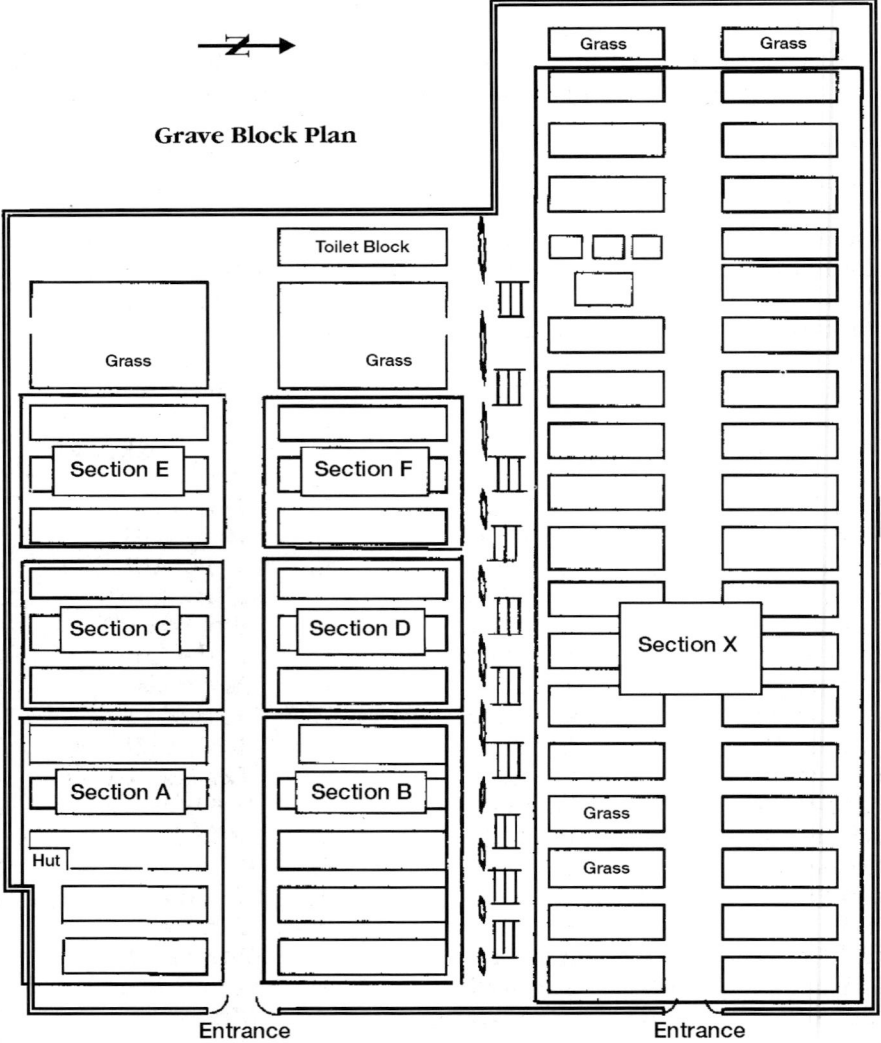

| | |
|---|---|
| Grass | Grass |

Toilet Block

Grass

Grass

Section E

Section F

Section C

Section D

Section X

Section A

Section B

Hut

Grass

Grass

Entrance

Entrance

## ~ ISLANDMAGEE NEW CEMETERY ~

Whitehead

~ LOW ROAD ~

Ballylumford

*Plan of Cemetery.*

# INDEX OF NAMES

**The figure in the bracket { } indicates the number of times that the surname occurs in the Section. Grave plot locations can be obtained by reference to the Section Map and Index.**

| | | | | | |
|---|---|---|---|---|---|
| Abbott | X | Barnett | D | Boyles {2} | X |
| Acheson | F | Bashford | X | Bradford | X |
| Adair {2} | F | Bass | C | Brady | X |
| Adams | F | Beasant | C | Branagh {2} | D |
| Adams {3} | X | Beattie | A | Branagh {2} | F |
| Adamson {3] | B | Beattie | B | Brennan {2} | B |
| Adamson {2} | F | Beattie | E | Brennan {3} | X |
| Agnew | F | Beattie | X | Briggs | X |
| Aiken | C | Beggs | X | Brookes | X |
| Aiken | X | Bell {3} | A | Brooks | F |
| Alexander | X | Bell | C | Broomfield {2} | B |
| Allen | C | Bell | E | Brown | A |
| Allen {2} | D | Bell {5} | X | Brown | C |
| Allen | X | Bennett | X | Brown {3} | X |
| Anderson {2} | X | Berry | C | Browne {2} | A |
| Arlow | C | Bingham | C | Browne {3} | B |
| Armour {2} | B | Bingham | F | Browne {2} | F |
| Armour | C | Birkmyre | B | Brownlee | X |
| Armour {3} | X | Black | E | Brownlie | A |
| Armstrong {3} | X | Black {2} | X | Bruce | A |
| Arnold {2} | X | Blair | C | Brunt {2} | X |
| Arthurs | A | Blake | X | Buchanan | A |
| Arthurs {4} | B | Blakely | E | Buckle {2} | X |
| Arthurs {3} | X | Blyth {2} | F | Budd | F |
| Atkinson {2} | X | Boal | X | Burns | X |
| Auld {2} | B | Boles | X | Burns | A |
| Auld | C | Bonar {5} | X | Burns | B |
| Auld {2} | D | Bonnar | C | Burns {2} | C |
| Baillie | D | Bonugli | B | Burnside | C |
| Baillio | X | Bosomworth | X | Burrows | X |
| Baird | D | Boucher | F | Bury | B |
| Baird {2} | X | Bowen {2} | A | Busby | B |
| Bannon | X | Bowman | X | Busby {2} | X |
| Barbour | X | Boyd {2} | B | Cairns | A |
| Barclay | X | Boyd {4} | X | Cairns | X |
| Barkley {2} | C | Boyle | X | Caldwell {3} | A |
| Barr | B | Boyd {4} | D | Calwell {3} | X |
| Bashford | F | Boyd | F | Cameron {3} | A |

2

| | | | | | |
|---|---|---|---|---|---|
| Cameron | B | Crafter | E | Ditty | X |
| Cameron {3} | C | Craig | D | Dixon | E |
| Cameron | E | Craig {2} | F | Dobbin | X |
| Cameron | X | Craig {3} | X | Dobson | D |
| Campbell | A | Crampton | X | Donaghy | X |
| Campbell {3} | B | Crawford {2} | B | Donald {2} | A |
| Campbell {2} | F | Crawford | C | Donald {2} | B |
| Campbell {8} | X | Crawford {5} | X | Donald {3} | X |
| Canning | X | Cresswell {2} | D | Donaldson | A |
| Carlisle {2} | B | Crooks | B | Donaldson | B |
| Carmichael | C | Crooks | X | Donaldson | E |
| Carson | C | Crossan | X | Donaldson | F |
| Carson | X | Crowhurst | X | Donnan | X |
| Casey {3} | F | Crozier | X | Donnelly | F |
| Cathcart | C | Cummings | F | Dorrans | X |
| Cathcart | X | Cunningham | X | Drillingcourt | X |
| Chambers {3} | X | Cuthbert | B | Drysdale | X |
| Chandler | A | Cuthbert | X | Duff {2} | A |
| Chapman | B | Dallas | F | Duff {4} | B |
| Clark | C | Dallas | X | Duff | X |
| Clarke | E | Davey | D | Duncan {2} | F |
| Clarke {2} | X | Davey | X | Duncan | X |
| Cleary | X | Davidson | X | Dunn | X |
| Cleland | X | Davies | A | Earls | C |
| Clements | C | Davis | X | Earls | X |
| Clements | X | Davison | A | Edens {2} | X |
| Clifford | X | Davison | X | Edgar | A |
| Clugston | X | Dawson | A | Egar | E |
| Coburn {3} | X | Dawson | D | Elliott | A |
| Coleman | E | Dawson | X | Elliott | X |
| Connelly {2} | F | Deane | X | English {6} | A |
| Connor {2} | B | Dempster | X | English {3} | B |
| Connor {4} | X | Devine | X | English | D |
| Cook | D | Devon | X | English {2} | E |
| Cooke {3} | X | Dick {2} | A | Esler | F |
| Cooper | E | Dick {11} | B | Espie | A |
| Corr | X | Dick {2} | D | Espie | A |
| Coulter {2} | X | Dick | C | Evans | X |
| Cowan | X | Dick | E | Farquharson | B |
| Cowell | X | Dick {6} | F | Fee {2} | X |
| Coyle {4} | X | Dick {4} | X | Feherty | C |
| Crabbe | F | Dinsmore {2} | E | Ferguson {4} | B |

3

| | | | | | |
|---|---|---|---|---|---|
| Ferguson | C | Gillespie | X | Hanna {2} | D |
| Ferguson {2} | X | Gilliland | C | Hanna {3} | X |
| Ferris | X | Gilliland | X | Hannah | X |
| Finlay | X | Gilmore | B | Hanvey | F |
| Flack | D | Gilmour {3} | X | Hanvey {2} | X |
| Flack | X | Gilroy | X | Harkness | X |
| Flack/Fleck {3} | D | Girvin | X | Harper | X |
| Fletcher | C | Glass {2} | X | Harrison {2} | B |
| Forbes | X | Goldie | C | Harte {2} | C |
| Ford {4} | B | Gordon {2} | A | Haveron {3} | A |
| Ford | D | Gordon {3} | F | Haveron {2} | X |
| Ford {3} | X | Gordon | X | Hawkins {3} | X |
| Forde {5} | B | Gourley | X | Hawthorne {2} | A |
| Forsythe | F | Gracey | X | Hawthorne {2} | B |
| Forsythe {4} | X | Graham {2} | A | Hawthorne | C |
| Foster | A | Graham {2} | B | Hawthorne | D |
| Foster {5} | X | Graham | C | Hay {2} | A |
| Fox | X | Graham {10} | X | Hay {2} | F |
| Foy | X | Grainger | X | Hayden {5} | D |
| Frackleton | D | Granger | D | Haydock {2} | C |
| Frackleton | X | Grant | B | Haydock {2} | D |
| Frayne {2} | A | Grant | X | Haydock | F |
| Frazer | B | Gray {4} | A | Heddles | A |
| Freil | X | Gray | B | Heddles {2} | B |
| Fullerton | X | Gray | F | Heddles {3} | X |
| Fullerton {2} | B | Gray {6} | X | Heggan | D |
| Fulton | F | Greaves | F | Heggan | X |
| Fulton | X | Greer | A | Heggen | X |
| Gallimore | F | Gregg {3} | X | Henderson {2} | B |
| Gamble {2} | E | Grubba | E | Henderson {2} | X |
| Gamble | F | Gupta | X | Henry {2} | A |
| Garrett | C | Guthrie | C | Henshaw | C |
| Garrett | X | Hack | D | Henshaw {2} | D |
| Geddes {2} | B | Hagan {2} | E | Heron | X |
| Gibson {2} | B | Hall | F | Hewitt | B |
| Gibson {2} | C | Hall {5} | X | Hewitt | X |
| Gibson {4} | X | Ham {2} | A | Heyburn {2} | X |
| Gilbert | X | Hamilton | A | Higginson {2} | B |
| Gillespie {2} | B | Hamilton {4} | B | Higginson | E |
| Gillespie {2} | D | Hamilton {4} | D | Higginson {4} | X |
| Gillespie {2} | E | Hamilton {3} | E | Hilditch {2} | X |
| Gillespie | F | Hamilton {4} | X | Hill {5} | A |

| | | | | | |
|---|---|---|---|---|---|
| Hill {2} | B | Jones {3} | E | Lemon | D |
| Hill {5} | D | Jones | F | Leslie {2} | X |
| Hill | E | Jones {6} | X | Lewis | D |
| Hill | F | Jordan | B | Lilley {2} | A |
| Hill {8} | X | Kane {3} | A | Lindsay | B |
| Hinton | F | Kane {5} | B | Linton | X |
| Hockings | X | Kane {2} | D | Logan {3} | X |
| Hogg | X | Kane {2} | F | Long {3} | A |
| Holmes {3} | A | Kane {7} | X | Long {2} | F |
| Holmes {3} | D | Kealey | X | Long {3} | X |
| Hood | B | Keatley {2} | X | Lorimer | X |
| Hood {2} | X | Keenan | X | Lough | D |
| Hope | X | Kell | F | Lowry {2} | B |
| Hopkins {2} | D | Kelly | C | Lowry {2} | X |
| Houston | F | Kerby | X | Lucas {2} | X |
| Houston {5} | X | Kernaghan | E | Lydon | X |
| Howlin | X | Kerr {3} | A | Lyle | X |
| Hughes | E | Kerr | C | Lynagh {2} | X |
| Hughes {2} | X | Kerr {6} | X | Lynn {3} | B |
| Hunter {2} | B | Kielty | X | Lynn | X |
| Hunter {3} | C | Kiley {2} | X | Lyttle | X |
| Hunter {3} | D | Kilpatrick {2} | X | Macaulay | X |
| Hunter {3} | X | Kirk | B | Macauley | B |
| Irvine | E | Kirk | D | Macauley | C |
| Irvine {2} | A | Knox | F | Macauley | D |
| Irvine {2} | D | Knox | X | Macauley {4} | X |
| Irvine {2} | X | Kyle | X | MacDonald {2} | A |
| Irwin {2} | F | Laing | X | MacDonald | X |
| Jackett | X | Laird | X | Macdonald {2} | F |
| Jackson {4} | A | Laird {2} | C | MacKenzie | X |
| Jackson {2} | B | Lamont | X | MacKeown | D |
| Jackson {2} | X | Lancaster | X | MacLaughlin | D |
| Jeffrey | X | Lappin | X | Macklin | E |
| Johnson | A | Latimer | A | Macrae {2} | C |
| Johnson {3} | X | Latimer {3} | B | Macready | A |
| Johnston {4} | B | Lattimore {2} | B | Magee | F |
| Johnston {3} | C | Laverty | X | Magill | A |
| Johnston | D | Lawler | X | Magill | C |
| Johnston | F | Lawrence | D | Magill | E |
| Johnston {4} | X | Leckie {3} | X | Magowan | F |
| Jones | C | Lees | D | Magowan | X |
| Jones {2} | D | Leitch | X | Maguire | X |

| | | | | | | |
|---|---|---|---|---|---|
| Mair | X | McClelland | B | McGuigan | X |
| Malcolm {2} | B | McClinton {2} | C | McHugh {2} | X |
| Mann | A | McCloy | A | McIlgorm {2} | A |
| Mann {2} | B | McCluney | E | McIlgorm | C |
| Mann {4} | X | McClung | X | McIlreavy | X |
| Marsh | B | McClure {3} | A | McIlroy | X |
| Marshall | B | McClure | F | McIlwain {2} | B |
| Martin | E | McClure | X | McIlwaine | X |
| Martin {2} | A | McClurkin | X | McIlwaine {2} | B |
| Martin {2} | D | McCluskey {2} | A | McKay {2} | B |
| Martin {2} | F | McCluskey | E | McKay | D |
| Martin {5} | X | McComb | E | McKay {2} | X |
| Mateer | X | McConachie | D | McKechnie | X |
| Mathews | A | McConkey | C | McKee {2} | C |
| Matson | X | McConnell {2} | B | McKee {2} | X |
| Mawhinney | F | McConnell | X | McKelvey {2] | X |
| Mawhinney {2} | X | McCorkell {2} | E | McKenzie | X |
| Maxwell {2} | B | McCormick {2} | X | McKeown {2} | C |
| Maxwell {2} | E | McCosh {2} | B | McKeown . | D |
| Maxwell {2} | X | McCosh | X | McKeown | X |
| Mayberry | X | McCoy | X | McKibben | X |
| Maybin | B | McCready | C | McKinley | B |
| McAdam {2] | D | McCreal | X | McKinstry | B |
| McAllister {2} | X | McCullough | X | McKinstry | F |
| McAloney | X | McCune | X | McKinstry | X |
| McAuley | X | McDevitte | X | McKinty | B |
| McBride {2} | A | McDonagh | C | McKinty {3} | X |
| McBride {2} | X | McDonald | X | McKnight | X |
| McBurney | C | McDowell | F | McLaughlin {2} | B |
| McCafferty | F | McDowell {2} | B | McLaughlin | X |
| McCallan | E | McDowell {3} | X | McLeer | X |
| McCallion | A | McElnea | C | McLeod | X |
| McCalmont | A | McFall | X | McLernon | X |
| McCalmont {3} | B | McFarlane {3} | X | McMaster | B |
| McCalmont {3} | D | McGee | X | McMaster | F |
| McCalmont | F | McGloughlin | A | McMaster {5} | X |
| McCalmont {7} | X | McGookin | B | McMaw {2} | E |
| McCammon {2} | X | McGookin | X | McMaw {4} | X |
| McCartney | X | McGowan | D | McMillan | X |
| McCaskey | X | McGowan | F | McMullan | X |
| McCavana | A | McGowan | X | McMurran | B |
| McClean | X | McGrady | C | McMurtry | A |

6

| | | | | | |
|---|---|---|---|---|---|
| McMurtry | B | Murdock {2} | F | Pollin | X |
| McMurtry {2} | X | Murray | C | Pollock | D |
| McNally | E | Nash | E | Pollock | X |
| McNaught | B | Neill {3} | X | Prenter | X |
| McNeice | X | Nelson {2} | A | Preston | X |
| McNeill | F | Nelson {2} | X | Pullin | D |
| McNeill {2} | X | Nesbitt | X | Ramsey | X |
| McNeilly {4} | B | Newbold | X | Rankin {2} | A |
| McPherson | E | Niblock {2} | A | Rankin {2} | B |
| McSpadden | X | Niblock {8} | B | Rankin {2} | X |
| McWilliam | X | Niblock {4} | E | Rea {2} | A |
| Mearns {3} | B | Niblock {4} | X | Rea | E |
| Meek | X | Nicol | A | Rea | X |
| Meeke | D | Nimick | X | Redford {2} | X |
| Meeke {2} | F | Nixon | X | Reid | C |
| Meneilly | B | Nolan | B | Reid | D |
| Mercer | X | Nolan | X | Reid | E |
| Michelbacher | B | Noonan | X | Reid | F |
| Millar | B | Noteman {2} | B | Reid {3} | X |
| Millar | D | Nuttall | X | Rendall {2} | B |
| Millar | X | O'Connell | F | Rendell | B |
| Mitchell {4} | E | O'Neill | X | Renwick | X |
| Monteith | B | Orr {7} | B | Reynolds {3} | X |
| Monteith | X | Orr | C | Richardson {2} | X |
| Montgomery {2} | A | Orr | X | Riddle | X |
| Montgomery | E | Orr-McAuley | X | Rides | X |
| Montgomery {10} | X | Osborne {2} | F | Riley | X |
| Moody | A | Palmer | D | Robinson {2} | B |
| Moody | X | Parke | A | Robinson {2} | C |
| Moore {3} | A | Patterson [2] | X | Robinson {2} | X |
| Moore {4} | X | Patton {2} | B | Rodgers {2} | X |
| Moorhead | C | Patton | X | Ross {5} | A |
| Moorhead | X | Paxton | X | Ross {9} | B |
| Morgan | F | Peoples {2} | C | Ross | D |
| Morrow | X | Perry | X | Ross | F |
| Morrow {2} | B | Phillips | X | Ross {8} | X |
| Morton | C | Phyllis | C | Rossall | B |
| Morton {2} | D | Picken {5} | X | Rossborough {2} | X |
| Mowat | X | Pink {2} | X | Rowe {2} | X |
| Mulholland | B | Pitcaithley {2} | X | Rowlatt {2} | E |
| Mulholland | X | Poag | X | Running | X |
| Mulvenna | D | Polglase | D | Rush {2} | E |

| | | | | |
|---|---|---|---|---|
| Taylor | E | Wells {2} | X |
| Telford | X | Welsh {3} | X |
| Templeton {3} | A | Whatley {2} | F |
| Templeton {2} | B | Whitall | X |
| Templeton {2} | C | White | E |
| Templeton {2} | E | White | X |
| Templeton | F | Whitehead | F |
| Templeton | X | Whitla | C |
| Thomas | X | Whittingham | X |
| Thompson | A | Williamson | D |
| Thompson {2} | B | Williamson {2} | E |
| Thompson | E | Wilson | C |
| Thompson {2} | X | Wilson {6} | A |
| Thomson {2} | B | Wilson {4} | B |
| Thornbury {3} | A | Wilson {6} | D |
| Tierney | X | Wilson {2} | E |
| Todd | F | Wilson {2} | F |
| Tomasso | X | Wilson {15} | X |
| Topping | X | Wisnom {2} | C |
| Toppon | E | Wisnom | D |
| Tumelty | X | Witherspoon | F |
| Tyrie | D | Wolfe | X |
| Tyrie | X | Wood {2} | X |
| Upton | X | Woodside {4} | X |
| Urquart {2} | X | Wotherspoon | F |
| Usher | C | Wright | D |
| Walker | A | Wright | C |
| Walker {2} | B | Wright [2] | B |
| Walker | X | Wright {2} | X |
| Waring | X | Young | F |
| Warren {2} | A | Young | X |
| Warren {2} | X | | |
| Warwick | E | | |
| Warwick | X | | |
| Watson {4} | X | | |
| Watt | B | | |
| Welch | X | | |

# GRAVESTONE
# INSCRIPTIONS
# AND
# INTERMENTS

The Society has transcribed and checked
all the information as carefully as possible
and sincerely hopes that any errors are minimal.

**Grave Plots Plan**

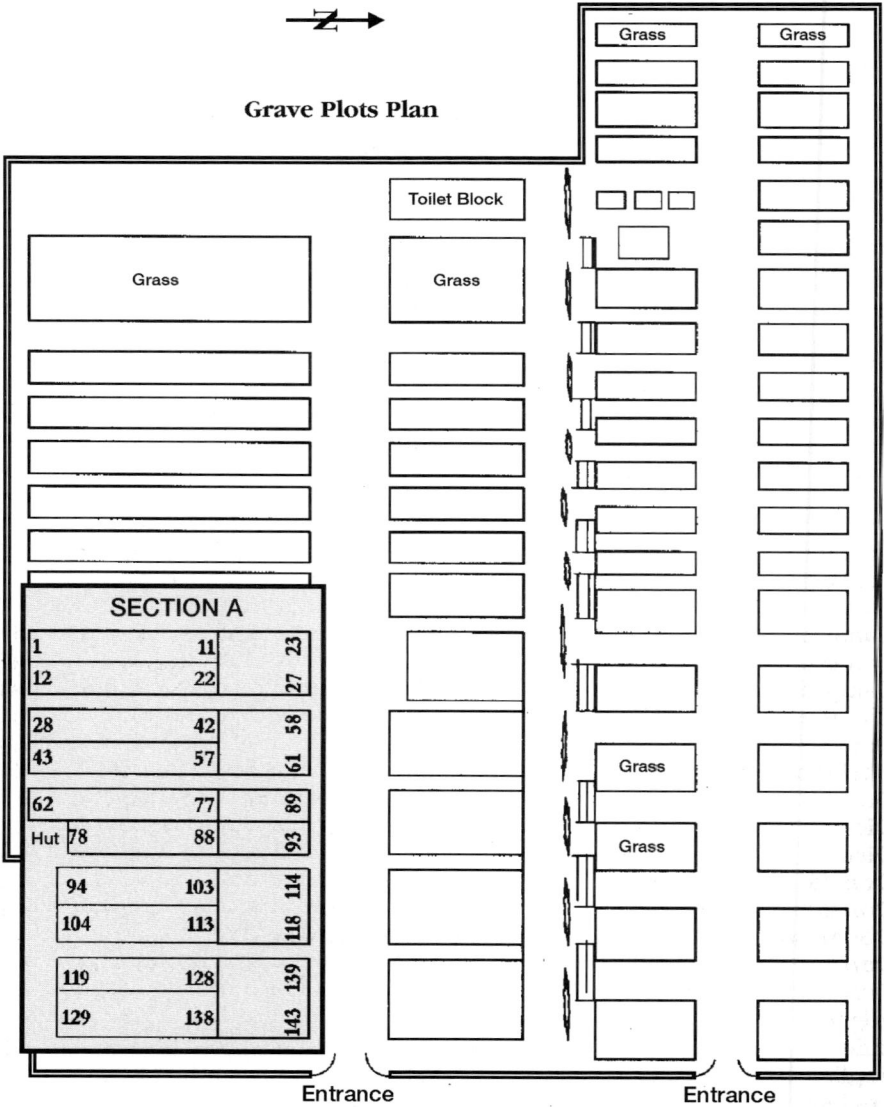

N →

| Grass | | Grass |
|---|---|---|

Toilet Block

| Grass | Grass |
|---|---|

SECTION A

| 1 | 11 | 23 |
| 12 | 22 | 27 |
| 28 | 42 | 58 |
| 43 | 57 | 61 |
| 62 | 77 | 89 |
| Hut 78 | 88 | 93 |
| 94 | 103 | 114 |
| 104 | 113 | 118 |
| 119 | 128 | 139 |
| 129 | 138 | 143 |

Grass

Grass

Entrance

Entrance

## ~ ISLANDMAGEE NEW CEMETERY ~

**Whitehead**

~ LOW ROAD ~

**Ballylumford**

←

→

# SECTION A

| Name | Plot | Name | Plot | Name | Plot | Name | Plot |
|---|---|---|---|---|---|---|---|
| Arthurs | 96 | Frayne | 90 | Kerr | 141 | Rea | 53 |
| Beattie | 78 | Frayne | 91 | Latimer | 65 | Rea | 54 |
| Bell | 12 | Gordon | 90 | Lilley | 127 | Ross | 17 |
| Bell | 13 | Gordon | 91 | Lilley | 128 | Ross | 18 |
| Bell | 93 | Graham | 33 | Long | 31 | Ross | 94 |
| Bowen | 38 | Graham | 34 | Long | 32 | Ross | 125 |
| Bowen | 39 | Gray | 90 | Long | 50 | Ross | 126 |
| Brown | 93 | Gray | 91 | MacDonald | 45 | Scott | 5 |
| Browne | 40 | Gray | 98 | MacDonald | 46 | Scott | 74 |
| Browne | 41 | Gray | 99 | Macready | 88 | Scott | 76 |
| Brownlie | 62 | Greer | 66 | Magill | 139 | Scott | 77 |
| Bruce | 52 | Ham | 12 | Mann | 42 | Simms | 137 |
| Buchanan | 131 | Ham | 13 | Martin | 33 | Simms | 138 |
| Burns | 80 | Hamilton | 97 | Martin | 34 | Skelton | 76 |
| Cairns | 78 | Haveron | 9 | Mathews | 6 | Skelton | 77 |
| Caldwell | 81 | Haveron | 10 | McBride | 33 | Sloan | 28 |
| Caldwell | 82 | Haveron | 11 | McBride | 34 | Smallwood | 80 |
| Caldwell | 83 | Hawthorne | 142 | McCallion | 63 | Smith | 86 |
| Cameron | 1 | Hawthorne | 143 | McCalmont | 59 | Smith | 87 |
| Cameron | 15 | Hay | 117 | McCavana | 56 | Smith | 108 |
| Cameron | 16 | Hay | 118 | McCloy | 29 | Smith | 109 |
| Campbell | 136 | Heddles | 47 | McClure | 9 | Smith | 110 |
| Chandler | 7 | Henry | 2 | McClure | 10 | Smith | 111 |
| Davies | 95 | Henry | 3 | McClure | 11 | Stewart | 137 |
| Davison | 58 | Hill | 21 | McCluskey | 105 | Stewart | 138 |
| Dawson | 79 | Hill | 22 | McCluskey | 106 | Strange | 75 |
| Dick | 14 | Hill | 24 | McGloughlin | 107 | Templeton | 8 |
| Dick | 56 | Hill | 25 | McIlgorm | 114 | Templeton | 12 |
| Donald | 60 | Hill | 103 | McIlgorm | 115 | Templeton | 13 |
| Donald | 61 | Holmes | 35 | McMurtry | 55 | Thompson | 102 |
| Donaldson | 23 | Holmes | 36 | Montgomery | 70 | Thornbury | 67 |
| Duff | 45 | Holmes | 37 | Montgomery | 71 | Thornbury | 68 |
| Duff | 46 | Irvine | 129 | Moody | 51 | Thornbury | 69 |
| Edgar | 116 | Irvine | 130 | Moore | 2 | Walker | 64 |
| Elliott | 89 | Jackson | 26 | Moore | 3 | Warren | 121 |
| English | 21 | Jackson | 27 | Moore | 29 | Warren | 122 |
| English | 22 | Jackson | 119 | Nelson | 100 | Wilson | 20 |
| English | 112 | Jackson | 120 | Nelson | 101 | Wilson | 43 |
| English | 113 | Johnson | 92 | Niblock | 123 | Wilson | 44 |
| English | 132 | Kane | 4 | Niblock | 124 | Wilson | 48 |
| English | 133 | Kane | 30 | Nicol | 85 | Wilson | 49 |
| Espie | 72 | Kane | 40 | Parke | 57 | Wilson | 76 |
| Espie | 73 | Kerr | 19 | Rankin | 40 | | |
| Foster | 104 | Kerr | 140 | Rankin | 41 | | |

A1

In fond memory of
**ROBERT**
Loved husband of
**Elizabeth CAMERON**
Died 17th Feby. 1950
Also the above named
**ELIZABETH**
Died 25th May 1997

- *Robert: Temple Effin, Whitehead.*
- *Elizabeth: Whitehead Private Nursing Home*

A2-A3

Placed in memory of
**Dr. FRANK MOORE**
**Ph.D, F.E.I.S., J.P.**
And of his wife
**ANNIE** died 15th November 1949
Their sons
**FRANKIE** died 21st August 1920
**ERNEST** died Christmas 1957
**HAROLD** died 6th June 1964
Their daughter
**ROBERTA** died November 1958
And all other members of their family
Interred here or elsewhere

Inside surround
**ENID MARGARET LAWRENCE**
**HENRY**
died 21st July 1986

Flower holder
In memory of
**HAROLD P. MOORE**

- *Miss E. M. L. Henry (age 79): Holywell Hospital, Antrim*

A4

In loving memory of
**SARAH WILSON NIBLOCK**
wife of
Alexander W. Kane
Died 21st January 1949
Aged 57 years
The above named
**ALEXANDER WILSON KANE**
Died 7th March 1969
Aged 78 years

- *Sarah: Upper Gransha, Islandmagee.*
- *Captain Alexander: The Acre, Mullaghdubh, Isalndmagee*

A5

In loving memory of
**MARTHA HAMILTON**
Dearly loved wife of
David R. Scott
At rest 3rd March 1960
The above **DAVID R. SCOTT**
At rest 9th August 1964
Say not goodnight but in some
brighter clime bid me good morning

A6

In affectionate remembrance of
**CHARLES**
Passed on 2nd July 1951
Loved husband of
Mary R. Mathews
Also the above
**MARY R. MATHEWS**
Passed on 18th October 1978

- *Charles and Mary (age 78): 5, Chester Ave. Whitehead*

A7

Sacred to the memory of
**MARGARET CHANDLER**
Who died 21st April 1948
and her husband
**JOSEPH CHANDLER R.N.**
Divisional Officer C.G., Clifden
Died 5th Feby. 1916
And was interred in Clifden, Co. Galway
Also their daughter **ALICE EVA**
Died 12th Feb. 1968
Until the day break and the
shadows flee away

- *Margaret (housewife, age 78): 4, Windsor Terrace Whitehead.*
- *Alice (age 78): The Beeches, Ballyclare*

A8

In loving memory of
**JOHN TEMPLETON M.B.E.**
Master mariner
Who died 5th July 1948 aged 71 years
His wife **MARY HENRIETTA**
Died 26th May 1955 aged 80 years
Faithful unto death

- *John: Ivy Cottage, Mullaghboy, Islandmagee*

A9-A10-A11

In
Loving memory of
**ABBIE McCLURE**
died 15th Feb. 1948
Also her sister **JANE HAVERON**
died 26th Aug. 1944
Also her husband
**ROBERT McCLURE**
died 11th April 1959
Also their son **ROBERT**
died 22nd January 1963
Their daughter **MARGARET**
died 25th May 1964
And their daughter **ISABEL**
died 12th September 1968
their daughter **MARY ELIZABETH**
died 8th March 1985
their daughter **WILHELMINA JANE**
died 24th Nov. 1985
**MARGARET DORA (DOREEN)**
wife of the above Robert
Died 14th May 1991 aged 80 years

- *Mrs. Jane Isabella Haveron: Ballystrudder, Islandmagee.*
- *Mary Elizabeth (single) and Wilhelmina Jane (single): 36 Adelaide Ave. Whitehead.*
- *Doreen: 17, Brooksland Park, Whitehead.*

A12-A13
In loving memory of
**ROBERT McC TEMPLETON,**
Master Mariner
Who died 21st August 1949
aged 68 years
And his wife **MARTHA TEMPLETON**
Who died 31st August 1960
aged 77 years
**MARGARET BELL,**
sister of Martha Templeton
Who died 3rd September 1964
**EDWARD W. HAM**
died 15th January 1979
**JANE BELL HAM**
died 2nd May 1997
**MARGARET EVELYN (PEGGY) BELL**
died 23rd June 1998

- *Martha and Robert McCalmont Templeton, and Margaret Bell: 3, Windsor Terrace, Whitehead.*
- *Edward Walter Ham (age 74): 21 Bridge End, Ballycarry.*
- *Mrs. Jean Ham (age 85): 9 Victoria Court, Whitehead.*
- *Peggy Bell (single): 74 Browns Bay Road, Islandmagee.*

A14

**DICK**
In loving memory of
**LETITIA DICK**
Died 1st May 1949
Also her husband **JOHN**
Died 26th April 1952

- *Letitia Dick (age 75, housewife): Mullaghboy, Islandmagee.*
- *John (age 84, carpenter): Portmuck, Islandmagee*

A15-A16
**CAMERON**
In loving memory of
**WILLIAM CAMERON**
Died 11th January 1948 aged 80 years
And his wife **WILHELMINA**
Died 6th August 1954 aged 69 years
Also their son
**JAMES ALLEN CAMERON**
Died 22nd July 1985 aged 74 years
Beloved husband of Madge

- *William and Wilhelmina Cameron: Temple Effin, Whitehead*
- *James: 45 Windsor Ave. Whitehead*

A17-A18
In loving memory of
**MATTHEW ROSS**
Who died 13th July 1947 aged 73 years
And his wife **AGNES ROSS**
Who died 6th Dec. 1959 aged 80 years
Also their son **WILLIAM JOHN**
Loved husband of Elizabeth Ross
Lost in the River Ribble on the
motor vessel Druid
22nd August 1962 aged 45 years

- *Captain Matthew Ross: Upper Gransha, Islandmagee*
- *Buried 3.8.2000*
**Miss MARTHA CAMPBELL ROSS**
*(age 90): Chester Park Nursing Home, Whitehead.*

A19
In fond remembrance of
**JOAN MARY KERR**
Died 9th April 1945 in her 19th year
And her father
**HUGH McC. KERR J.P.**
Died 10th July 1960 in his 79th year
And her mother
**ESSIE FLORENCE KERR**
Died 2nd Jan. 1978 in her 83rd year
**KERR**

- *Captain Hugh McC. Kerr and Joan Kerr (single): Vohmar, Islandmagee*

A20

In fond memory of
**SUSAN**
beloved wife of **James WILSON**
Died 26th March 1955 aged 74 years
**JAMES WILSON**
Died 6th June 1968 aged 79 years
**WILSON**

• *James (engineer) and Susan Wilson:*
  *3 Royal Terrace, Whitehead*

A21-A22

In loving memory of
**ANNA BELLA HILL**
Who died 1st January 1942 aged 63 years
Wife of Thomas Hill, master mariner
Also their son
**JOHN GIBSON HILL C.B.**
Loving husband of Marian
Died 18th January 1976
Aged 64 years
And their daughter
**ELEANOR MARGARET ENGLISH**
Died 5th December 1996 aged 80 years
**HILL**

• *Anna Bella Hill: Wyncroft, Balfour Ave.*
  *Whitehead.*

• *John Gibson Hill (retired civil servant,*
  *death recorded as 1975): Hillcrest, York*
  *Ave. Whitehead.*

• *Mrs. English (widow, Congregationalist):*
  *17 Alexander Ave. Whitehead*

A23

In loving remembrance of
My dear husband
**WILLIAM HUGH KERR DONALDSON**
Who died 25th October 1944
Loves last gift remembrance

• *William (school teacher): The Moat,*
  *Islandmagee.*

A24-A25

In loving memory of
**WILLIAM ROBERT**
Infant son of
**Margaret and James HILL**
Died 28th July 1943 aged 6 weeks
Also the above named **MARGARET**
Died 5th April 1975 aged 70 years
And her dear husband **JAMES**
Died 30th December 1996 aged 90 years

• *William Robert Hill: Upper Gransha,*
  *Islandmagee*

• *James and Margaret McMaster Hill:*
  *176, Middle Road, Islandmagee*

A26-A27

In loving memory of
**MARTHA JACKSON**
Who died the 16th of March 1938
And her husband
**GEORGE ALEXANDER JACKSON**
Died on the 21st March 1950
And their son
**JOHN DONALDSON JACKSON**
Died 21st April 1970
**JACKSON**

• *Martha and John Donaldson Jackson (age*
  *77, married): The Moat, Ballydown,*
  *Islandmagee.*

• *Buried 19.3.1982* **Mrs. WILHELMINA**
  **MARGARET JACKSON,** *(age 87, widow):*
  *22 Ballylumford Road, Islandmagee*

A28

**CHRISSIE SLOAN**
Died 1st October 1950
Lovingly Remembered
Cecil
Desmond and Sylvia

• *Mrs. Christina Sloan, housewife:*
  *Parkview, Islandmagee*

A29

**ANNA JANE MOORE**
Died 20th January 1952
Wife of Nathaniel Moore
Also their daughter **JEAN. H**
Died 1st January 1949
Wife of **Fred McCOY**
And the above
**NATHANIEL MOORE**
Died 17th Nov. 1967
**MOORE**

- *Anna Jane: Port Road, Islandmagee.*
- *Mrs. Jean Hunter McCloy: Hunterville, Whitehead.*
- *Nathaniel (merchant tailor, age 94): Clanferran, Ballystrudder, Islandmagee*

A30

**KANE**
In Loving Memory of
A devoted husband and father
**WILLIAM KANE**
Who died 15th February 1970
And our dear mother **MINA BELLA**
Who died 3rd March 1981

- *William Kane (age 72, rtd. Master Mariner): Hopefield, Mullaghdubh, Islandmagee.*
- *Mina (age 73, Presbyterian): 6, Donegall Cres. Whitehead*

A31-A32

Erected by John Long
In Loving Memory of his father
**JOHN LONG**
Who died 19th August 1948,
Aged 73 years
Also his mother
**ISABELLA BRANNON (LONG)**
Died 9th April 1959
Aged 85 years
Also their daughter **LIZZIE**
Died 7th July 1973
The above **JOHN LONG**
Died 29th January 1988

- *John (father) seaman: Mullaghdubh Islandmagee*
- *Lizzie: 2, Kilton Lane Islandmagee.*
- *John (son), age 86, Holywell Hospital, Antrim*

A33-A34

On surround
In Loving Memory of
**EDMUND A. GRAHAM**
Who died on the 28th February 1947

In Loving Memory of
**EVELYN MARTIN**
died 2nd July 1987
**NORMAN MARTIN**
died 29th April 1990

- *Edmund Graham (bank official): Redlands, Whitehead*
- *Cremated remains of Evelyn Martha Jane Martin (home duties) and Norman Martin; Cheadle, Cheshire, England*
- *Buried 22.7.1994 cremated remains of **Mrs. MURIEL McBRIDE** (age 73, housewife): 79, Lovell Ave. Mill Valley, Mann, California 94941-6*

A35-A36-A37

In Loving Memory of
**FRANCES GORDON HOLMES**
Born August 6th 1885,
died January 20th 1951
Also
**MARRIOTT GORDON HOLMES**
Born January 13th 1878, died
October 31st 1967

- *Miss F.G. Holmes and M.G. Holmes (farmer): The Gobbins, Isalndmagee*

A38-A39

Erected by
**GEORGE BOWEN**
In Loving Memory of his wife
**ELLEN BOWEN**
Who died 4th March 1926
And his wife
**MARGARET JANE BOWEN**
Who died 17th June 1963
**GEORGE BOWEN**
Who died 22nd April 1977
And his daughter
**ISOBEL**
Who died 19th April 1994

- *Ellen Bowen (age 51): Mullaghdubh, Islandmagee*
- *George (age 94): Magheramorne House.*
- *Miss Isobella Ellen Duff Bowen (age 79): 7, Riverdale House, Dunmurry, Belfast*

A40-A41

**BROWNE**
In Loving Memory of
**ARTHUR** beloved husband of
**MARY BROWNE**
Died 8th January 1931 aged 44 years
The above named **MARY BROWNE**
Died 18th March 1976 aged 83 years
In Memory of my darling wife
**HILDA RANKIN** (nee **KANE**)
Niece of the above
Died 11th October 1996 aged 79 years

- *Arthur (mariner): Marburn, Islandmagee.*
- *Hilda is Mrs. Jeannie Hill Rankin: 6, Willowvale Cres. Islandmagee*

A42

In Loving Memory of
**JOSEPH**
Beloved husband of
**Elizabeth MANN**
Who lost his life when MV Inverilen
was Torpedoed in the Atlantic,
3rd February 1943
Aged 46 years

A43-A44

In Loving Memory of
**ANNIE**
Beloved wife of **George WILSON**
died 7th Sep. 1949
The above **GEORGE WILSON**
died 23rd Nov 1950
Their son **HERBERT H. WILSON**
Called home 16th September 1971
Dearly loved husband of
**MADGE WILSON**
Who died 12th May 1989
Worthy of everlasting remembrance
**WILSON**

- *Herbert Hemingway Wilson (age 73, painting contractor) and Mrs. Margaret Wilson (Madge age 91, buried 7.9.1990): 6, Marine Parade, Whitehead.*

## A45-A46

In Memory of
**MARGARET CURRIE** (nee **Leighton**)
Beloved wife of John Allen Duff
Born 2nd March 1871 died 8th June 1947
The above **JOHN ALLEN DUFF**
Born 19th May 1870
died 7th February 1950
Also their son-in-law
**GEORGE OSWALD MACDONALD**
(Master Mariner)
Born Aug. 1895 - died Aug. 1972
Also a beloved wife and daughter
**MARY ALLEN MACDONALD**
Born 6th March 1903
died 4th August 1986

- *John: Hollymount, Whiteabbey.*
- *George buried 10.8.1972 (age 76): 55, Islandmagee Road, Whitehead.*
- *Mary (housewife, age 83): Flat 32, Fergus Fold, Carrickfergus*

## A47

- *Buried 5.2.1947* **WILLIAM J. HEDDLES** *(bus driver): Alexander Ave. Whitehead*

## A48-A49

In fond memory of
**ALFRED**
Loved husband of **Agnes WILSON**
Died 1st October 1959
The above **AGNES WILSON**
Died 11th November 1972
And their son **ALFRED E. WILSON**
Died 12th September 1985
Dearly loved husband of
Andrene Wilson

- *Alfred (postman) and Agnes: Broadview, Ballystrudder, Islandmagee.*
- *Alfred Edward (pilot station officer): 51, Larne Road, Carrickfergus*

## A50

**LONG**
In Loving Memory of
**BESSIE ALLEN LONG**
who died 1st July 1945

- *Bessie (age 75): Upper Gransha, Islandmagee*

## A51

In Memory of
**ELIZABETH MOODY**
died 8th Nov. 1948 aged 60 years
And her husband
**WILLIAM JOHN MOODY**
died 13th March 1961 aged 75 years

- *Elizabeth (housewife): Gransha, Islandmagee*

## A52

Sacred
To the memory of my husband
**ROBERT BRUCE**
Who died 23rd April 1944

- *Robert: Kilcoan, Islandmagee*

## A53-A54

**REA**
In fond remembrance of
our dear daughter
**MARY J. (MOLLIE)**
Who died 7th February 1927
aged 17 years
Also her dear mother **JEANNIE**
Who died 15th April 1951
And her father **ROBERT**
Who died 9th April 1971
Also **MAUREEN ELIZABETH**
who died 3rd July 1941
Beloved daughter of
Robert and Norah Rea

- *Mary Jane (Mollie): Ballystrudder, Islandmagee.*
- *Robert (age 86): 46, Cedar Ave. Belfast*

## A55

- *Buried 18.11.1929* **JAMES McMURTRY** *(age 68, mariner): Gransha, Islandmagee.*
- *Buried 8.5.1932* **JOHN McMURTRY:** *Erection, Islandmagee*

## A56

**DICK**
In Loving Memory of
**CATHERINE**
Beloved wife of John Dick
Died 6th July 1932
Above named **JOHN DICK**
died 9th December 1945
Also his second wife **SARAH**
Died 8th November 1982

- *Sarah is Sara McCavana (widow, age 76): 21, Summerhill Park, Belfast*

## A57

**PARKE**
In affectionate remembrance of
**MARTHA**
Dearly beloved wife of Thomas Parke
Died 12th October 1929 aged 72 years
Also the above **THOMAS PARKE**
Died 24th August 1939 aged 85 years
And their daughter **RUBY**
Died 1st January 1989 aged 98 years
Peace Perfect Peace

- *All: The Hill, Islandmagee.*
- *Thomas (rtd. School Master, recorded age 86). Ruby (single, recorded age 99).*

## A58

- *Buried 23.8.1941*
  **JAMES LINDSAY DAVISON** *(customs and excise officer): Kings Road, Whitehead*

## A59

In affectionate remembrance of
My dearly loved husband
**JAMES McCALMONT**
Who was drowned 11th Dec. 1937
aged 57 years
And **MARGARET ELIZABETH**
loved wife of the above
Died 28th December 1950 aged 72 years
Also their son **JAMES STANLEY**
Died result of an accident
20th November 1977 aged 58 years
Sometime we'll understand

- *James (Master Mariner): 90, Victoria Gardens, Belfast.*
- *James Stanley (clerk): 105, Islandmagee Road, Whitehead*

## A60-A61

In Memory of
**THOMAS ALEXANDER DONALD**
Who died 5th November 1951
And his wife **JESSIE M.**
Who died 2nd February 1963
The Lord is my Shepherd

## A62

In memoriam
**MARY A. BROWNLIE**
**LAWRENCE W. BROWNLIE**
1951

- *Mary Ann (buried 24.1.1951, housewife): Clonallen, Islandmagee*

## A63

**McCALLION**
In Loving Memory of
My dear husband
**JOHN**
Died 27th Aug. 1951

## A64

**WALKER**
In Loving Memory of
My dear husband
**SAMUEL**
Died 15th Jan. 1951

- *Samuel: 29, Edward Road, Whitehead.*
- *Buried 3.10.1973*
  ***Mrs. MARTHA WALKER** (age 81,
  housewife): 11, Edward Road, Whitehead*

## A65

**LATIMER**
In Loving Memory of
A devoted husband
**JOSEPH EDWARD LATIMER**
15th September 1973
and his ever loving wife
**MARY LAVINIA**
14th July 1988

- *Mary (age 75) and Joseph (age 62,
  business manager): 22, Cable Road,
  Whitehead*

## A66

**GREER**
In Loving Memory of
our darling son
**JOSEPH VALENTINE (VAL)**
Aged 17 years
Who was drowned in a
yachting accident
In Belfast Lough on 27th May 1950
Also his father **JOSEPH VALENTINE**
Who died 23rd December 1979
aged 83 years

- *Val: Kaleena, Victoria Ave. Whitehead.*
- *Buried 9.6.1989* ***Mrs. MARGARET GREER**
  (age 90): Whitehead Private Nursing Home*

## A67-A68-A69

- *Buried 10.2.1947*
  ***Mrs. EMMA L. THORNBURY**
  (housewife): Boghall, Islandmagee*
- *Buried 7.4.1972*
  ***ELIZABETH THORNBURY**
  (age 78, housekeeper): Ballystrudder
  Gardens, Islandmagee.*

## A70

In Memory of
**HUGH MONTGOMERY**
Who died 30th September 1943
And his wife **SARAH JANE**
Who died 2nd Feb. 1947

## A71

In Loving Memory of
my dear husband
**ROBERT C. MONTGOMERY**
Died 28th March 1974
Also our dear son **ROBERT D.**
Died 9th January 1947
Also **ELIZABETH T.**
Wife of Robert C. Montgomery
Died 3rd January 1981
Thy will be done

- *Robert Cosgrove Montgomery (age 84,
  blacksmith) and Elizabeth (age 82):
  19, Loughview Bungalows, Islandmagee*
- *Robert D. (sailor): Methodist Cottage,
  Islandmagee*

A72-A73

In Loving Memory of
**RICHARD ESPIE**
Who died 4th December 1943
His wife **HARRIET**
Who died 16th March 1969
Their daughter **MINNIE GRAHAM**
Who died 16th March 1971
Their son **RICHARD**
Who died 3rd October 1979
Their son **SAMUEL RAINEY**
Who died 1st Oct. 1982
Their daughter
**MARGARET BURNSIDE**
Who died 3rd April 1986
Their son **JOHN ESPIE**
who died 19th August 1991
**ESPIE**

- *Richard (railway official), Harriet (age 91), Minnie (single, age 64, home duties), Son Richard (age 68), Samuel (age 67) and Margaret (single, age 73): 17, Windsor Ave. Whitehead.*

- *John (age 71): 16 Coole Park, Newtownabbey*

A74

In Loving Memory of
**JOSEPH SCOTT**
Who died 19th October 1945
and his son
**JOHN MOLSEED SCOTT**
Killed in action at sea
24th Feb. 1945 aged 36
Also his wife **LOUISA SCOTT**
Who died 11th Jany. 1953
Also their son **JAMES**
Who died 29th April 1994
**SCOTT**

- *Joseph: Edward Road, Whitehead.*
- *James (age 88): 3, York Ave. Whitehead*

A75

In Memory of
**HUGH STRANGE**
Who died 5th Aug. 1943
And his wife
**ADA STRANGE**
Died 6th Oct. 1948
Erected by
Thomas H. Robinson

- *Hugh (farmer): Ballymoney, Islandmagee*

A76-A77

In Remembrance of
**WILLIAM L. SKELTON**
Who died 24th Oct. 1942 aged 68 years
And his wife **ELLEN JANE**
Died 5th March 1965 aged 86 years
Also their daughter **SALLY**
Died 13th January 1981 aged 70 years
Beloved wife of **James SCOTT**
Their daughter **NORAH**
died 12th Oct. 1991
**SKELTON**

- *William (solicitor): York Lodge, York Ave. Whitehead.*

- *Sally is Sarah McMurtry Scott (home duties): 3, York Ave. Whitehead.*

- *Norah (age 77, single): 1 Prince of Wales Ave. Whitehead*

- *Buried cremated remains 11.12.2002* **Mrs. MARY ANN WILSON** *(age 92): 30, Ballymacreely Road, Killinchy*

A78

In Memory of
**WILLIAM CAIRNS**
husband of Isabell Cairns
Died 28th Oct. 1953
His brother-in-law
**JAMES BEATTIE**
Died 11th Dec. 1950
Also the above named **ISABELL**
Died 7th August 1971

- *William (labourer): Whitehouse, Islandmagee.*

- *Isabella (age 80): 30 Windsor Crescent, Whitehead*

A79

In Loving Memory of
**JOHN DAWSON**
Who died 29th March 1954
And his wife **CHARLOTTE**
died 7th December 1943

- *John (sailor): Millbay, Islandmagee.*
- *Buried 16.2.1963 **JOHN DAWSON** (Junior): Millbay*

A80

In Loving Memory of
**THOMAS**
Beloved husband of **Letitia BURNS**
Died 2nd February 1943
And their daughter
**ELIZABETH SMALLWOOD**
Died 31st Aug. 1921 and was interred
In Elmwood Cemetry Ontario Canada

- *Thomas and Letitia (housewife, buried 22.5.1948): Millbay, Islandmagee*

A81

In Loving Memory of
**FRANCIS CALDWELL**
Died 12th June 1969
His wife **MARGARET**
Died 23rd Oct 2000
Their infant daughter
**MYRTLE**
Died 24th Jan. 1942

- *Francis Davison Caldwell (Master Mariner, age 58): Lower Gransha, Islandmagee.*
- *Margaret (age 81): 8, Ballystrudder gdns. Islandmagee.*
- *Myrtle: "Roydene", Ballymuldrough, Islandmagee*

A82-A83

Erected by Hugh Caldwell
In Loving Memory of his mother
**MARY ELIZABETH CALDWELL**
Who died 16th July 1940 aged 60 years
And his father
**SAMUEL CALDWELL,** 2nd Officer
Who died through sinking of
S.S. Teelin Head, on
22nd Jan 1918 aged 40 years
interred in Portsmouth
also his brother **SAMUEL JOHN,**
3rd Officer died through bombing
of H.V. Atheltemplar, 1st March 1941
aged 22 years interred in Leith

On surround
**JAMES CALDWELL**
loved husband of Agnes
died 4th January 1961
**HUGH C. CALDWELL**
died 5th September 1967 aged 58 years

- *Mary (widow): Mullaghdubh, Islandmagee.*
- *Hugh C. (seaman): Cloughfin, Islandmagee*

A84 unused

A85

In Loving Memory of our father
**JAMES NICOL**
Who died 17th January 1938,
and our brothers
**THOMAS F.** killed in action
18th May 1915
And **JOHN M.B.E. M.N.,**
killed at sea
By enemy action 19th March 1943
And our mother **AGNES NICOL**
Died 31st July 1948
And her son **WILLIAM,**
died 19th June 1963
Devoted husband of
**MARGARET NICOL**
**NICOL**

- *James and Agnes: Bentra, Whitehead*

A86-A87

### SMITH
In Loving Memory of
Our dear son **PARKE**
Died 27th December 1937,
aged 18½ years
Also his father **ALFRED HENRY**
died 26th September 1964
Devoted husband of **Meta SMITH**
And his mother **META**
died 2nd December 1966
Loves last gift – Remembrance

- *Thomas Parke Smith (schoolboy):*
  *The Hill. Islandmagee.*
- *Meta is Martha Emily (age 79):*
  *17 Ravenhill Park, Belfast*

A88

In Loving Memory of
**Rev. HENRY HUGH MACREADY**
Born 5th December 1864 -
died 17th December 1937
Minister of 2nd Islandmagee
Presbyterian Church for 46 years
And of **EVE MARIE,** his wife
Died 12th July 1944

- *Rev. Macready (age 72)*

A89

In Loving Memory of
**MARGARET ELLIOTT**
Who died 3rd October 1938
And her husband **ROBERT ELLIOTT**
Died 14th January 1966

- *Margaret: 362 Brownsbay, Islandmagee.*

A90-A91

### GORDON
In Loving Memory of
**JOSEPH PINNINS GORDON**
Died 16th April 1959
His son
**WILLIAM JOHN GRAY GORDON**
Killed in action 8th June 1940
Also his sister-in-law **ELLEN GRAY**
Died 12th March 1959
Also his wife **JAMESINA**
Died 24th September 1989

- *Flower container: In loving memory of*
  ***WILHELMINA R. FRAYNE***
- *Jamesina (age 103): 27 Hillside Park,*
  *Whitehead*

A92

### JOHNSON
In Loving Memory of
**RACHEL JOHNSON** nee Nurse Gray
Died 5th October 1937
Like her divine Master she went
about doing good
And her husband
**THOMAS STEWART JOHNSON**
Died 21st January 1957

- *Rachael: 26 Glentilt St. Belfast*

A93

### BROWN
In Loving Memory of
**FREDERICK BROWN**
Died 11th July 1929
And his wife **ISABELLA**
Died 22nd July 1964
Also their daughter
**SARAH IRENE BELL**
Died 6th June 1981

- *Frederick (tailor age 39): 30 Rathcool St.*
  *Belfast*

## A94

- *Buried 1.6.1949* **Mrs. ROSS** *(housewife): Lower Gransha, Islandmagee*

## A95

- *Buried 25.1.1947* **Mrs. L. DAVIES** *(housewife): Portmuck, Islandmagee*

## A96

**ARTHURS**
In
Loving Memory of
My dear husband
**ROBERT THOMAS**
Who died 12th May 1961
Also his beloved wife
**CATHERINE AMELIA**
Who died 12th June 1991
The Lord is my Shepherd

- *Robert (labourer): Millbay, Islandmagee.*
- *Catherine: 35 Ballystrudder Gardens, Islandmagee.*

## A97

- *No date recorded for burial of* **ROBERT HAMILTON:** *10, Forth Parade, Springfield Road, Belfast.*
- *Buried 4.11.1967* **MARION ELIZABETH HAMILTON** *(age 80): Hawthorn House, Carrickfergus*

## A98-A99

**GRAY**
In Loving Remembrance of
**THOMAS NELSON**
Who died 11th October 1963
Also his wife **SARAH JANE**
Who died 3rd April 1977

- *Thomas: Millbay, Islandmagee*
- *Sarah (age 91): 83, Millbay Road, Islandmagee*

## A100-A101

In Loving Memory of
**JOHN NELSON**
Who died 26th August 1945
aged 37 years
Also his wife **NORA**
Died 29th March 1975
Some time we'el understand

- *John (recorded age 38, engineer) and Nora (age 64): Millbay, Islandmagee*

## A102

**THOMPSON**
In Loving Memory of our dear parents
**RICHARD**
died January 1952 aged 54 years
**MARY ELIZABETH**
died July 1971 aged 72 years
(Interred Australia)
their sons
**RICHARD**
died March 1990 aged 67 years
(Interred Manchester)
**WILLIAM DONALD**
died August 1944 aged 2½ years
**JAMES HILL DONALD**
died May 1992 aged 68 years
(Interred Ballywalter, Bangor)

- *William: 41, Canning St. Belfast*

## A103

In Loving Memory of
**MARY McKEEN HILL**
Died 30th September 1979

- *Mary (single, age 89): 59, Edward Road, Whitehead*

## A104

- *Buried 9.4.1948* **Mrs. ABIGAIL GREER FOSTER** *(housewife): Ardrahan Cottage, Bentra, Whitehead*

## A105-A106
In Loving Memory of
**WILLIAM GIBB McCLUSKEY**
Who died 10th September 1946
Also his wife **ELIZABETH**
Who died 14th January 1950

- *Elizabeth: Millbay, Islandmagee*

## A107

- *Buried 15.5.1943*
  ***THOMAS McGLOUGHLIN:***
  *Cloughfin Islandmagee.*
- *Buried 12.6.1975*
  ***Mrs. JAMESINA McGLOUGHLIN***
  *(age 82): Castlerocklands, Carrickfergus*

## A108-A109-A110-A111
In Memory of
**Dr. GEORGE SMITH**
Who died 2nd September 1942
Aged 43 years
And his father
**EDWARD COEY SMITH**
Who died 7th February 1944
Aged 79 years
And his mother
**SARA SMITH**
Who died 13th February 1967
Aged 95 years
**NORMAN HOUSTON SMITH**
Who died 22nd July 1988
**SMITH**

- *George C. Smith*
  *(medical doctor, recorded age 38):*
  *New Road, Donaghadee.*
- *Norman (age 79):*
  *42, Brownsbay Road, Islandmagee*
- *Buried 17.1.2002*
  ***Mrs. NORAH SMITH,*** *(age 84):*
  *4, Willowvale Park, Islandmagee*

## A112-A113
**ENGLISH**
In Loving Memory of
**JOHN A. ENGLISH**
died 19th March 1955
His wife **MARY ANN**
died 13th April 1960
And their son
**ALEXANDER HATRICK**
died 16th July 1971
And his wife **JEANETTE**
died 24th November 1993

- *Alexander (age 65, farmer): Brownsbay, Islandmagee.*
- *Jeanette (age 83): 11, Brownsbay Drive, Islandmagee*

## A114-A115
In Loving Memory of
**MATTHEW McILGORM**
Who died 5th October 1937
aged 88 years
And his nephew **ROBERT**
loved husband of
Maggie M.O. McIlgorm
died 11th Nov. 1964
Aged 75 years
**MARGARET J. McILGORM**
died 1st June 1965
**FLORRIE A. McILGORM**
died 26th July 1975
**CHRISTINA McILGORM**
died 11th February 1977
**MAGGIE M.O.**
wife of Robert died 1st July 1972

- *Matthew (rtd. Master Mariner, age 88): Ballydown, Islandmagee.*
- *Robert (grocer), Margaret J. and Maggie M.O: The Hill, Islandmagee.*
- *Florence Agnes (age 76): 51 Glenvale Park, Glynn*

## A116
**GEORGE EDGAR**
Who died 19th May 1932
And **MARGARET** his wife
Who died 4th February 1944

- *George: 12a Shaftesbury Square, Belfast*

A117-A118
Erected by Thomas Hay
In Loving Memory
of his devoted mother
**SARAH HAY**
Who died on 27th October 1936
aged 86 years

Calm on the bosom of thy God
Fair spirit rest thee now
Even while with us thy footstep trod
His seal was on thy brow

Dust, to it's narrow house beneath
Soul, to it's place on high
They that have seen thy look in death
No more may fear to die

Also his father
**JOHN HAY**
Who was lost at sea on
8th October 1884 aged 42 years
**THOMAS HAY**
Died 13th May 1950 aged 74 years
Because I live ye shall live also
John 14, 19

- *Sarah: 2, Windsor Terrace, Whitehead*

A119-A120
**JACKSON**
**ANDREW ROSS** 1869-1943
**ELIZABETH KERR** 1866-1948
**JANE** 1898-1981

- *Andrew (farmer, buried 2.2.1943):*
  *Portmuck, Islandmagee*
- *Elizabeth (married, buried 10.2.1948):*
  *Portmuck*
- *Jane (single, age 82, buried 23.2.1981):*
  *32 Portmuck Road, Islandmagee*

A121-A122
In Memoriam
**ROBERT AUGUSTUS M. WARREN**
Died 13th January 1947 aged 71 years

A123-A124
In Loving Memory of
**Captain ALEXANDER NIBLOCK O.B.E.**
Who died suddenly 4th January 1947
Also his wife **ROBINA**
Who died 12th April 1964
Absent but not forgotten

- *Last known residence: Montrose,*
  *Islandmagee*

A125-A126
In Loving Memory of
**ELIZABETH ROSS**
Who died 13th August 1946
aged 60 years
Also **CAPTAIN THOMAS ROSS**
Who died 31st October 1952
aged 70 years

- *Mrs. Ross: Iona, Islandmagee*

A127-A128
In loving memory of
**MARY LILLEY**
Who died on the 17th July 1945
Also her son
**WILLIAM FREDERICK LILLEY**
Who died on the 16th Feb. 1951
**MARGARET ISABEL** 1894-1982
**MARY EILEEN** 1897-1991

- *Margaret Isabel Lilley*
  *(age 86, buried 16.4.82):*
  *54 Cable Road, Whitehead.*
- *Mary (single, age 93, buried 20.2.91):*
  *Joymount House, Carrickfergus*

A129-A130
**IRVINE**
In
Loving memory of my dear husband
**JOHN EDWARD**
Died 15th March 1982 aged 79 years
Also our twin sons who died in infancy
**ELLEN JANE** wife of above
Who died 9th January 1995 aged 88 years
At rest

- *Twins Samuel Hill and John Edward,*
  *(buried 22.1.43): Ballyharry, Islandmagee.*
- *John and Ellen (recorded age 87):*
  *1, Mullaghboy Bungalows, Islandmagee*

## A131

- *Buried 14.7.45*
  **Mrs. GEORGINA BUCHANAN:**
  *The Hill, Islandmagee*

## A132-A133

**ENGLISH**
In
Loving Memory of
**SARAH**
Who died 20th May 1963
Beloved wife of
Alexander English
The above **ALEXANDER ENGLISH**
Died 12th Jan. 1983

- *Alexander (age 91):*
  *135a Islandmagee Road, Whitehead*

## A134 unused

## A135 unused

## A136

Erected by
Gilmore Campbell
In memory of his wife **ANNIE M.E.**
Who died 28th Sept. 1943
Also the above
**GILMORE CAMPBELL**
Died 11th May 1968 aged 92 years

- *Annie and Gilmore (recorded age 90):*
  *Erection Villas, Islandmagee*

## A137-A138

In Loving Memory of
My dear wife
**MARGARET STEWART**
Died 17th Sept.1982 aged 81 years
And her husband **NELSON**
Died 24th Dec.1986 aged 83 years
Their daughter **MARGARET SIMMS**
Died 13th Nov.1978
And her beloved husband
**RICHARD GORDON SIMMS**
Died 27th June 1997

- *Margaret and Nelson: 29, Bay Park,*
  *Larne*
- *Buried 29.4.43* **Baby STEWART:**
  *Mullaghdubh, Islandmagee*

## A139

In Loving Memory of
**PATRICK MAGILL**
Who was lost at sea
11th December 1937
And his wife **SARAH MAGILL**
died 6th March 1957

## A140-A141

In Loving Remembrance of
**WILLIAM (BILLY) KERR**
Who died on the 29th July 1946
in his 9th year
Also his father **WILLIAM**
Who died 20th April 1979
aged 89 years
Also his mother **ANNABELLA**
Who died 6th March 1991
aged 87 years

- *Last known residence:*
  *"Ferndene" Islandmagee*

## A142-A143

In Loving Memory
of my dear husband
**ROBERT JOHN HAWTHORNE**
Who passed away 25th Aug. 1940
aged 48 years
During his passage home from Aruba
And was interred in Arlington Cemetry
New Jersey U.S.A.
Also his dear wife **AGNES JANE**
Died 22nd June 1972
Devoted mother of Roy, Mary and Joy

- *Agnes (age 78): Sunnymount,*
  *36 Ballylumford Road, Islandmagee*

## Grave Plots Plan

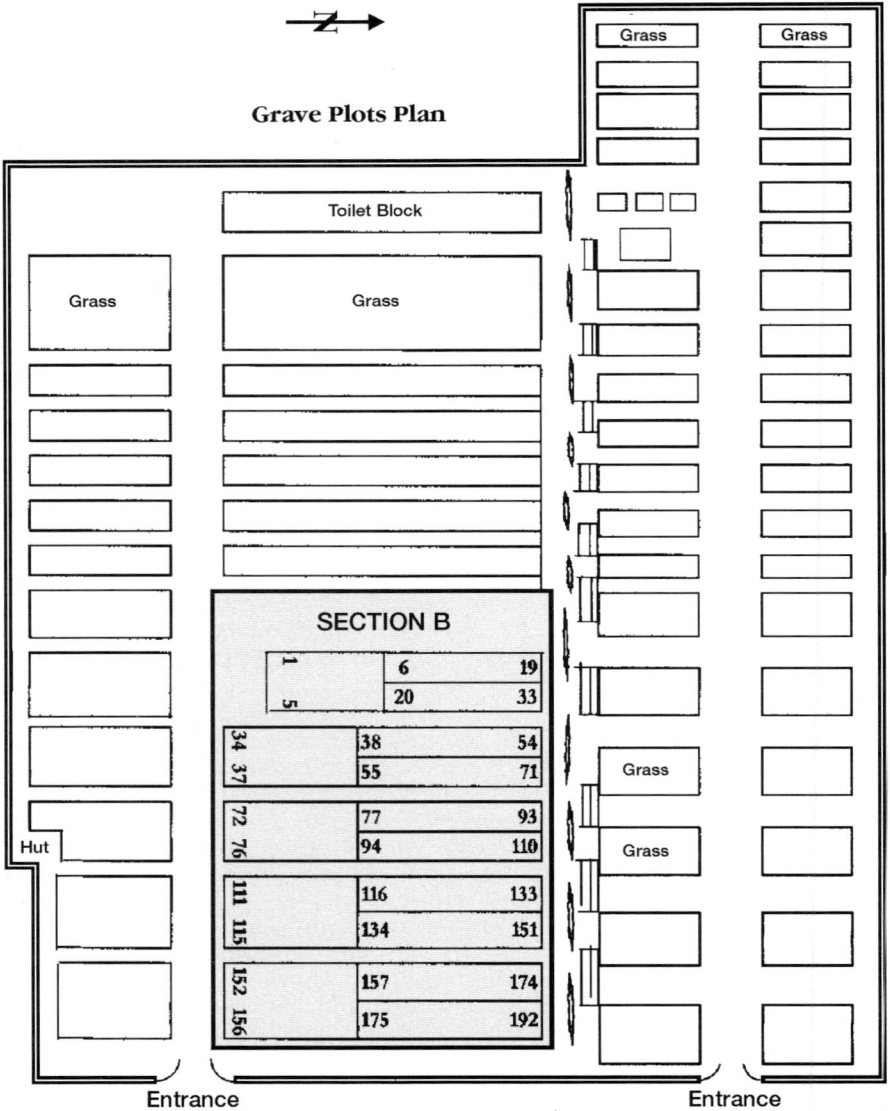

Grass Grass

Toilet Block

Grass

Grass

SECTION B

| 1 | | 6 | 19 |
| 5 | | 20 | 33 |
| 34 | | 38 | 54 |
| 37 | | 55 | 71 |
| 72 | | 77 | 93 |
| 76 | | 94 | 110 |
| 111 | | 116 | 133 |
| 115 | | 134 | 151 |
| 152 | | 157 | 174 |
| 156 | | 175 | 192 |

Grass

Grass

Hut

Entrance

Entrance

## ~ ISLANDMAGEE NEW CEMETERY ~

**Whitehead**

~ LOW ROAD ~

**Ballylumford**

# SECTION B

| Name | Plot | Name | Plot | Name | Plot |
|------|------|------|------|------|------|
| Adamson | 125 | Davies | 84 | Geddes | 131 |
| Adamson | 126 | Davis | 191 | Geddes | 132 |
| Adamson | 173 | Dick | 62 | Gibson | 145 |
| Armour | 179 | Dick | 63 | Gibson | 146 |
| Armour | 180 | Dick | 69 | Gillespie | 33 |
| Arthurs | 4 | Dick | 107 | Gillespie | 49 |
| Arthurs | 5 | Dick | 108 | Gilmore | 152 |
| Arthurs | 98 | Dick | 110 | Graham | 161 |
| Arthurs | 99 | Dick | 116 | Graham | 162 |
| Auld | 34 | Dick | 117 | Grant | 111 |
| Auld | 35 | Dick | 134 | Gray | 15 |
| Barr | 47 | Dick | 135 | Hamilton | 32 |
| Beattie | 188 | Dick | 140 | Hamilton | 31 |
| Birkmyre | 174 | Dick | 141 | Hamilton | 86 |
| Bonugli | 154 | Donald | 92 | Hamilton | 87 |
| Boyd | 127 | Donald | 93 | Harrison | 100 |
| Boyd | 128 | Donaldson | 160 | Harrison | 101 |
| Brennan | 150 | Duff | 73 | Hawthorne | 189 |
| Brennan | 151 | Duff | 74 | Hawthorne | 190 |
| Broomfield | 122 | Duff | 75 | Heddles | 6 |
| Broomfield | 123 | Duff | 76 | Heddles | 7 |
| Browne | 52 | English | 3 | Henderson | 129 |
| Browne | 53 | English | 122 | Henderson | 130 |
| Browne | 55 | English | 123 | Hewitt | 119 |
| Browne | 56 | Farquharson | 13 | Higginson | 189 |
| Burns | 13 | Ferguson | 57 | Higginson | 190 |
| Bury | 10 | Ferguson | 58 | Hill | 111 |
| Busby | 22 | Ferguson | 155 | Hill | 112 |
| Cameron | 83 | Ferguson | 156 | Hood | 164 |
| Campbell | 11 | Ford | 182 | Hunter | 31 |
| Campbell | 12 | Ford | 183 | Hunter | 32 |
| Campbell | 24 | Ford | 184 | Jackson | 100 |
| Carlisle | 44 | Ford | 181 | Jackson | 101 |
| Carlisle | 45 | Forde | 139 | Johnston | 19 |
| Chapman | 166 | Forde | 168 | Johnston | 143 |
| Connor | 191 | Forde | 169 | Johnston | 158 |
| Connor | 192 | Forde | 185 | Johnston | 159 |
| Crawford | 70 | Forde | 186 | Jordan | 28 |
| Crawford | 71 | Frazer | 153 | Kane | 59 |
| Crooks | 136 | Fullerton | 50 | Kane | 60 |
| Cuthbert | 160 | Fullerton | 51 | Kane | 170 |

| Name | Plot | Name | Plot | Name | Plot |
|------|------|------|------|------|------|
| Kane | 171 | McLaughlin | 105 | Rendell | 3 |
| Kane | 172 | McLaughlin | 106 | Robinson | 100 |
| Kirk | 165 | McMaster | 72 | Robinson | 101 |
| Latimer | 38 | McMurran | 133 | Ross | 25 |
| Latimer | 39 | McMurtry | 18 | Ross | 26 |
| Latimer | 40 | McNaught | 174 | Ross | 27 |
| Lattimore | 147 | McNeilly | 96 | Ross | 41 |
| Lattimore | 148 | McNeilly | 97 | Ross | 42 |
| Lindsay | 42 | McNeilly | 122 | Ross | 43 |
| Lowry | 166 | McNeilly | 123 | Ross | 64 |
| Lowry | 167 | Mearns | 77 | Ross | 113 |
| Lynn | 77 | Mearns | 78 | Ross | 114 |
| Lynn | 78 | Mearns | 79 | Rossall | 174 |
| Lynn | 79 | Meneilly | 30 | Smiley | 105 |
| Macauley | 48 | Michelbacher | 14 | Smiley | 106 |
| Malcolm | 8 | Millar | 29 | Smyth | 61 |
| Malcolm | 9 | Monteith | 85 | Smyth | 77 |
| Mann | 29 | Morrow | 161 | Smyth | 78 |
| Mann | 144 | Morrow | 162 | Smyth | 79 |
| Marsh | 147 | Mulholland | 119 | Smyth | 82 |
| Marshall | 176 | Niblock | 16 | Steele | 1 |
| Maxwell | 113 | Niblock | 17 | Steele | 2 |
| Maxwell | 114 | Niblock | 34 | Steen | 105 |
| Maybin | 163 | Niblock | 35 | Steen | 106 |
| McCalmont | 20 | Niblock | 36 | Stewart | 147 |
| McCalmont | 21 | Niblock | 37 | Stewart | 148 |
| McCalmont | 124 | Niblock | 137 | Stewart | 153 |
| McClelland | 47 | Niblock | 138 | Templeton | 94 |
| McConnell | 179 | Nolan | 109 | Templeton | 95 |
| McConnell | 180 | Noteman | 67 | Thompson | 46 |
| McCosh · | 157 | Noteman | 68 | Thompson | 154 |
| McCosh | 175 | Orr | 69 | Thomson | 90 |
| McDowell | 80 | Orr | 88 | Thomson | 91 |
| McDowell | 81 | Orr | 89 | Walker | 119 |
| McGookin | 176 | Orr | 94 | Walker | 120 |
| McIlwain | 65 | Orr | 95 | Watt | 54 |
| McIlwain | 66 | Orr | 103 | Wilson | 23 |
| McIlwaine | 96 | Orr | 104 | Wilson | 102 |
| McIlwaine | 97 | Patton | 50 | Wilson | 177 |
| McKay | 142 | Patton | 51 | Wilson | 178 |
| McKay | 143 | Rankin | 158 | Wright | 122 |
| McKinley | 115 | Rankin | 159 | Wright | 123 |
| McKinstry | 141 | Rendall | 122 | | |
| McKinty | 149 | Rendall | 123 | | |

B1-B2

In loving memory of
**ALEXANDER** loved husband of
Ruby M. Steele
Died 16th April 1969 aged 79 years
**RUBY M. STEELE**
died 20th Nov. 1980 aged 85 years
Loved parents of
Samuel, James and Rene
**SAMUEL ALEXANDER STEELE**
Dearest and loving husband of May
Died 11th October 1994 aged 75 years

- *Alexander (general merchant) and Rubena Margaretta: Brownsbay.*
- *Samuel (recorded age 84): 23 Brownsbay Road, Islandmagee*

B3

In loving memory of
**ANNIE ENGLISH**
Who died 20th May 1945
**JOHN,**
loved husband of Marion Rendell
Died 5th September 1960
His wife **MARION,**
died 4th October 1980

B4-B5

In loving memory of
**ROBERT T. ARTHURS**
Who died 4th October 1925
Aged 65 years
Also his wife **HELEN**
Died 12th December 1959
Aged 96 years
**ARTHURS**
"Thy will be done"

- *Robert Thomas (ship owner): Druids Altar, Islandmagee.*
- *Helen: Strangford Ave. Belfast*

B6-B7

In loving memory of
**DANIEL HEDDLES**
Died 22nd Feb. 1922 aged 66 years
Also his wife **MARGARET**
Died 20th Oct. 1933 aged 77 years
And their son **STEWART**
Died 9th April 1964 aged 64 years
Also his wife **MAUD**
Died 7th Jan. 1986 in her 86th year
**HEDDLES**

- *Margaret (recorded age 78) and Stewart: Craigendoran. Islandmagee.*
- *Maud: 195 Gobbins Road, Islandmagee*

B8-B9

In loving memory of
our darling son
**FRANCIS INGRAM MALCOLM
(FRANK)**
Who died 22nd Nov. 1933
aged 2 years
Also his father **JAMES MALCOLM**
Who died 16th June 1964
And his mother **FRANCES ANNA**
Died 12th December 1989
**MALCOLM**

- *Frank: 2, Victoria Terrace, Whitehead.*
- *Frances (age 84): 31 Ashley Park, Bangor*

B10

**BURY**
In loving memory of
our dear mother
**JANE BRENNAN BURY**
Who died 18th January 1959
Erected by her daughters Mary
Margaret (Peg) and Frances
"Ever remembered"

B11-B12
### CAMPBELL
In loving memory of my dear wife
**MARIANNE CAMPBELL**
Died 25th March 1935 aged 61 years
Also my son **SAMUEL EDGAR**
died 12th March 1915
Interred in Ballyprior aged 4 years
And my son **THOMAS HEGGAN**
died 19th May 1923
And was buried at sea, aged 17 years
And **WILLIAM** husband of the
above Marianne Campbell
Died 25th March 1958 aged 86 years
**MARY AGNES CAMPBELL**
Died 20th April 1984 aged 71 years
Beloved wife of David Campbell

- *Marianne (Mary Ann):*
  *Seamore, Ballymoney Islandmagee.*
- *Mary: 193 Gobbins Road, Islandmagee*

B13
Erected in memory of our beloved Aunt
**MARTHA BURNS**
Died 28th February 1954 aged 89 years
Also her niece
**MARY FARQUHARSON**
Died 4th December 1977
And her husband
**ANDREW FARQUHARSON**
Died 10th September 1977

- *Martha and Mary (age 75):*
  *260, Househillwood Road, Craigbank,*
  *Glasgow*

B14
### MICHELBACHER
In loving memory of
**FREDERICK MICHELBACHER**
Died 28th September 1945
Also his beloved wife **MARGARET**
Died 6th March 1966

- *Frederick William: Balfour Ave.*
  *Whitehead*

B15
### GRAY
I know that my Redeemer liveth
**JOHN GRAY**
17th December 1947
**MARY CARSON GRAY**
11th March 1972

- *John (chemist): 51, Antrim Road Belfast.*
- *Mary (married, age 85, housewife):*
  *585, Oldpark Road, Belfast 14*

B16-B17
In loving memory of
**JAMES NIBLOCK**
Who passed away 18th October 1945
Aged 41 years
Also his wife **FRANCES**
Who passed away 27th March 1989
Aged 77 years

- *James (sailor): Hillcrest Mullaghdubh,*
  *Islandmagee.*
- *Mary Frances: 8, Alexandra Court,*
  *Whitehead*

B18
Erected by
**WILLIAM B. McMURTRY**
In loving memory of
my dear wife
**ANNIE**
Died 18th Nov. 1935 aged 74 years
**McMURTRY**

- *Last known residence: Copeland View,*
  *Islandmagee*

B19
In loving memory of mother
**AGNES JOHNSTON**
Died 2nd Dec. 1931
Also father **JAMES JOHNSTON**
Died 3rd Nov. 1935

- *Agnes: Copeland View, Islandmagee*

B20-B21

1925
## McCALMONT
In loving memory of
**WILLIAM McCALMONT**
Died 17th December 1925 aged 64 years
And his wife **JANE**
died 6th April 1940
And their son **ROBERT**
died 3rd December 1970
And **JEMIMA** wife of the above
**ROBERT**
Died 9th March 1997 aged 95 years
Peace perfect peace

- *William (Master Mariner) and Robert (marine engineer): Ballydown, Islandmagee.*
- *Jemima: 11, Lough Road, Islandmagee*

B22

- *Buried 26.1.26 **WILLIAM JOHN BUSBY** (age 49, mariner): Gransha, Islandmagee*

B23

- *Buried 23.2.26 **THOMAS WILSON** (age 41, Master Mariner): Ballybuttle Millisle*
- *Buried 5.10.77 **AGNES WHITESIDE WILSON** (age 94): Northfield House, Donaghadee*

B24

Erected
In loving memory of
My dear wife
**JENNY CAMPBELL**
Who died 18th April 1926
Aged 58 years
Also **THOMAS H. CAMPBELL**
Who died 11th March 1946
Aged 79 years
And his wife
**CHARLOTTE CAMPBELL**
Who died 4th February 1956
Aged 59 year
**CAMPBELL**

- *Jenny: Mullaghboy, Islandmagee*

B25-B26

In
Loving memory of
**SAMUEL J. ROSS**
Who died 12th May 1926
Aged 20 years
Also his mother
**ELIZA JANE ROSS**
Who died 12th Oct. 1937
Aged 69 years
And his father
**SAMUEL J. ROSS**
Who died 8th Aug. 1948
Aged 80 years
And his sister
**MARGARET**
Died 26th October 1976
Aged 81 years
He giveth his beloved sleep
**ROSS**

- *Samuel James McIlwaine Ross (mariner): Ballydown, Islandmagee.*
- *Margaret: Castle Rocklands, Carrickfergus*
- *Samuel J. (father, Master Mariner)*

B27

In loving memory of
**ELLEN ROSS**
Who died 28th December 1949
Aged 53 years
Also her husband
**THOMAS McCREADY ROSS**
Died 7th Oct. 1971 aged 73 years
**ROSS**

- *Ellen: "Norwyn" Brownsbay, Islandmagee*
- *Thomas, (rtd. Master Mariner): Sunnymount, Islandmagee*

B28

In loving memory of
**ALEXANDER JORDAN**
Who departed this life
On 1st August 1926
Aged 79 years

- *Alexander (printer): Gransha,*
  *Islandmagee*

B29

Erected
by
Elizabeth Millar
In loving memory of
Her husband
**WILLIAM SHAW MILLAR**
Who died 26th Dec. 1926
Aged 60 years
Also their son **WILLIAM SHAW**
Who died at sea
20th Sept. 1919 aged 20 years
the above named
**ELIZABETH MILLAR**
Died January 1943
**MILLAR**

- *William (father, mariner): Gransha,*
  *Islandmagee*
- *Buried 24.8.59* ***Captain JAMES MANN***
  *Master Mariner: Isle House, Islandmagee*

B30

Erected
by
Lizzie and John Meneilly
The above **JOHN MENEILLY**
Died 6th April 1936
Also the above named
**LIZZIE MENEILLY**
Died 17th Feby. 1938

- *John and Elizabeth: Mullaghboy,*
  *Islandmagee*

B31-B32
**HAMILTON**
In loving memory of
**ANNLEE**
Much loved and only daughter of
Andrew and Emmeline G. Hamilton
Who entered the fuller life
16th August 1929
In her 17th year
With Christ which is far better
Phil.1.23

Around the surround:
**EMMELINE GERTRUDE**
Beloved wife of Andrew Hamilton
Died 11th May 1956

**ANDREW HAMILTON, M.M.**
Died 27th December 1957

**EDITH E. HUNTER**
Died 6th December 1936

**HELENA M. HUNTER**
Died 1st April 1940

**JOHN GILLESPIE HAMILTON**
(1912 - 1992)
Twin of Annlee
And husband of Agnes Etta
(1914 - 1989)

- *Anne Greenlees Hamilton (Annlee):*
  *"Rosselle" Whitehead.*
- *Edith E. (recorded as Edith Anna Hunter,*
  *age 62, shopkeeper) and Helena Maud:*
  *Brightside, Balmoral Ave. Whitehead*

B33

In loving memory of
**JOHN C. GILLESPIE**
Who died 6th September 1933
And his wife
**MARY L. GILLESPIE**
Who died 19th March 1940
Erected by John C. Hamilton

- *Mary Louisa: Mount Randal, Whitehead*

B34-B35

1929
In
loving memory
of
**ELEANOR MARGARET AULD
(PEGGY)**
died 25th February 1927
aged 21 years
**AGNES M. NIBLOCK**
Died 11th June 1951
Aged 74 years
**WILLIAM NIBLOCK**
Master Mariner
Died 18th August 1953
Aged 77 years
**Wm. LAURENCE NIBLOCK**
Died 5th Sept. 1990
Aged 78 years
**MARY (MAISE) NIBLOCK**
Died 25th Feb. 1999
Aged 83 years
**NIBLOCK**

- *Peggy (single): Cloughfin, Islandmagee.*
- *Agnes Murray and William: Aldersyde, Island'nagee.*
- *Laurence and Mrs. Maise: 8, Gobbins Path Islandmagee*

B36-B37

**NIBLOCK**
In
Loving remembrance of
My dear husband
**SAMUEL W. NIBLOCK**
Who died 26th July 1928 aged 35 years
Also **MAUD W.** wife of the above
Samuel W. Niblock
Died 23rd June 1956 aged 63 years

- *Samuel William (Mariner): Cloughfin, Islandmagee*

B38-B39-B40

**LATIMER
MARGARET ANN LATIMER**
Died 1st October 1958
**ELIZA LATIMER**
Died 9th April 1939
**HELEN LATIMER**
Died 9th July 1941

B41

In remembrance of
**JOHN A. ROSS**
Entered into rest Jan 2 1940
aged 46 years
And his wife **WINIFRED MARY**
Died Jan 31 1980 aged 88 years
In Gods keeping

- *John (bank official): The Crag, Beach Road, Whitehead*

B42

In remembrance of
**WILLIAM ROSS**
Born 1898 - died 1975
Aged 76 years
And his wife **SARAH (SADIE)**
Died 12th May 1992 aged 91 years
Also their daughter
**JENNY (JEAN) LINDSAY**
Died 17th October 1992
aged 65 years

- *William, buried 26.1.75: 76, West St. Ballycarry.*
- *Sadie: Chester Park Nursing Home, Whitehead.*
- *Mrs. Jean Lindsay (surname): 3, Sunnylands Pass, Carrickfergus*

B43

In affectionate remembrance of
**JAMES ROSS**
Who gave his life for his country
28th July 1940
and his wife
**AGNES ISOBEL**
Died 10th August 1969

- *James (sailor) and Agnes: Bentra, Whitehead*

**B44-B45**
In loving memory of
**JAMES CARLISLE**
Died 9th September 1946
Also his wife **MARGARET**
died 1st January 1948
Also their son
**HERBERT STEVENSON CARLISLE**
Died 31st August 1987 aged 76 years
Also his wife **DAPHNE**
Died 2nd March 1992 aged 72 years

- *Margaret B. Carlisle: Cable Rd. Whitehead.*
- *Herbert: 7, Donegal Park, Whitehead.*
- *Daphne Breadon Carlisle: Park Manor Private Nursing Home, Ballycastle*

**B46**

**THOMPSON**
In loving memory of
**DAVID**
Dearly loved husband of Bertha
Died 22nd June 1993
Infant daughter **SARAH GLENYS**
Died 8th September 1946
Baby son **JOHN ROSS**
died 28th November 1962

- *David (age 77): 26, Island Rd. Ballycarry.*
- *Sarah: Mullaghdubh, Islandmagee*

**B47**

**McCLELLAND**
In loving memory of
My dear parents
**THOMAS**
Died 29th December 1949
**ELIZABETH**
Died 19th November 1950
Also my dear husband
**JAMES C. BARR**
Died 20th January 1985
Till the day dawns

- *Thomas (engine driver, date of burial recorded as 1950) and Lizzie: The Hill, Islandmagee.*
- *James Campbell Barr (age 74): 25, Sheringhurst Park, Belfast.*
- *Buried 23.6.99 **Mrs. ELIZABETH BARR** (age 88): Chester Park Nursing Home, Whitehead*

**B48**

**MACAULAY**
In loving memory of
**ROBERT**
Died 1st November 1987
Beloved husband of Sarah (Cis)
Also their infant twin daughter
**SARAH ELIZABETH**
Died 19th October 1942
Also the above named
**SARAH (CIS)**
Died 20th May 1996

- *Robert (age 77): 10a, Kilton Lane, Islandmagee.*
- *Cis (age 83): Spa Nursing Home, Ballynahinch.*
- *Buried 7.6.43 **Baby MACAULAY**: 5, Derg Villas, Strabane*

**B49**

**GILLESPIE**
In memory of
**ELIZABETH**
Dearly loved wife of Robert
Died 26th November 1993
Also the above named **ROBERT**
A much loved husband and father
Died 21st December 1994

- *Elizabeth (age 79, Presbyterian) and Robert (age 92): Chalet 15, Castlerocklands, 22, Belfast Rd. Carrickfergus*

**B50-B51**

**FULLERTON**
To the fond memory of my husband
**JOHN FULLERTON**
Kilcoan, Islandmagee
Who died 15th May 1946 aged 85 years
**HENRIETTA SHAW**
beloved wife of above
Who died 16th June 1967 aged 96 years
**EDWARD PATTON B.Agr.**
dear husband
Of Mary and son-in-law of above
Died 24th March 1977 aged 71 years

- *John, farmer*

B52-B53

In loving memory of
**CHARLOTTE BROWNE**
Who died 6th April 1941 aged 52 years
**Captain SAMUEL BROWNE O.B.E.**
Born 18th January 1885
Passed away 30th December 1951
And their youngest son
**GORDON E. BROWNE L.T.C.L.**
Died 10th February 1967 aged 34 years

- *Charlotte (married), Samuel (Master Mariner) and Gordon (recorded age 33, music teacher): Elmdene, Cable Rd. Whitehead*

B54

In remembrance of
**JAMES WATT**
Who died 23rd April 1945
Aged 73 years
Also his wife
**MARY ISOBEL**
Who died 20th April 1955

- *James (carpenter): Sunnybank, Ballydown, Islandmagee*

B55-B56

**BROWNE**
In
Loving memory of
A devoted husband and father
**JAMES WILSON BROWNE**
Who died 16th July 1957
Also his father **WILLIAM BROWNE**
Who died 21st February 1932
Also his mother **SARA BROWNE**
Who died 21st November 1944

- *William McKee Browne (age 69, farmer): Ballystrudder, Islandmagee.*
- *Buried 24.6.79 **Mrs. ISABELLA BROWNE** (age 71)*
- *Buried 29.8.99 **DAVID WILSON BROWNE** (age 52, farmer): 1, Lough Drive, Islandmagee*

B57-B58

Erected
By
Daniel Ferguson
In loving memory of his wife
**JANIE CALDWELL**
Who died 24th March 1927
The above named
**DANIEL FERGUSON**
Died 6th May 1961
Also his daughter
**ROSE (ROLLIE)**
Died 21st August 1945

- *Janie Caldwell Ferguson (age 47): 8, Golf Terrace, Portrush.*
- *Daniel (rtd. Stationmaster): 42, Hopefield Ave. Belfast*

B59-B60

**KANE**
In memory of
Our only and dearly beloved son
**JOHN FREDERICK**
Who died 14th August 1927
Aged 23 years
And his father **JOHN KANE**
Who died 1st June 1960 aged 84 years
And his mother
**JANE CAMPBELL KANE**
Who died 14th April 1963
Until the day dawn

- *John Frederick (mariner) and John (mariner): Millbay, Islandmagee*

B61

**SMYTH**
In loving memory of
**Capt. DAVID**
(Master Mariner)
Died 1st August 1983
And his wife **ANNIE JANE**
Died 27th December 1988

- *David (age 84): 7, Downshire Gdns. Carrickfergus.*
- *Annie (age 91): 2, Downshire Gdns. Carrickfergus*

**B62-B63**
### DICK
In loving memory
of
**WILLIAM DICK**
Who died 22nd October 1927
And his wife **MARY ELIZABETH**
Who died 20th December 1927
**DENNIS MAGILL DICK**
Who died 3rd May 1941
**MARY (MOLLIE) DICK**
Died 9th January 1962
**WILLIAM DICK**
died 15th March 1980
**MATILDA DICK**
died 24th October 1995

- *William (age 63, shipwright) and Mollie (married): 27, Newington Ave. Belfast.*
- *The second William (age 81): 2, Shanlieve Pk. Belfast*
- *Mrs. Matilda Dick (age 72): Abbeyfield, Portstewart*

**B64**
### ROSS
Erected in memory of
**MARY ROSS**
Who died 8th July 1928
Also her sister **MINA ROSS**
Who died 22nd July 1934

- *Mary (age 49, single): Cloughfin, Islandmagee*

**B65-B66**
### McILWAIN
In loving memory of **JOHN**
Beloved husband of Isabella McIlwain
Who died 16th January 1929
aged 53 years
Also their beloved son **ISAAC**
Who died 4th July 1929 aged 21 years
The above named
**ISABELLA McILWAIN**
Died 8th June 1940 aged 59 years
Also their son **WILLIAM McILWAIN**
Drowned at Bowling Harbour
11th January 1942 aged 37 years
At rest with Jesus

- *John (mariner): Ballydown, Islandmagee.*
- *Buried 31.1.93 **Mrs. MARY McILWAIN** (wife of William, age 82): 28, Millbay Rd. Islandmagee*

**B67-B68**
### NOTEMAN
In loving memory of **WILLIAM**
Died 24th Feb. 1930
His wife **ISABELLA**
Died 11th June 1932
Also their son **WILLIAM**
Died 29th October 1975
And his wife **MARGARETTA**
Died 28th August 1988

- *William (age 73, farmer) and son William (age 91): Ballyharry, Islandmagee.*
- *Isabella: Ballygowan, Islandmagee.*
- *Margaretta (age 87): 125, Low Rd. Islandmagee*

B69

**ORR**
In fond memory of
**JOHN ORR**
Who died 8th April 1960 aged 85 years
**MARY ORR** (nee **DICK**)
Died 28th Nov. 1966 aged 86 years
**SARAH ORR**
Died 20th August 1998 aged 93 years
Peace perfect peace

- *Mary: 16, Cheviot Ave. Belfast.*
- *Sarah Jane Orr (single): Lisburn Nursing Home*

B70-B71

In remembrance of
**JOHN CRAWFORD**
Who died 15th September 1949
Also his son **WILLIAM** who died
21st March 1929
Also his wife **ESTHER** who died
13th March 1970

- *John (farmer), William (age 7) and Esther (age 82): Ballycronanmore, Islandmagee.*
- *Buried 12.6.89*
  ***MISS ELIZABETH CRAWFORD** (age 74): 22, Ballystrudder Gdns. Islandmagee*

B72

On surround
**CLARA A.A. McMASTER**
died 7th July 1956
**JAMES JOSEPH**
died 19th June 1955

B73-B74

**DUFF**
Erected by Samuel Duff
In memory of his beloved wife
**ISABELLA DUFF**
Who died 14th November 1946
The above **SAMUEL DUFF**
died 24th December 1966

- *Samuel (age 83): 8, Cable Rd. Whitehead.*
- *Isabella (housewife): Whitehead*

B75-B76

**DUFF**
Erected in memory of
Our father and mother
**JOHN AULD DUFF**
born 1830 died 1932
**ELEANOR STEELE DUFF**
born 1884 died 1937
And our brother
**DAVID WILSON DUFF**
Born 1927 died 1937
**JOHN MURRAY DUFF**
born 1918 died 1941
**KATHLEEN DUFF**
born 1915 died 1942
**MARGARET BROWNE DUFF**
born 1914 died 1946

- *John Auld (grocer, buried 1.4.1932): 2, Causeway Villas, Ballycarry*
- *Eleanor (buried 13.11.1937): 171, University Street, Belfast*
- *Margaret (Housekeeper, buried 10.12.1946): 1. St. Judes Ave, Ormeau Road, Belfast*

B77-B78-B79
In loving memory of
**JANE SMYTH**
Who died 28th August 1937
Also her husband
**ROBERT JOHN SMYTH**
Who died 18th April 1940
Also their daughter
**ELIZABETH ELLEN**
who died in infancy
**RAYMOND LYNN**
died 31st July 1982
**SMYTH**

On surround
In loving memory of
**THOMAS HENRY MEARNS**
died 13th January 1975
And his wife
**JEAN GRAY MEARNS**
died 22nd September 1975

In loving memory of
**ROBENA LYNN** died 28 Sept. 1961
And her husband **JAMES EDWARD**
Died 16th February 1970

- *Jane Smyth (age 56) and Mrs. Robena Lynn: Portmuck, Islandmagee*
- *Edward Raymond Carson Lynn (age 47, buyer): 39, Wedderburn Av., Finaghy*
- *James Edward Lynn (age74): 55, Graymount Crescent, Belfast*
- *Thomas (age 70, Presbyterian, ret. machinest) and Jean (Jane) (age 73, Presbyterian, housewife): Minnowburn House, Milltown Road, Belfast*

B80-B81
**McDOWELL**
In loving memory of
**WILLIAM** died 16th April 1985
Beloved husband of Ruby
Who died 24th December 1999
Also his son **WILLIAM CLIVE**
Died 22nd April 1940 aged 3½ years
And his mother **MARY**
Died 25th November 1975 aged 92 years
The Lord is my shepherd

- *William (age 75): 143, Islandmagee Road, Whitehead*
- *Ruby (age 87): Ravenhill Nursing Home, Carrickfergus*
- *William Clive and Mary (recorded age 91): 5, Alexandra Ave, Whitehead*

B82
**SMYTH**
In loving memory of
A devoted husband and father
**HERBERT SMYTH**
Died 11th April 1980
Also a devoted wife and mother
**MARTHA SMYTH**
Died 3rd June 1988

- *Herbert (age 71, Presbyterian): 17, Lumfiord Ave, Whitehead*
- *Martha (age 81, Presbyterian): Holywell Hospital*

B83
**CAMERON**
In loving memory of
A devoted husband and father
**WILLIAM CAMERON,** Master Mariner
Died 19th April 1972
Also a devoted wife and mother
**MATILDA CAMERON**
Died 13th July 1982

- *William (age 71) and Matilda (age 80): 111, Islandmagee Road, Whitehead*
- *Buried 23.6.1936*
  ***WILLIAM LAURENCE CAMERON**
  (infant): "Wilyth" Doagh*

B84

## DAVIES
**ERNEST EDWARD**
died 28th August 1943
**JANE SHANKS**
died 10th March 1967

- *Ernest: Wilmont, Ballystrudder, Islandmagee*
- *Mrs. Jane Shanks Davies (age 89): Clanferran, Ballystrudder, Islandmagee*

B85

- *Buried 1.1.1945* ***JOHN MONTEITH:*** *Egremont, Cable Road, Whitehead*
- *Buried 28.2.1969* ***Mrs. KATHLEEN MONTEITH:*** *1, Barnhill Terr., Curran Road, Larne*

B86-B87

## HAMILTON
**ROBERT HAROLD (ROY)**
Beloved son of George and Agnes
Died 11th July 1946 aged 9 weeks
**STEPHEN ROBERT**
Beloved son of Robert and Sandra
Died 2nd June 1978 aged 1 year
**GEORGE FERGUSON,**
Master Mariner
Devoted husband and father
Died 30th January 1998 aged 86 years

- *Roy: Prospect House, Kilcoan, Islandmagee*
- *George Ferguson Hamilton: Ben Madigan Nursing Home, Whiteabbey*

B88-B89

In loving memory of
**HUGH ORR**
Who died 16th November 1945
Also his mother **MARGARET**
Who died 25th April 1951
And his father **EPHRAIM**
Who died 4th June 1956
His sister **ELEANOR**
Who died 30th December 1988
His sister **MARY**
Who died 24th February 1994
**ORR**

- *Hugh (sailor): Upper Gransha, Islandmagee*
- *Eleanor (single, age 89): 14A Ransevyn Park, Whitehead*
- *Mary (single, age 91): Ravenhill Private Nursing Home, Greenisland*

B90-B91

In loving memory of
**JOSEPH HENRY**
Beloved husband of
Ellen Thomson
Called home 7th Dec. 1947
The above **ELLEN THOMSON**
Called home 14th Jan. 1968
**THOMSON**

- *Joseph Henry Thomson: Cartref, Cable Road, Whitehead*
- *Ellen (age 91): 21 Promenade, Whitehead*
- *Flower holder – To father from Nan, Malcolm and Nora*

B92-B93
## DONALD
In loving memory of my dear husband
**JAMES TEMPLETON DONALD**
Died 24th March 1956
Also our dear sons
**IVAN** died in infancy 9th March 1948
**JAMES LESLIE**
died as the result of an accident
2nd April 1970 aged 24 years
Devoted wife and mother
**KATHLEEN McCLELLAND DONALD**
died 13th July 2001

- *Ivan: Portmuck, Islandmagee*
- *James Leslie (merchant navy officer): Hylands, Portmuck, Islandmagee*
- *Mrs. Kathleen McClelland Donald (age 94): 34 Portmuck Road, Islandmagee*

B94-B95
In loving memory of
Our dear son **HILL**
Who died the result of an accident
on the 9th February 1930
also my dear husband
**JAMES TEMPLETON**
died 28th May 1951
also his wife **JANE**
died 18th Sept. 1960
and their son **THOMAS**
(Master Mariner)
died 10th February 1969
**HUGH DOUGLAS ORR**
Died 16th September 1979
And his wife **MINNIE**
died 11th May 1988
## TEMPLETON

- *William Hill Templeton (age 17): Ashvale, Mullaghboy, Islandmagee*
- *Thomas Templeton (age 62) and Hugh Orr (age 79): Arran, Mullaghboy*
- *Minnie Orr (age 84): 11, Brownsbay Drive, Islandmagee*

B96-B97
## McILWAINE
In fond and loving memory of
**MARY PURDY**
Beloved wife of Andrew McIlwaine
Who died 27th October 1930
Aged 49 years
Also my dearly loved father
The above **ANDREW McILWAINE**
Who died 15th Feb. 1956 aged 81 years
Also their daughter **KATHLEEN**
Who died 8th Sept. 1982 aged 78 years
Also their grandson
**FRANCIS McILWAINE McNEILLY**
Died 22nd July 1984 aged 51 years
Loves last gift remembrance

Flower holder
In memory of
our Mum and Brother

- *Mary: Ferndene, Islandmagee*
- *Francis (single): 42 Laharna Avenue, Larne*

B98-B99
In loving memory of
**SAMUEL JOHN ARTHURS**
Died 3rd August 1936 aged 80 years
## ARTHURS

- *Samuel (Captain): St. Johns, Islandmagee*
- *Buried 3.12.1952*
  **Mrs. ELIZABETH ARTHURS:**
  *St. Johns Islandmagee*

B100-B101

In loving memory of
**THOMAS TWEED JACKSON**
Who died on the 18th March 1931
And his wife **SARAH JANE**
Who died on the 3rd June 1967
And their son
**THOMAS TWEED JACKSON**
Who died on the 10th Sept. 1985
And their daughter
**MARTHA ROBINSON**
Who died on the 30th September 1995

- *Thomas (publican) and Sarah (age 90): Millbay, Islandmagee*
- *Son Thomas (age 65) and Martha (age 83, married, Robinson is surname): 77 Lynn Road, Larne*
- *Buried 11.10.2000*
  ***Mrs. NELLIE HILL HARRISON** (nee JACKSON, age 83, housewife): 6, Loughview Bungalows, Islandmagee*

B102

- *Buried 19.1.1932*
  ***Captain JOHN WILSON** (age 71, Master Mariner): Ailsa View, Ballyharry, Islandmagee*

B103-B104

In loving memory of
**Rev. SAMUEL HENRY ORR**
Who died at Whitehead
21st July 1933
also his wife **MARY ALBIN**
who died 25th August 1936
and their son **FREDERICK WILLIAM**
who died 24th July 1954
Thy will be done

- *Rev. Orr (age 80, Church of Ireland), Mary (age 83) and Frederick: 2 Eastbourne Villas, Whitehead*

B105-B106

In loving memory of
**DAVID STEEN**
Born December 26th 1851
Died November 21st 1931
For 54 years minister of
First Presbyterian Church
Islandmagee
And his wife
**MATILDA WILSON**
Who died 15th August 1949
And their daughter
**AMY ELIZABETH SMILEY**
Who died 14th November 1950
Also their son
**THOMAS WILSON RENNIE STEEN**
Who died 7th March 1975
And son-in-law
**ERNEST McLAUGHLIN**
Who died 8th March 1983
Also his wife
**MARGARET TEGLA**
Died 12th September 1986
He giveth His beloved sleep
**STEEN**

- *Matilda and Amy: Cable Road, Whitehead*
- *Thomas (age 71, farmer): Erection House, Islandmagee*
- *Ernest (age 82, bank manager) and Margaret (age 85): 165 Ravenhill Road, Belfast*

B107-B108
In memoriam
Sacred to the memory of
**AGNES**
Beloved wife of Captain John Dick
Who entered into eternal rest
23rd January 1931 aged 53 years
also their beloved daughter
**EILEEN**
Who died 21st May 1907 aged 1½ years
Also the above
**Captain JOHN DICK**
Who entered into rest
14th December 1959
His son
**Commodore WILLIAM DICK**
Died 24th March 1983
"Oh for the touch of a vanished hand
and the sound of a voice that is still"
also his beloved wife **ISABELLA**
died 29th June 1986
a devoted mother

- *Agnes Heddles Dick: 1, Causeway Villas, Ballycarry Station*
- *Captain Dick (age 82): 27 Ophir Gardens, Belfast*
- *Commodore Dick (age 79): 13 Lestannon Ave. Whitehead*
- *Isabella (age 74)*

B109
In loving memory of
**KATE ELLEN NOLAN**
Died 2nd July 1932

- *Mrs. Nolan (age 71): Ardmore, Balfour Ave. Whitehead*

B110
Erected by Robert Dick
In loving memory of his wife
**CATHERINE DICK**
Who died 23rd October 1949
The above **ROBERT DICK**
Who died 18th October 1955

- *Catherine (housewife): Ballylumford, Islandmagee*

B111
In loving memory of
**THOMAS HILL**
Died 20th April 1956 aged 72 years
Also his son **THOMAS**
Died 19th January 1931 aged 23 years
And his wife **SARAH**
Died 9th August 1959 aged 75 years
And their daughter **LILY GRANT**
Died 4th August 1978 aged 67 years

- *Thomas: Kilcoan Cottage, Islandmagee*
- *Lily is Eliza Mary (housewife): 5, Reids Road, Islandmagee*

B112
**HILL**
In loving memory of
A dear husband and father
**SAMUEL**
Died 6th June 1976
Also infant son **ROBERT JAMES**
Died 12th January 1953
A dear wife and mother
**MARY JANE (MAISIE)**
Died 10th April 1979

- *Samuel (age 63, timber worker) and Maisie (age 62): 8, Ballystrudder Gardens, Islandmagee*

B113-B114
**ROSS**
In loving memory of
**JAMES** (Master Mariner)
Died 3rd May 1955
Also his wife **JANE**
Died 20th September 1970
And their daughter
**SARAH ELIZABETH MAXWELL**
Died 20th September 1932

- *Jane (age 84, housewife): 13B Islandmagee Road, Whitehead*
- *Sarah Elizabeth Smyth Maxwell (surname, age 21): Clanchatten St. Belfast*

B115

In loving memory of
**ELEANOR MARTHA (ELLIE)**
Who died 13th June 1932
Peace perfect peace
**McKINLEY**

- *Ellie (age 40, Manageress of Towel
  company): Upper Gransha, Islandmagee*

B116-B117

In loving memory of
**MARY AMELIA**
beloved wife of F.C. DICK
Died 16th September 1946
Also **FRANCIS CHALMERS DICK**
(Master Mariner)
Died 30th July 1960
Their son **WILLIAM FRANCIS**
Died 4th November 1985
And his loving wife
**MARY JANE (MOLLIE)**
Died 2nd October 1990
**DICK**

- *Mary: Ballymoney House, Islandmagee*
- *William (age 72) and Mollie (age 66):
  30 Mullaghboy Road, Islandmagee*

B118

- *Fallen grey headstone with surround and
  flower container **McCANDLESS***

B119

- *Buried 20.11.1961 **Mrs. M. WALKER**:
  22 Adelaide Ave. Whitehead*
- *Buried 1.1.1985 **WILLIAM JAMES HEWITT**
  (age 65): 29 Rawbrae Road, Whitehead*
- *Buried 7.9.1991
  **Mrs. MARY ELIZABETH MULHOLLAND**
  (age 40): 30 Ransevyn Park, Whitehead*

B120

- *Buried 25.2.1945 **THOMAS WALKER**:
  St. Elmo, York Ave. Whitehead*

B121 unused

B122-B123

Erected by Margaret Wright
In memory of her beloved son
**ANDREW McN. WRIGHT,**
Master Mariner
Who lost his life by enemy action
In France 8th March 1945
Her beloved daughter **STELLA**
died 29th Aug. 1943
And her beloved husband
**JAMES WRIGHT**
Who died 21st July 1945
The above named
**MARGARET WRIGHT**
Died 10th June 1953
Loves last gift remembrance

On surround
In loving memory of two dearly
loved parents and grandparents
**STEWART** and **TILLIE McNEILLY**
died 3-5-1989 and 10-1-1996
Forever in our thoughts

- *Mrs. Stella Broomfield (age 19) and James:
  Whitehouse, Kilcoan, Islandmagee*
- *Margaret: Middle Road, Islandmagee*
- *Stewart: 41 Windsor Ave. Whitehead*
- *Tillie; Joymount House Carrickfergus*
- *Buried (circa 1940's)
  **Miss ANNIE ENGLISH**: Greenmount,
  Ballydown, Islandmagee*
- *Buried 7.10.1980
  **Mrs. MARION RENDALL** (age 81):
  26 Ballylumford Road, Islandmagee*

B124

**McCALMONT**
In loving memory of
**JOHN McCALMONT,** Master Mariner
Died 1st Jany. 1943 aged 34 years
Safe in the arms of Jesus

- *Last known residence: Riverside,
  Cloughfin, Islandmagee*

## B125-B126

**ADAMSON**
On surround
**FLORENCE EVELYN ADAMSON**
B. 31st December 1876 D. 1st May 1947
**THOMAS SHANNON ADAMSON**
B. 1st Sept. 1876 D. 24th Dec.1942
**GEORGE ORR ADAMSON**
B. 23rd June 1911 D. 6th July 1951

- *Thomas (death recorded as 1943): Rathmoyle, Cable Road, Whitehead*

## B127-B128

In memory of
**ROBERT DAVID BOYD**
Born 5th December 1929
Died 8th March 1935
And his father
**WILLIAM HOUSTON BOYD**
Died 28th June 1962
Also his mother
**HANNAH BOYD**
Died 10th September 1994

- *Robert: 481 Holloway Road, London N19*
- *William (age 80, Doctor): 36 Malone Hill Park Belfast*
- *Hanna Rosana (age 96): 16 Rosepark, Belfast*

## B129-B130

**HENDERSON**
In loving memory of
A devoted husband and father
**JOHN** (Master Mariner)
Died 8th October 1946

- *Last known residence: 4, Cardigan Drive, Belfast*
- *Buried 8.10.2002 **JOHN HENDERSON** (age 66, Sea Captain): 1, Island Village, Islandmagee*

## B131-B132

- *Buried 1.12.1947*
  ***FREDERICK T. GEDDES:***
  *The Crag, Beach Road, Whitehead*
- *Buried 10.1.1967*
  ***Mrs. SARAH NEVIN GEDDES** (age 76): same address*
- *Buried 22.10.1970*
  ***FREDERICK DERMOT GEDDES** (age 56, wages clerk): same address*

## B133

- *Buried 12.11.1949*
  ***GEORGE McMURRAN:***
  *Railway Cottages Whitehead*
- *Buried 2.1.1960*
  ***Miss ELIZABETH McMURRAN:** same address*

## B134-B135

**DICK**
In loving memory of
**CHARLES**
Died 2nd April 1977
**WINIFRED**
Died 10th June 1988

- *Charles (retired harbour pilot) and wife Winifred: 81, Merville Garden Village, Whitehouse*
- *Buried 9.5.1932 **HUGH DICK** (age 79, school attendance officer): Ballymoney House, Islandmagee*
- *Buried (no date)*
  ***PRISCILLA AUGUSTA DICK:** same address*

## B136

In loving memory of
**WILLIAM CROOKS**
Who died 2nd January 1933
And his wife **MINNIE CROOKS**
Died 16th February 1965

- *William (age 61, landstewart): Castle Chester, Whitehead*

B137-B138

In loving memory of
**ROBERT FERRIS NIBLOCK**
Who died 4th May 1934 aged 22 years
Also his mother **MARTHA NIBLOCK**
Who died 24th January 1939
aged 69 years
And his father **JOHN NIBLOCK,**
Master Mariner
Who died 19th October 1941
aged 78 years
Also their son
**ALEXANDER NIBLOCK**
**Lt. Comdr. R.N.R.**
Who died 5th October 1996
aged 89 years

- *Robert (mariner), Martha and John:*
  *St. Michaels, Ballylumford, Islandmagee*
- *Alexander: 3, Quarterland Road,*
  *Islandmagee*

B139

- *Buried 9.12.1934* ***STEWART FORDE***
  *(mariner): c.o Mrs. McAuley, Thornhill,*
  *Islandmagee*

B140

- *Buried 6.3.1932 (date on B141 is 1937)*
  ***ROSINA ALEXANDRIA DICK*** *(married):*
  *Ferndene, Islandmagee*

B141

In loving memory of
**JOHN McKINSTRY**
Who died 23rd October 1949
Also his wife **MARY E.** died 8th
February 1954
And her sister **ROSINA A. DICK**
died 4th March 1937

B142

In memory of
A loving mother and father
**JANE LEWIS McKAY**
Died 1st September 1949 aged 55 years
**ARTHUR HILL McKAY**
Died 4th March 1957 aged 71 years

- *Jane and Arthur (carpenter):*
  *Carnspindle, Islandmagee*

B143

In loving memory of
**Capt. ANDREW McKAY**
Lost at sea 27th May 1940
And his wife **MARY JOHNSTON**
died 4th march 1961
Also their son **CHARLES**
died 5th December 1989

- *Andrew: Gransha, Islandmagee*
- *Charles (age 61): 96, Low Road,*
  *Islandmagee*

B144

In loving memory of
**WILLIAM** beloved husband of
**Hannah MANN**
Who died 7th October 1934
aged 51 years
The above named **HANNAH**
beloved wife and mother
Died 19th March 1974
aged 90 years

- *William (recorded age 53, farmer):*
  *Sunnyside, Ballygrainey, Co. Down*

B145-B146

In
Loving memory of
**WILLIAM ERNEST**
Second son of
William and Sarah Gibson
Died 23rd September 1936
**WILLIAM GIBSON,**
Master Mariner, M.B.E.
Died 25th March 1960
Also his wife **SARAH**
Died 26th January 1961
At rest
**GIBSON**

- *William Ernest (age 29, sailor):*
  *Stratton, Glenkeen Ave. Jordanstown*

**B147-B148**
Erected by
**John Marsh STEWART O.B.E.**
In memory of his parents
**WILLIAM**
7th August 1883 - 9th March 1941
interred here
**ELIZABETH  LATTIMORE**
(nee **Marsh**)
8th July 1887 - 15th April 1982
interred in Glynn

- *William (age 57, mill manager):*
  *Ivy Lodge, Mill Road, Whitehouse*

**B149**
In loving memory of
**EVELYN**
Died 4th March 1959
wife of **JAMES McKINTY**
And **MARGARET McKINTY**
A devoted mother
Died 12th September 1968
Also **JAMES**
husband of Evelyn
Died 18th January 1983

- *Evelyn (housewife): Boghall, Islandmagee*
- *Margaret (age 86, housewife):*
  *11 Chichester Gardens, Whitehead*
- *James (age 78): Whitehead*

**B150-B151**
In loving memory of
**ROBERT BRENNAN**
Who died 1st March 1943
aged 63 years
And his wife **ANNIE ELIZABETH**
Died 13th July 1965 aged 83 years
Their son **ROBERT**
Died 20th July 1988
Beloved husband of Isobel
**BRENNAN**

- *Robert (farmer): Bentra, Ballycarry*
- *Son Robert (age 68): 8, Brooklands Drive,*
  *Whitehead*

**B152**
In memory of
**ELSIE**
The beloved wife of
The **Rev. Samuel Gilmore**
Who died 8th February 1933
Also his 2nd wife **JESSIE ELIZ.**
Died 18-1-98
In Thy light shall we see light
**GILMORE**

- *Elsie (age 35): Benmore, Islandmagee*
- *Jessie (age 90): 15A Chester Ave.*
  *Whitehead*

**B153**
Here lies the body of
**ISABEL**
Beloved wife of
The **Rev. W.F.S. STEWART**
Died 22nd Jan. 1945
And her parents
**WILLIAM AND HELEN FRAZER**

- *Isabel: The Manse, Whitehead*
- *Helen buried 15.2.1963*

**B154**
**STAFFORD THOMPSON**
Who died on the 15th July 1942
His wife **SUSAN MAUDE**
Died 20th Sept. 1968
**HELEN BONUGLI** 1918 - 1993
**GIUSEPPE BONUGLI**
Born 8th April 1915 -
died 5th Aug. 1996

- *Stafford M. Thompson (engineer, death*
  *recorded as 1943): Ivanhoe, Edward Road,*
  *Whitehead*
- *Susan (age 73): The Beeches, Ballyclare*
- *Buried 3.2.1993 Helen (age 74):*
  *10, Chelmsford Place, Larne*
- *Giuseppe (age 81): 10, Chelmsford Place,*
  *Larne*

B155-B156

In loving memory of
**WILLIAM SMYTH**
Second son of
James and Martha Ferguson
Lost at sea by enemy action
2nd March 1941
Aged 19 years
His father **JAMES FERGUSON**
died 26th July 1958
**THOMAS A. D. FERGUSON**
Son of James and Martha Ferguson
Died 20th June 1976 aged 51 years
Beloved husband of Elizabeth Martin
**MARTHA FERGUSON**
died in Canada
26th Sept. 1983 aged 84 years
Loves last gift - Remembrance

On second stone
Foster–son of James and Martha
**A.F. JAMES (FRANK)**
Master Mariner died 17th Oct. 1997.

- *Arthur Francis James Ferguson (age 77):*
  *13, Islandmagee Road, Whitehead*

B157

- *Buried 6.12.1940* **Infant McCOSH:**
  *Ballymuldrough, Islandmagee*

- *Buried 4.8.1985*
  **Mrs. ELIZABETH McCOSH, (ZABETH)**
  *(age 73): 3, Malone Ave. Whitehead*

- *Buried 15.1.1990* **CECIL McCOSH,**
  *(age 86): 80 Low Road, Islandmagee*

B158-B159

In loving memory of
**JAMES RANKIN, M.N.**
Died 7th December 1944 aged 61 years
Also his beloved wife
**MARY AGNES** (nee **SMYTH**)
Died 24th March 1985 aged 91 years
Their son-in-law
**JAMES OSBORNE JOHNSTON**
Died 1st March 1995 aged 86 years
And his loving wife
**JESSIE AUDREY SMYTH**
Died 12th May 1995 aged 79 years

- *James Rankin (ships steward):*
  *2, Balmoral Ave. Whitehead*

- *Mary: Moyle Hospital*

- *James Johnston and Jessie:*
  *7, Craigyhill Bungalows, Larne*

B160

**DONALDSON**
In loving memory
**ALEXANDER** 1881-1946
**JANE** 1892-1985
Son **JOHN** 1918-1957
Son-in-law
**JACK CUTHBERT** 1910-1964

- *Alexander (sailor, buried 11th April):*
  *Balloo, Islandmagee*

- *Mrs. Jane Weir Donaldson (buried 9th Feb.*
  *age 92): Joymount House, Carrickfergus*

B161-B162

**MORROW**
In loving memory of
**ERNEST**
Died 4th June 1965
Loves last gift – remembrance

Flower holder
In loving memory of my mother
**MARY GRAHAM 1897 – 1985**

- *Mary (buried 24th Dec, age 88):*
  *39 Ferndene Gardens, Dundonald*

- *Buried 8.5.2002 (cremated remains)*
  **THOMAS GRAHAM,** *(age 72):*
  *21 Galloway, Newtownards*

**B163**

- Buried 15.10.1947 ***ROBERT MAYBIN:***
  *2, Windsor Ave. Whitehead*

**B164**

In loving memory of
**JOHN INGLEBY HOOD**
Who died 11th May 1948
And his wife **PATSY**
Who died 22nd June 1947

- *John (ferryman) and Patricia:*
  *The Ferry, Islandmagee*

**B165**

**KIRK**
In loving memory of
A dear husband and father
**JOHN**
Who died 13th January 1987
And son **MAURICE**
Who died 16th April 1947 aged 3 years
Also daughter
Who died in infancy 10th March 1943
Interred in St. Johns Churchyard

- *John (age 74):*
  *52, Islandmagee Road, Whitehead*
- *Maurice: Millbay Islandmagee*

**B166-B167**

In loving memory
of
**ARCHIE CARR LOWRY**
Born 11th Jan. 1892
died 13th Sept. 1947
And his dear wife
**IDA MARY** (nee **CHAPMAN**)
Born 26th Aug. 1904
died 23rd Nov. 1985

- *Archie (flax merchant, age 53):*
  *Golf Bungalow, Ferris Bay, Islandmagee*
- *Ida (age 82): The Villa, Mill Road, Doagh*

**B168-B169**

- Buried 12.10.1944 ***ARCHIBALD FORDE***
  *(labourer): Kilcoan Beg, Islandmagee*
- Buried 8.12.1980
  ***Mrs. SARAH ELIZABETH FORDE*** *(home
  duties): 198, Larne Road, Carrickfergus*

**B170-B171**

In fond remembrance of
**HILL KANE** beloved husband
of Agnes Kane
Who died on board the
M.V. Elmbank on the
12th February 1940 aged 40 years
and was buried at sea
his wife **AGNES ISABELLA**
died 8th Dec. 1976
their son **GEORGE** Master Mariner
beloved husband of Bonita
and a dear father
died 5th Nov. 1987 aged 54 years

**B172**

In fond remembrance of
**SAMUEL MILLIKEN KANE**
Dearly loved husband of
**ISOBEL KANE**
Who was lost at sea owing to
Enemy action
On the 16th Feb. 1942
Aged 28 years
Also his cousin
**JOHN MANN KANE**
Master mariner
Died 11th June 1991

B173

In loving memory of
**HAROLD ALLISTER ADAMSON**
M.M.
Who died 19th September 1960
aged 45 years
And his son **HAROLD ALLISTER**
died 14th June 1948
**MOYA ADAMSON**
a loving wife and mother
died 10th February 1998 aged 84

- *Harold (Captain): Larne*
- *Son Harold (infant): 2, Balmoral Ave. Whitehead*

B174

(on surround):
In memory of **WILLIAM ROSSALL**
Died 7th August 1946
And his wife **FRANCES ELIZABETH**
Died 18th October 1948
**ELSIE BIRKMYRE**
Died 26th January 1990
**ANNIE McNAUGHT**
Died 2nd April 1991

- *William (policeman): Ferris Bay, Islandmagee*
- *Mrs. Birkmyre (age 90): Greenisland House, Carrickfergus*
- *Mrs. McNaught (age 86): Gilleroo Lodge, Larne*

B175

In loving memory of
**MARGARET PURDY McCOSH**
Died 7 March 1934
And her son
**THOMAS HAMILTON McCOSH**
Lost at sea 17 Dec. 1940
Also her husband
**ALEXANDER McCOSH**
Died 28 January 1953
Also their sons
**WILLIAM SHAW McCOSH**
Died 15 March 1985
**JOHN PURDY McCOSH**
died 21 Dec. 1989
Loves last gift - remembrance

- *Margaret (age 54): Ballymuldrough, Islandmagee*
- *William (age 72): Holywell Hospital*
- *John (age 83): 35, Rossmore Green, Greenisland*

B176

**McGOOKIN**
In loving memory of
A devoted wife and mother
**ELLEN**
Died 21st March 1979
Also her mother
**AGNES MARSHALL**
Died 4th January 1936
Also her husband
**JAMES McGOOKIN**
Died 12th January 1994

- *James (age 74, presbyterian) and Ellen: 23, Elmwood Park, Woodburn, Carrick*
- *Agnes (age 44): Millbay, Islandmage*

B177-B178
In loving memory of
**AGNES JANE (NESSIE) WILSON**
Died 22nd Nov. 1936 aged 4 years
Also her father **JOHN WILSON**
Died 14th December 1955
aged 55 years
Also **ELLEN**
wife of the above John
Died 2nd January 1988 aged 87 years
Also their son-in-law **WILLIAM**
Died 19th September 1995
aged 64 years

- *Nessie and John (labourer): Newchurch, Islandmagee*
- *Ellen: 8, Ballystrudder Gardens, Islandmagee*
- *William Wilson: 113, Low Road, Islandmagee*

B179-B180
Erected by
Joseph and Esther Armour
In loving memory of their son
**JOSEPH**
Died 27 Sept. 1938 aged 20 years
And his mother
**ESTHER ARMOUR**
Died 1st Sept. 1974 aged 77 years
The above **JOSEPH ARMOUR**
Died 14 March 1976 aged 88 years

Flower holder
In loving memory of
**ELIZABETH McCONNELL**
(nee **ARMOUR**) 1926 – 2000
and her beloved husband
**DAVID** 1930 – 1994

- *Joseph (son): 1, Portland Terrace, Magheramorne*
- *Joseph (recorded age 87)*

B181
- *Buried 3.8.1940* **Mrs. RUTH FORD:** *Roseplace, Ballystrudder, Islandmagee*

B182
- *Buried 12.3.1941* **JAMES FORD** *(sailor): Kilcoanbeg, Islandmagee*

B183-B184
**FORD**
In loving memory of
**MOLLY** beloved wife of Samuel
Died 25th October 1972 aged 64 years
The above mentioned
**SAMUEL FORD**
Died 13th November 1977
aged 73 years
**SAMUEL IVAN FORD**
loving husband and father
Died 1st December 1995 aged 66 years
The Lord is my shepherd

- *Molly (Mary) and Samuel (age 74): Denmark Cottage, 150, Low Road, Islandmagee*
- *Samuel Ivan: 88, Ballystrudder Gardens, Islandmagee*

B185
- *Buried (no date)* **WILLIAM FORDE:** *Kilcoanbeg, Islandmagee*
- *Buried 12.12.1976* **Mrs. ANNIE JANE FORDE,** *(age 82): 35 Bridewell Drive, Carrickfergus*

B186
- *Buried 18.8.1940* **ARCHIBALD FORDE,** *(age 71): Kilcoanbeg, Islandmagee*

B187 unused

**B188**

### BEATTIE

In loving memory of
Our dear father
**GEORGE HERBERT**
Died 30th November 1968
Also our dear mother
**ELIZABETH ANN**
D.ed 30th September 1969
Their children
**VIOLET**
Died 1st July 1942
**BERTIE**
Died 2nd July 1947

- *George (age 74) and Elizabeth (age 74): 2, Sunningdale Park, Belfast*
- *Violet (age 8): Ballyharry, Islandmagee*

**B189-B190**

In memory of
My beloved husband
**WILLIAM HIGGINSON**
Died 19th May 1941
Also his loving wife **AGNES**
Died 4th Sept. 1971 in her 99th year

- *William (age 79, farmer): Dundressan, Islandmagee*
- *Agnes: 40, Ballystrudder Road, Islandmagee*
- *Buried 27.3.1974*
  **SAMUEL BOYD HAWTHORN,**
  *(age 70, seaman): 40, Ballystrudder Road, Islandmagee*

**B191**

### CONNOR

**GERALD LINDSAY** bro. of Roy
Who died 16th February 1940
Aged 47 years
**MABEL JANE** sister of Roy
Who died 22nd January 1952
Aged 69 years
**EMILY MARIAN** sister of Roy
Who died 26th April 1961
Aged 84 years
**Lieut JAMES ROY LINDSAY CONNOR**
Irish Fusiliers
who died 5th June 1957
Aged 61 years
also his wife
**KATHLEEN MARY** (nee **Davis**)
who died 23rd September 1938
Aged 33 years
and their son
**PATRICK SHANE** mariner
who died 2nd September 1999
Aged 68 years
The sea is still.
The winds in silence rest
Yet speaks the voice of grief
within my breast

- *Gerald: Avoca, Ballycarry*
- *Patrick Shane Connor (recorded age 67, seaman): 28 Morrison House, Grays, Essex*
- *Miss Mabel Jane Connor: Hillhead, Ballycarry*

**B192**

- *Buried 29.9.1938*
  ***Mrs. KATHLEEN CONNOR,*** *(age 36): Bogend, Islandmagee*
- *Buried 29.4.1961* ***Miss CONNOR:*** *Ballycarry*

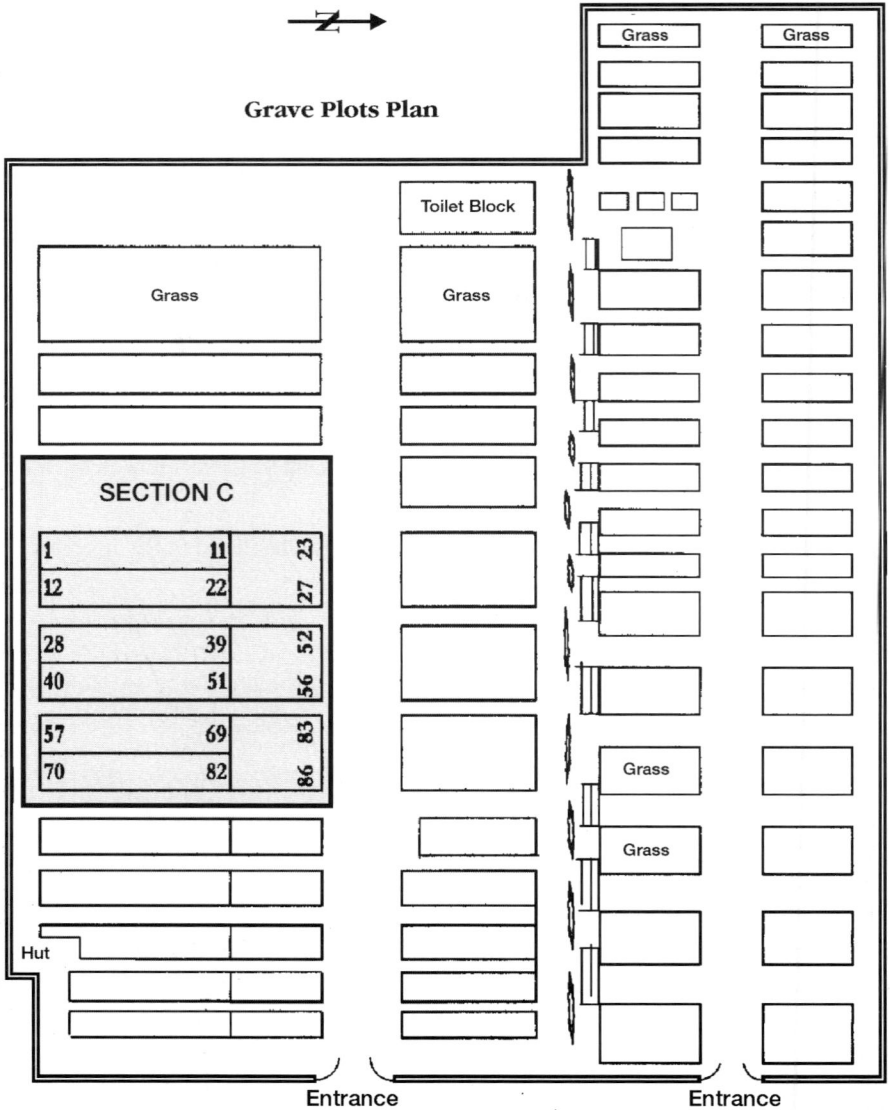

**Grave Plots Plan**

N →

Grass | Grass

Toilet Block

Grass | Grass

SECTION C

| 1 | 11 | 23 |
| 12 | 22 | 27 |
| 28 | 39 | 52 |
| 40 | 51 | 56 |
| 57 | 69 | 83 |
| 70 | 82 | 86 |

Grass | Grass

Grass

Hut

Entrance          Entrance

# ~ ISLANDMAGEE NEW CEMETERY ~

**Whitehead** ←          ~ **LOW ROAD** ~          **Ballylumford** →

# SECTION C

| Name | Plot | Name | Plot | Name | Plot |
|------|------|------|------|------|------|
| Aiken | 26 | Gibson | 10 | McElnea | 56 |
| Allen | 6 | Gibson | 11 | McGrady | 61 |
| Arlow | 66 | Gilliland | 30 | McIlgorm | 31 |
| Armour | 54 | Goldie | 68 | McKee | 37 |
| Auld | 67 | Graham | 52 | McKee | 83 |
| Barkley | 32 | Guthrie | 71 | McKeown | 81 |
| Barkley | 80 | Harte | 17 | McKeown | 82 |
| Bass | 46 | Harte | 18 | Moorhead | 24 |
| Beasant | 50 | Hawthorne | 36 | Morton | 42 |
| Bell | 49 | Haydock | 13 | Murray | 47 |
| Berry | 44 | Haydock | 58 | Orr | 12 |
| Bingham | 84 | Henshaw | 45 | Peoples | 64 |
| Blair | 7 | Hunter | 10 | Peoples | 65 |
| Bonnar | 34 | Hunter | 11 | Phyllis | 28 |
| Brown | 43 | Hunter | 19 | Reid | 29 |
| Burns | 72 | Johnston | 7 | Robinson | 59 |
| Burns | 78 | Johnston | 70 | Robinson | 73 |
| Burnside | 22 | Johnston | 73 | Smyth | 4 |
| Cameron | 8 | Jones | 41 | Smyth | 55 |
| Cameron | 85 | Kelly | 77 | Steele | 51 |
| Cameron | 86 | Kerr | 54 | Stewart | 14 |
| Carmichael | 84 | Laird | 74 | Stewart | 63 |
| Carson | 67 | Laird | 75 | Strahan | 21 |
| Cathcart | 9 | Macauley | 39 | Strahan | 35 |
| Clark | 12 | Macrae | 85 | Strahan | 48 |
| Clements | 57 | Macrae | 86 | Templeton | 5 |
| Crawford | 76 | Magill | 53 | Templeton | 69 |
| Dick | 20 | McBurney | 62 | Usher | 62 |
| Earls | 40 | McClinton | 17 | Whitla | 38 |
| Feherty | 23 | McClinton | 18 | Wilson | 33 |
| Ferguson | 27 | McConkey | 62 | Wisnom | 74 |
| Fletcher | 70 | McCready | 29 | Wisnom | 75 |
| Garrett | 43 | McDonagh | 25 | Wright | 56 |

C1-C2 unused

C3 unused (fallen stone)

C4

### SMYTH
### JOHN WILSON
Died 16th March 1983
Beloved husband of **MURIEL**
Who died 14th February 1987

- *John (Church of Ireland, age 75) and
  Muriel Hester (Church of Ireland, age 79):
  8, Lestannon Ave. Whitehead*

C5

- *Buried 12.1.1977*
  ***ROBERT ALFRED TEMPLETON,***
  *(Presbyterian): 8, Killeaton Cres,
  Dunmurry*
- *Ashes buried 8.7.1991*
  ***OLIVE MARY TEMPLETON** (age 82),
  died in Lagan Valley Hospital, Lisburn*

C6

In fond memory of
### GRACE ANNA
Beloved wife of **W.J.C. ALLEN**
Died 12th May 1970
Also her husband **WILLIAM**
Died 7th March 1981

- *Grace (Housewife, Presbyterian):
  Hazeldene, Cloughfin, Islandmagee*
- *William J. G. (age 70, Presbyterian,
  widower): 13, Middle Road, Islandmagee*

C7

In Loving Memory
### DAVID BLAIR
1902-1977
### AMELIA BLAIR
1903-2002

- *Buried 30.9.1977 David
  (age 75, Presbyterian, married):
  47 Lisowen Street, Belfast.*
- *Buried 14.9.2002 Amelia (age 98, widow):
  Manor Court Nursing Home, Dungannon.*
- *Buried 3.1.1975*
  ***ELIZABETH TEMPLETON JOHNSTON**
  (age 68, Presbyterian, housewife):
  137 Ardenlee Ave, Belfast.*

C8

In
Loving memory of
### JEAN
Died 31st Aug. 1973
Loved wife of
### Thomas CAMERON

- *Jean (age 49, Congregationalist):
  18, Gobbins Path, Islandmagee*

C9

- *Buried 22.8.1969*
  ***AGNES EDITH CATHCART,***
  *(age 69, Methodist, housewife):
  2, Lumford Ave. Whitehead*
- *Buried 24.9.1969 **JAMES CATHCART,**
  (age 92, Presbyterian): 2, Lumford Ave.
  Whitehead*

C10-C11

### GIBSON
In loving memory of
My dear wife
### JEAN
Died 15th March 1985 aged 79 years
Also her sister **MARTHA HUNTER**
Died 12th March 1966 aged 65 years
**Capt. ROBERT THOMAS GIBSON**
husband of the above Jean
Died 4th May 1986 aged 87 years

- *Jean (recorded as 80 years),
  Martha (single) and Robert:
  9, Lynda Ave. Jordanstown*

C12

- *Buried 15.7.1969 **JOHN S. CLARK**
  (age 60, Church of Ireland, Mercantile
  Marine): 119 Islandmagee Road,
  Whitehead*
- *Buried 30.7.1979 **CHRISTINA E. ORR**
  (age 90, Presbyterian):184 Gobbins Road,
  Islandmagee*
- *Buried 25.1.1990 **Mrs. SHEELAH CLARK**
  (age 76, Presbyterian): 184, Gobbins Road,
  Islandmagee*

C13

- *Buried 6.1.1976*
  ***Miss ELIZABETH HAYDOCK***
  *(age 81, Church of Ireland):
  78, Cable Road, Whitehead*

**C14**

### STEWART
In loving memory of
**WILLIAM JOHN STEWART**
(Master Mariner)
Born 11th January 1900
died 5th December 1972
And his wife **MONA VASHTI DICK**
Born 25th September 1911 died
25th April 1992

- *William (Presbyterian): Hillmount,
  Islandmagee*
- *Mona Vashti Dick Stewart (age 81,
  Presbyterian): 6, Ashvale Park
  Islandmagee*

**C15** unused

**C16** unused

**C17-C18**
Flower holders
**MICHAEL JAMES HARTE**
died 24th May 1984 aged 3 months

- *Michael: 33, Knockdhu Park, Larne*
- *Buried 30.3.1968 **SAMUEL McCLINTON,**
  (age 57, Methodist, married):
  Drumgurland, Islandmagee*
- *Buried 25.2.1996
  **ELIZABETH (LILY) McCLINTON,**
  (age 79, Methodist, widow):
  4, Windsor Park, Whitehead*

**C19**

### HUNTER
In loving memory of our dear father
**WILLIAM McKAY HUNTER**
Died 7th July 1947 and was interred
in Tentir Churchyard North Wales
Also our dear mother
**MARGARET ELIZABETH HUNTER**
Died 1st August 1966

- *Margaret E. Mc. Hunter
  (age 67, Presbyterian, housewife):
  6, Glenkeen Drive, Greenisland*

**C20**

In
Fond memory of
**MARY**
Loved sister of Thomas Dick
Died 16th June 1966
Also her brother
**THOMAS J. DICK**
Died 22nd October 1970

- *Mary (spinster) and Thomas (age 80):
  5, Loughview Bungalows, Islandmagee*

**C21**

### STRAHAN
In loving memory of
Our dear sister
**MARIA**
Died 27th April 1966
And **MARTHA**
Died 2nd November 1972

- *Maria (single, shopkeeper) and
  Martha (single, age 76, home duties):
  Upper Gransha, Islandmagee*

**C22**

- *Buried 3.11.1965 **ALFRED BURNSIDE:**
  50a, Islandmagee Road, Whitehead*

**C23**

In loving memory of
**JOHN JAMES FEHERTY, R.N.**
Who died 4th Feb. 1964
aged 86 years
And his beloved wife
**ANNIE GERTRUDE**
Who died 6th Oct. 1967
aged 74 years

- *John (retired coastguard) and Annie
  (housewife): Ferris Bay, Islandmagee*

## C24

**MOORHEAD**
In loving memory of
Our dear parents
**WILLIAM JOHN**
Died 14th May 1963
**LIZA ANN**
Died 3rd August 1975
Also their daughter-in-law
**MARIE**
Died 19th December 2001
Loving wife and mother, sadly missed
Forever in our thoughts

- *William and Marie (age 65):
  75 Fortwilliam Parade, Belfast*

## C25

In loving memory of
**ETHEL FRANCES**
Beloved wife of
John Robert McDonagh
Died 14th December 1978 aged 84 yrs.
Also the above named
**JOHN ROBERT McDONAGH**
Died 19th September 1981
aged 88 years

- *Ethel (housewife): 33, Lestannon Ave.
  Whitehead*

- *John: 15, Ransevyn Court, Whitehead*

## C26

**AIKEN**
In loving memory of
**DAVID**
Beloved husband of Eva
Died December 3rd 1975
And the above named **EVA**
Who died April 3rd 1983

- *David and Eva (age 72):
  3, Milebush Crescent, Carrickfergus*

## C27

In loving remembrance
of
**THOMAS FERGUSON,**
Master Mariner
Who died 1st August 1962
And his loving wife
**ROBERTA J.**
Who died 22nd October 2002
aged 94

- *Thomas: Kilcoanbeg, Islandmagee*
- *Roberta Jackson Ferguson (age 94):
  Chester Private Nursing Home, Whitehead*

## C28

**PHYLLIS**
In memory of
**MATILDA**
Died 1st September 1978
Devoted wife of
**WALTER**
Died 26th June 1988
At rest

- *Matilda (age 79):
  23, Glenville Road, Whiteabbey*

- *Walter (age 87, Presbyterian):
  Moylinney House, Rathcoole*

## C29

In
Loving memory of
**ROBINA REID** nee **McCREADY**
Born in Islandmagee
6th September 1896
died 21st December 1973
also her brother
**WILLIAM A. McCREADY**
Died 1st February 1982
Aged 72 years

- *Robina (age 77, Presbyterian, married)
  and William Albert (Presbyterian, single):
  647, Shore Road, Jordanstown*

C30

On surround
**MARY E. GILLILAND**
Died 3rd May 1981 aged 89 years
**JAMES GILLILAND**
Died 4th April 1969 aged 77 years

- *Mary Ellen (Presbyterian) and James (Presbyterian, painter and decorator): 12, Abbeyville St., Newtownabbey, Whiteabbey*

C31

**McILGORM**
In loving memory of
**ELIZABETH E. (LILY)**
Who died 28th December 1978
Beloved wife of
**HUGH McILGORM J.P.**
Who died 1st November 1992
Aged 95 years
Resting where no shadows fall

- *Lily (Presbyterian): 36 Chaine Memorial Road, Larne*
- *Hugh (Presbyterian): York House, Portrush*

C32

In loving memory
**WINIFRED MARGARET BARKLEY**
Died 2nd August 1985
Also her husband
**ALEXANDER (ALEX) BARKLEY**
Died 30th December 1996

- *Winifred (age 66, Presbyterian): 33a Marine Parade, Whitehead*
- *Alex (age 84, Presbyterian): Tamlaght Private Nursing Home, Carrickfergus*

C33

In
Loving memory of
**JOHN** beloved husband of
**Barbara WILSON**
Died 21st May 1966

- *John (Carpenter): 6, Ransevyn Drive, Whitehead*
- *Buried 2.3.1991 **Mrs. BARBARA WILSON** (age 80) same address*

C34

- *Buried 8.9.1965 **Miss ANNIE BONNAR:** Steela Mairs, Blackhead, Whitehead*
- *Buried 5.2.1972*
  ***Miss ELIZABETH BONNAR** (age 78): same address*

C35

In fond memory of
**SARAH KANE**
Beloved wife of John Strahan
Died 8th January 1969
The above **JOHN STRAHAN**
Died 21st May 1972

- *Sarah (date of death recorded as 1971, Presbyterian, sub post mistress) and John (age 74, Presbyterian, garage owner): 4, Causeway Villas, Ballycarry Station*

C36

**HAWTHORNE**
In loving memory of
My dear husband **JACK**
Died 22nd June 1965
His wife **EILEEN**
Died 21st May 1981
Memories grow deeper as life travels on

- *Jack (John) and Eileen (age 70): 22, Ashley Drive Belfast BT9*

C37

**McKEE**
In loving memory of
**JOHN ADRAIN**
Died 23rd October 1992

- *John (age 73, Presbyterian, single): Holywell Hospital, Antrim*

C38

## WHITLA
In loving memory of
**JOHN GEORGE**
husband of Maud
Died 14th January 1965
Also **MAUD**
Died 16th December 1990
The Lord is my Shepherd

- *John (clerk): 3, Mullaghboy Bungalows, Islandmagee*
- *Buried 30.3.1991* **Mrs. MAUD WHITLA** *(age 88): High Peak Nursing Home, Culcheth, Warrington*

C39

## MACAULEY
In loving memory of
My dear husband
**WILLIAM**
Died 11th August 1963

- *William: 252, Merville Garden Village, Newtownabbey*
- *Buried 12.6.1988* **Mrs. VICTORIA MAY MACAULEY,** *(age 91): Rathmoyle Nursing Home, Larne*

C40

- *Buried 23.8.1964* **Mrs. MARGARET EARLS** *(Housewife): Upper Gransha, Islandmagee*

C41

## JONES
In loving memory of
**ERNEST HENRY (HARRY)**
died 9th April 1971
Loved husband of Kathleen Jones
Also in fond remembrance
of the above
**KATHLEEN JONES**
died 11th November 1989

C42

In loving memory of
**BRUCE WALLACE MORTON**
Temple-Effin
Died 8th September 1964
Also his beloved wife
**ANNIE MORTON**
Died 12th March 1966
R.I.P.

C43

Cherished memories
**SAMUEL CECIL**
17-9-1925 - 23-6-1993
dearly loved husband of
**Ellen** (nee **Brown**)
8-6-1890 - 23-11-1963
father **SAMUEL BROWN**
11-2-1877 - 12-4-1940
Interred in Glynn
mother **MARY JANE BROWN**

The Lord is my Shepherd
**GARRETT**

Black polished end piece
**Dad**
**Elaine       Vivienne**

Flower holder
**MARY JANE BROWN**
died 23rd Nov. 1963

- *Samuel Garrett (age 67): 34, Woodland Gardens, Lambeg, Lisburn*
- *Mary Jane: 22, Gardenmore Place, Larne*

C44

## BERRY
In loving memory of
**NORMAN**
Died April 6 1965
And his beloved wife **LILLIE**
Died 9th May 1980

- *Norman: 10, Lenamore Ave. Jordanstown*
- *Lilian (Lillie) (age 74, buried 28th May): 34, Sycamore Drive, Jordanstown*

C45

### EDWIN HENSHAW
Died 26th February 1965

- *Edwin S. (civil servant): 6, Lumford Ave. Whitehead*

C46

- *Buried 20.8.1963 **PHILIP M. BASS,** (retired farmer): Drumkeen, The Roddens, Larne*
- *Buried (no date) **Mrs. BRIDIE BASS,** (housewife): same address*

C47

In loving memory of
### PHILIP MURRAY
Much beloved husband of
Mary Ellen Bass
Died 17th August 1963
His devoted wife **MARY ELLEN**
Died 1st April 1965

C48

### STRAHAN
In
Loving memory of
My dear husband
### ROBERT
Who died 22nd April 1963
His wife **MARTHA**
Who died 25th March 1969

- *Robert (bus inspector) and Martha Jane (age 72, housewife): 27, Edward Road, Whitehead*

C49

### BELL
In loving memory of
### JOHN BELL
Died 22nd March 1963
And his wife **MARGARET**
Died 30th January 1980
Also their son
### WILLIAM ROBERT (BOBBIE)
Died 31st March 1993 aged 70 years

- *John (plasterer); Millbay, Islandmagee*
- *Margaret (age 87, home duties): 14a Chichester Park, Whitehead*
- *Bobbie: 42a Islandmagee Road, Whitehead*

C50

- *Buried 1.2.1963 **Miss ETHEL BEASANT:** Upper Gransha, Islandmagee*

C51 (fallen stone)

- *Buried 7.9.1962 **Mrs. MARY STEELE** (housewife): 35 Ballystrudder gardens, Islandmagee*

C52

In fond memory of
### WILLIAM STANLEY
Loved husband of **Vera GRAHAM**
Died 4th April 1961

- *William: Wilmont, Ballystrudder, Islandmagee*

C53

- *Buried 22.11.1961 **WILLIAM MAGILL** (labourer): 19, Loughview Bungalows, Islandmagee*

## ARMOUR
In loving memory of
**ALEXANDER KERR**
Died March 1961
**SARAH BROWN ARMOUR**
Died April 1978
**THOMAS KERR ARMOUR**
Died May 1998
We hold you close
Within our hearts
And there you shall remain
To walk with us
Throughout our lives
Until we meet again

- *Buried 31st March 1961, Alexander Kerr (labourer): Millbay, Islandmagee*
- *Buried 26th April 1978, Sarah (age 59, married): Millbay, Islandmagee*
- *Buried 17th May 1998, Thomas (age 82): Whitehead Private Nursing Home*

## SMYTH
In fond memory of
**ALLISON** loved husband of
Sarah Smyth
Died 28th January 1961
Also **ROSALIND** their darling daughter
Died 8th March 1969

- *Allison (bank official): 89, Islandmagee Road, Whitehead*
- *Rosalind (age 8): 36, Strathmore Park North, Belfast*
- *Buried 16.10.2001 **Mrs. SARAH SMYTH**, (age 86): 28 Massey Court, Belfast*

## WRIGHT
In loving memory of
My dear husband
**RAYMOND**
Who died 14th Feb. 1988
Also **MARY McELNEA**
who died 8th Sept. 1960
And her husband **DAVID**
who died 9th April 1967

- *Raymond Ernest (age 64, warehouse manager): 60, Middle Road, Islandmagee*
- *Mary (housewife) and David (age 79, baker): 1, Kilton Cottage, Mullaghdubh, Islandmagee*

In fond memory of
**KATHLEEN ISOBEL**
Loving wife of
**Robert J. CLEMENTS**
Died 7th June 1963
Also her dear husband
**ROBERT JAMES (BOBBY)**
Died 27th March 2002

- *Kathleen and Robert (age 87): 45, Edward Road, Whitehead*
- *Buried 5.4.2001 **Mrs. EDITH CLEMENTS**, (age 80): same address*

- *Buried 10.2.1963 **Mrs. ANNIE ELIZABETH HAY**, (housewife): Knockgallagh, Whitehead*
- *Buried 20.3.1970 **JOHN HAY**, (age 70): same address*

- *Buried 22.1.1963 **SAMUEL ROBINSON**: 24 Windsor Crescent, Whitehead*
- *Buried 2.6.1979 **Mrs ETHEL MAY ROBINSON**, (age 83): 15, Ransevyn Court, Whitehead*

Unused

C61

## McGRADY
### WILLIAM H. McGRADY M.B.E.
Master Mariner
Died 5th January 1963
Beloved husband of Florence
His wife **FLORENCE MARY**
Died 7th October 1965

- *William and Florence: 7, Slievedarragh Park Cavehill Road, Belfast*

C62

In fond memory of
### JOHN
Loved husband of **Irene USHER**
Died 25th June 1962
Also **MARGARET I. McBURNEY**
Died 28th December 1989

- *John Usher and Mrs. McBurney (age 67): 25, Lestannon Ave. Whitehead*
- *Buried 12.7.1987 **Baby McCONKEY:** Moyle Hospital, Larne*
- *Buried 10.12.1988 **Baby McCONKEY:** City Hospital, Belfast*

C63

## STEWART
In
Loving remembrance
of my dear husband
The **Rev. WILLIAM F. S. STEWART M.Litt D.D.**
Who passed home 12th January 1962
32 years Minister of
Whitehead Presbyterian Church
his beloved wife
### MARGARET REDMOND STEWART
Who passed home 20th February 1991

- *Rev. Stewart: The Manse Whitehead*
- *Mrs Stewart (age 87): 17, Fortwilliam Parade, Belfast*

C64-C65

## PEOPLES
In loving memory of **STEWART**
Darling eldest son of
W.J. and M.E. Peoples
Died 26th December 1962
Aged 17½ years
Also his father **WILLIAM JAMES**
Died 10th March 1970 aged 55 years

- *William Stewart (farmer) and father William (farmer, recorded as age 56): Sans Souci ,Islandmagee*

C66

## ARLOW
In loving memory
of
### WILLIAM ARLOW
Died 10th February 1962
And his beloved wife
### LOUISE MADELINE
Died 8th April 1992

- *William Edward: 3, Lumford Ave. Whitehead*
- *Louise (age 90): Chester Nursing Home, Whitehead*

C67

- *Buried 18.1.1962* **Miss RABIE I. CARSON,** *(Retired Companion): Port Davey House Whitehead*
- *Buried 16.6.1969* **Miss MARGARET WILSON AULD,** *(age 92): Seamore House Dunmurry*

C68

- *Buried 23.2.1963* **Squadron Leader ALAN GOLDIE:** *Portmuck, Islandmagee*

C69

## TEMPLETON
In
Affectionate remembrance of
### ROBERT
Loved husband of Ella
Died 7th August 1961 aged 57 years
The above **ELLA**
Died 2nd December 1995 aged 85 years

- *Robert (Mariner): Bonnyrigg, Sycamore Drive, Jordanstown*
- *Eleanor (Ella, recorded age 86): Ravenhill Private Nursing Home, Carrickfergus*

C70

### JOHNSTON
In loving memory of my dear husband
### GEORGE
Died 14th December 1962
Also his wife
### ELLEN JUNE
Died 8th November 1995

- *George: 147, Islandmagee Rd, Whitehead*
- *Ellen (age 93): Chester Park Nursing Home, Whitehead*
- *Buried 6.8.1980*
  ***Miss CELENA FLETCHER:***
  *3, Brooklands Crescent, Whitehead*
- *Buried 2.7.1986*
  ***LOFTUS HAMILTON HUGH FLETCHER**
  (age 88, widower): 27, Brookslands Crescent, Whitehead*

C71

### GUTHRIE
In
Loving memory of
My dear wife and our beloved mother
### MARY GUTHRIE
Who died 15th February 1962
Also her devoted husband
and our dear father
### JAMES GUTHRIE
Who died 1st July 1965

- *Mary (Minnie): Cloughfin, Islandmagee*

C72

In loving memory
of
### SAMUEL BURNS
Died 10th January 1962
### ISOBEL
Dearly loved wife of above named
Died 4th December 1979
Aged 69 years

- *Samuel (builder): 27, Alexandra Ave. Whitehead*
- *Margaret Isobel: 6, Moylinney Park, Muckamore*

C73

- *Buried 23.12.1961*
  ***Miss MARGARET JOHNSTON** (age 21): 30a, Windsor Ave. Whitehead*
- *Buried 21.10.1967*
  ***WALTER HENRY JOHNSTON** (age 60, car park attendant): same address*

C74-C75

In fond memory of
### ROBERT
Loved husband of **Sally LAIRD**
died 27th November 1966
Also **HELEN** mother of Robert
died 27th November 1961
Also the above named **SALLY**
died 20th June 1984

- *Robert (age 58, Presbyterian, master builder): Cloughfin Islandmagee*
- *Mrs. Helen Wisnom: same address*
- *Sally (age 76, Presbyterian, widow): 14, Gobbins Road Islandmagee*

C76

### CRAWFORD
Ever remembered
On surround **JAMES CRAWFORD**
died 19th November 1961

- *James (labourer): Green Lodge, Lower Gransha, Islandmagee*

C77

In
Memory of
**EDWIN A. R. KELLY**
Died 6th October 1961
Aged 90 years

- *Edwin: Esplanade Hotel, Whitehead*

C78

- *Buried 18.8.1961* ***WILLIAM H. BURNS:*** *6, Windsor Parade, Whitehead*

C79 unused

C80

**BARKLEY**
In loving memory of
**JAMES**
Died 31st July 1961
His wife **ELLEN**
Died 6th February 1969
And their son
**DAVID JAMES** (Master Mariner)
Died 30th December 1981

- *James: 33a Marine Parade, Whitehead*

C81-C82

**McKEOWN**
In
Loving memory of
A devoted wife and mother
**ELIZABETH McKEOWN**
Who died 3rd October 1960
Also her husband
**ROBERT JAMES McKEOWN**
Who died 16th May 1969

- *Elizabeth and Robert (engine driver): 4, Balmoral Ave. Whitehead*
- *Buried 9.5.2002* ***DAVID GIRVAN McKEOWN*** *(age 71): 6, Chichester Park, Whitehead*

C83

**McKEE**
In loving memory of
our dear parents
**ROBERT**
Died 5th Nov. 1969
**SARAH ELIZABETH**
Died 2nd Feb. 1973
And their daughter
**DOROTHY**
Died 13th June 1960

- *Robert (age 83, ships carpenter) and Dorothy Elizabeth (single): Ballydown, Islandmagee*
- *Sarah (age 86): 96, Millbay Rd, Islandmagee*

C84

**CARMICHAEL**
In loving memory of my dear sister
**AGNES WILSON CARMICHAEL**
Died 29th April 1960
This stone was erected by
**ISABEL McPHAIL CARMICHAEL**
Died 11th February 1966
and at rest here
Remembering also their sister
**CATHERINE McARTHUR BINGHAM**
nee **CARMICHAEL**
Died October 1958 and buried nearby

- *Agnes (single): 29, Balfour Ave. Whitehead*

C85-C86

Erected by John A. Cameron
In memory of his wife **ANNIE**
Died 4th March 1960 aged 70 years
The above **JOHN A. CAMERON**
(Master Mariner)
Died 24th July 1963 aged 78 years
Also their daughter
**KATHLEEN E. MACRAE**
Died 7th August 1979
And her husband
**JOHN DONALD (JOCK) MACRAE**
Died 28th October 1994

- *Annie, Kathleen Elizabeth and Jock (age 83): 36 Marine Parade, Whitehead*

**Grave Plots Plan**

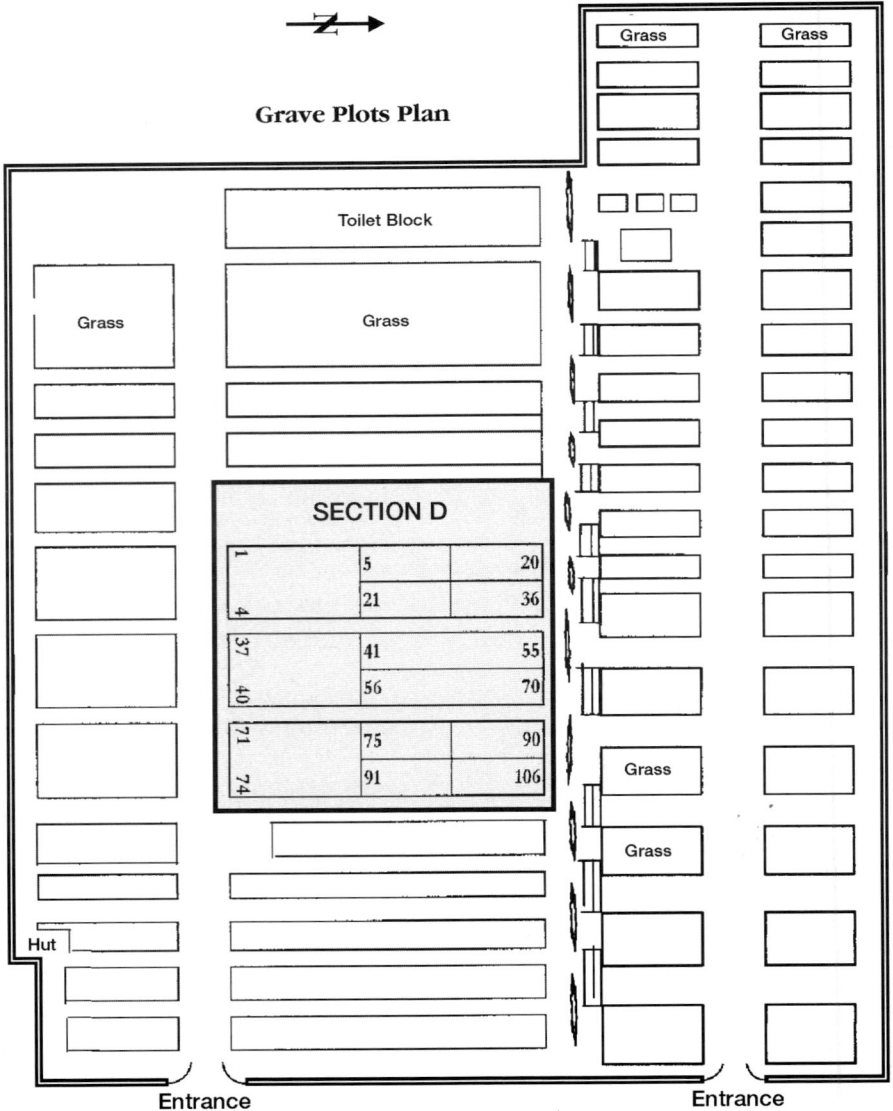

N →

| Toilet Block |
| Grass | Grass |

## SECTION D

| 1 | 5 | 20 |
| 4 | 21 | 36 |
| 37 | 41 | 55 |
| 40 | 56 | 70 |
| 71 | 75 | 90 |
| 74 | 91 | 106 |

Grass

Grass

Grass

Grass

Grass

Grass

Hut

Entrance

Entrance

## ~ ISLANDMAGEE NEW CEMETERY ~

**Whitehead** ←

~ **LOW ROAD** ~

**Ballylumford** →

# SECTION D

| Name | Plot | Name | Plot | Name | Plot |
|---|---|---|---|---|---|
| Allen | 84 | Hayden | 17 | McAdam | 48 |
| Allen | 85 | Hayden | 18 | McCalmont | 30 |
| Auld | 69 | Hayden | 19 | McCalmont | 44 |
| Auld | 70 | Hayden | 20 | McCalmont | 98 |
| Baillie | 83 | Haydock | 78 | McConachie | 80 |
| Baird | 46 | Haydock | 79 | McGowan | 56 |
| Barnett | 88 | Heggan | 64 | McKay | 2 |
| Boyd | 6 | Henshaw | 49 | McKeown | 28 |
| Boyd | 62 | Henshaw | 50 | Meeke | 41 |
| Boyd | 73 | Hill | 10 | Millar | 91 |
| Boyd | 90 | Hill | 11 | Morton | 71 |
| Branagh | 52 | Hill | 12 | Morton | 72 |
| Branagh | 53 | Hill | 13 | Mulvenna | 105 |
| Cook | 91 | Hill | 14 | Palmer | 61 |
| Craig | 89 | Holmes | 8 | Polglase | 7 |
| Cresswell | 42 | Holmes | 57 | Pollock | 102 |
| Cresswell | 43 | Holmes | 86 | Pullin | 58 |
| Davey | 74 | Hopkins | 67 | Reid | 45 |
| Dawson | 80 | Hopkins | 68 | Ross | 104 |
| Dick | 94 | Hunter | 31 | Scott | 16 |
| Dick | 95 | Hunter | 32 | Scott | 17 |
| Dobson | 38 | Hunter | 33 | Scott | 18 |
| English | 27 | Irvine | 36 | Scott | 19 |
| Flack | 103 | Irvine | 37 | Scott | 20 |
| Flack/Fleck | 96 | Johnston | 60 | Senior | 96 |
| Flack/Fleck | 97 | Jones | 96 | Senior | 97 |
| Flack/Fleck | 100 | Jones | 97 | Sproule | 77 |
| Ford | 2 | Kane | 54 | Steele | 35 |
| Frackleton | 66 | Kane | 55 | Streight | 46 |
| Gillespie | 81 | Kirk | 90 | Swan | 63 |
| Gillespie | 82 | Lawrence | 21 | Tyrie | 21 |
| Granger | 33 | Lees | 93 | Williamson | 34 |
| Hack | 29 | Lemon | 87 | Wilson | 23 |
| Hamilton | 3 | Lewis | 86 | Wilson | 24 |
| Hamilton | 4 | Lough | 34 | Wilson | 39 |
| Hamilton | 54 | Macauley | 92 | Wilson | 40 |
| Hamilton | 55 | MacKeown | 1 | Wilson | 59 |
| Hanna | 81 | MacLaughlin | 51 | Wilson | 65 |
| Hanna | 82 | Martin | 75 | Wisnom | 99 |
| Hawthorne | 73 | Martin | 76 | Wright | 15 |
| Hayden | 16 | McAdam | 47 | | |

**D1**

In loving memory of
**ELEANOR MacKEOWN**
Died 1 Nov 1947 aged 81 years
And her husband
**JOHN MacKEOWN**
Died 7th April 1951 aged 81 years

**D2** unused

**D3-D4**

In loving memory of
**SMYLEY**
Beloved son of
**Alex** and **Jennie HAMILTON**
Lost at sea January 1938 aged 22 years
And their children
**MARY, ROBERT AND JANE**
Interred in New Churchyard
The above **JENNIE HAMILTON**
died 21st March 1945
Aged 63 years
The above **ALEXANDER HAMILTON**
died 19th November 1947

- *Buried 27.6.1940 **JOHN McKAY** (sailor): 34 Windsor Ave. Whitehead*
- *Buried 2.10.1972 **AGNES FORD** (age 82, housewife): 68, Windsor Ave. Whitehead*

**D5** unused

**D6**

**BOYD**
In loving memory of
**SAMUEL H.**
Died Oct. 1946
And his dear wife
**ELEANOR L.**
Died Dec. 1985

- *Samuel Hugh: Kings Lea, Kings Road, Whitehead*
- *Eleanor (age 91): 60, Rawbrae Road, Whitehead*

**D7**

In loving memory of
**CORINE EMILY POLGLASE**
Who died 13th November 1943
aged 69 yrs.

- *Corine (married): Windsor Ave. Whitehead*
- *Buried **Miss CORALIE LILLIAN POLGLASE**, (age 82): Whitehead Nursing Home*

**D8**

**THOMAS S.S. HOLMES**
Born 6th Oct. 1883
Died 27th August 1964
"Impossible to forget"

**D9** unused

**D10-D11-D12-D13-D14**

In memory of
**ROBERT HILL**
born 1849 died 1937
**WILLIAM H. HILL**
born 1853 died 1940
**JAMES B.K. HILL**
born 1868 died 1944
**MARY B. HILL**
born 1859 died 1946
**FRANCIS H.H. HILL**
born 2nd Nov 1865 died 8th Dec. 1961
**HILL**

- *Robert (buried 22.1.1937): Gloonan Lodge, Ahoghill*

**D15**

Erected by
Thomas H. Wright
In loving memory of his mother
**ANNA R. H. HILL WRIGHT**
Who died 3rd of September 1935

- *Anna Roberta Holmes Hill Wright (recorded as buried 16.8.1935, age 60): Gloonan Lodge, Ahoghill*

## D16-D17-D18-D19-D20
In memory of
**THOMAS SCOTT**
born 1849 died 1940
**HENRIETTA S. SCOTT**
born 1848 died 1936
**HARIET HILL HAYDEN**
born 1880 died 1966
**EVELYN MAY SCOTT**
born 1885 died 1970
**ROSINA HOLMES SCOTT**
Died 30th January 1972 aged 97 years
**SCOTT**

- *Henrietta S. H. Scott (buried 19.3.1936, age 88, married), Evelyn (buried 7.11.1970, age 72, single) and Rosina (Roslin) (buried 22.2.1972, age 85, single): Hannaville, Greenisland*

## D21
**TYRIE**
In loving memory of
A dear husband and father
**JOHN**
Died 2nd March 1987
Also our dear mother
**MARY JANE**
Died 2nd May 1991
"I am the Resurrection
and the Life"

- *John (age 76) and Mary (age 80): The Beeches, Ballyclare*
- *Buried 10.12.1941* **THOMAS J. LAWRENCE,** *(age 66): Seaview Cottage, Drumgurland. Islandmagee*

## D22 unused

## D23-D24
- *Buried 12.8.1945* **HUGH WILSON,** *(farmer): Ballymuldrough, Islandmagee*
- *Buried 9.3.1970* **Mrs. MARGARET ISABELLA WILSON,** *(age 83): same address*
- *Buried 10.3.1979* **HUGH WILSON,** *(age 64, farmer): 325, Middle Road, Islandmagee*
- *Buried 8.5.1979* **Miss ISABELLA WILSON** *(age 62): same address*
- *Buried 21.6.1996* **WILLIAM WILSON,** *(age 74, farmer): same address*

## D25 unused

## D26 unused

## D27
**ENGLISH**
In memory of
our dear parents
**THOMAS**
Died 8th May 1941
**ELIZABETH**
Died 19th March 1983
Their daughter
**SALLY**
Died 24th December 1927
And son **WILLIAM R.N.**
Lost at sea H.M.S. Daring
18th February 1940

- *Thomas (ex-service man): Parkmount Cottage, Ballyharry, Islandmagee*
- *Elizabeth (age 92): Royal Victoria Hospital Belfast*

## D28
**McKEOWN**
In loving memory of
**BERTIE**
Died 10th February 1967
Aged 45 years
"The Lord is my Shepherd"

- *Robert James (Bertie) (driver): 49, Station Road, Greenisland*
- *Buried 17.3.1947* **JAMES McKEOWN:** *Balmoral Avenue, Whitehead*

**D29**

- *Buried 26.1.1949*
  **WILLIAM GILFORD HACK**
  *(confectioner): Shaftesbury Sq. Whitehead*
- *Buried 1.12.1961* **GEORGINA HACK:**
  *Shaftesbury Square, Whitehead*
- *Buried 15.3.1979*
  **JOHN NEVILLE M. GILFORD HACK**
  *(age 64): 5, Victoria Ave. Whitehead*

**D30**

McCALMONT
In fond memory of
**JOHN McCALMONT**
Who died 10th August 1956
Aged 74 years
And his wife
**SARAH McCALMONT**
Who died 2nd August 1962
Aged 85 years
"Ever Remembered"

**D31-D32**

On surround
**HUNTER**
**MAVIS** loved wife of Michael
Died 20th June 1979
**JOHN STEPHEN**
Infant son of Michael and Mavis
Died 20th January 1950 aged 1 day
**NORA**
Died 10th Feb. 1978
Aged 89 years
**JOHN ANDREW**
Loved husband of Nora
Died 1st March 1963

- *Mavis Hunter (age 59): 9, Cable Road, Whitehead*
- *Nora Hunter: 1, Balfour Ave. Whitehead*

**D33**

**GRANGER**
In memory of
**MINNIE GRANGER**
Died 19th November 1960
**JOHN Wm. GRANGER**
Died 13th June 1961
Beloved parents of Mavis Hunter

- *Minnie and John: 1, Balfour Ave. Whitehead*

**D34**

Flower holder
**JOHN LOUGH**
born Edinburgh
Nov. 29th 1890 – died 1948
And his wife
**CHARLOTTE LAURENSEN**
nee **WILLIAMSON**
Born Edinburgh July 26th 1886 –
died 1954

- *John: 2, Alexandra Ave. Whitehead*

**D35**

- *Buried 29.3.1950*
  **Miss ELIZABETH STEELE:**
  *Wembley Cottage, Islandmagee*

**D36-D37**

In loving memory of
**THOMAS MATTHEW IRVINE**
Who died on the 25th August 1939
And his wife **MARGARET IRVINE**
Who died on the 5th October 1953

- *Thomas: 2, Adelaide Gardens, Whitehead*

**D38**

In loving memory of
A darling wife and mother
**LILY DOBSON** 27th March 1949
And **ADAM B. DOBSON**
Beloved husband and father
18th March 1954
Also their children
**ERIC F. DOBSON**
5th December 1989
**DOROTHY** 23rd March 1999

- *Lily: Wavecrest, Whitehead*
- *Dorothy Madeline (single, age 97): 19, Balmoral Ave. Whitehead*

**D39-D40**

- *Buried 5.11.1935*
  **JAMES MULHOLLAND WILSON,**
  *(schoolboy): Nith View, Pine Terrace, Silloth, Cumberland, England*

D41
## A.H. MEEKE M.D., M.B.
- *Buried 28.12.1935 **ARTHUR HENRY** (age 80, Doctor): The Mount, Whitehead*
- *Buried 20.3.1939 **DEBORAH MEEKE**: same address*

D42-D43
In loving memory
of
My dear mother
**ELIZA JANE CRESSWELL**
Who died 4th January 1935
Also my dear sister **ETHEL**
Who died 25th October 1941
Also my dear brother
**JOHN LEONARD**
Lost at sea during the Great War
20th February 1919
Till the day break and the
shadows flee away
- *Eliza (widow): Craigallen, Kilton, Islandmagee*

D44
**McCALMONT**
Sacred to the memory of
**MARY McCALMONT**
Died 25th April 1934 aged 65 years
Also her husband
**ROBERT McCALMONT**
Master Mariner
Died 28th Sept. 1945 aged 84 years
Their son **JOSEPH**
Died 18th December 1977
aged 85 years
Till we meet
- *Mary: 48, Hillman Street, Belfast*

D45
**REID**
In loving memory of
**ELIZABETH**
Beloved wife of William Reid,
Whitehead
Died 26th December 1938
aged 73 years
And her husband **WILLIAM REID**
Died 23rd March 1954 aged 91 years
Also their dear son
**LEONARD WILLIAM REID**
Died 6th May 1981 aged 83 years
And his devoted wife
**ANNIE ELIZABETH**
Died 12th January 1988
aged 78 years
- *Elizabeth and William (tobacconist): Lynwood, Chester Ave. Whitehead*
- *Leonard (recorded age 82): 7, Carrickburn Road, Carrickfergus*
- *Annie: Carrickfergus Hospital*

D46
**BARBARA CATHERINE STREIGHT**
18-12-1939
**ELIZABETH MARY BAIRD**
30-1-1942
**ROBERT ALEXANDER BAIRD**
29-5-1957
Dominus Regit ME
- *Barbara (age 45, married): Ardnaree, Cable Road, Whitehead*
- *Buried 7.10.1992 **Miss GERTRUDE STREIGHT** (age 95).*

D47-D48
**McADAM**
In memory of
**JOHN McADAM Sgt. Pilot R.A.F.**
Killed in action 20th February 1941
aged 21 years
Also **ROSE McADAM**
Died 8th April 1941 aged 43 years
**JOHN LUSK TORRENS McADAM**
**O.B.E. M.C.**
Died 2nd July 1960 aged 67 years
- *John (1941): York Villa, Cable Road, Whitehead*

D49-D50
In loving memory
of
**JOSEPH McKEOWN HENSHAW**
Who died 20th April 1943
**HENSHAW**

Stone slab with anchor crest
**D. HENSHAW**
Leading Airman R.N. FX. 85331
H.M.S. "Daedalus"
15th December 1941 age 19
He died that we should live

- *Desmond (recorded age 20): Islandview, Whitehead*

- *Buried 28.4.1972*
  ***LILIAN ANN JANE HENSHAW** (age 86, housewife): Clonmore House, Rathcoole, Newtownabbey*

D51
In loving memory of
**Rev. DAVID MACLAUGHLIN
B.D., Ph.D, D.C.F.**
Who died 1st February 1942,
his eldest son
**Lieut. ALEXANDER WILSON**
No.1 Sqdr. R.F.C.
Presumed dead October 1917,
his youngest son
**JAMES EDWARD** who died of
gunshot wounds 25th April 1947
And was interred in Malacca Jahore
His beloved wife **ANNIE**
Died 17th August 1961 in her 97th year
His daughter **NORAH ISOBEL**
Died 25th May 1972 in her 76th year
Thy will be done

- *Rev. David Maclaughlin: Innisfree, Balfour Ave. Whitehead*

- *Norah (Single): Windermere, Rostrevor*

D52-D53
In
Loving memory of
**THE BRANAGH FAMILY**
Erected by
Edith Branagh

- *Buried 31.8.1942*
  ***MINNIE AGNES BRANAGH:**
  Rosemary, Cable Road, Whitehead*

- *Buried 1.12.1989*
  ***Miss EDITH BRANAGH** (age 105):
  Chester Park Nursing Home, Whitehead*

D54-D55
On surround
"This is the victory even our faith"
In loving memory of
**AGNES ETTA HAMILTON**
devoted wife of John
died 31st Oct. 1989
In remembrance of
**Rev. GEORGE KANE** Sen. Minister
of Saltersland Pres. Church who
entered into rest 19th May 1948
In remembrance of
**A. LOUISE SHANNON KANE**
who entered into rest
15th December 1943
Their dtr. **ISABEL KANE**
died 16th December 1987
dear sister of Etta and John

- *Rev. and Mrs. Louise Kane: Brightside, Balmoral Ave. Whitehead
  (Note – burial dates are recorded as:
  Rev. Kane 17.12.1943 and
  Mrs. Kane 21.5.1948)*

- *Miss Emily Isabella Kane (age 71):
  8, York Ave. Whitehead*

D56
In loving memory of
**THOMAS GILMORE McGOWAN**
Who entered into rest 12th July 1938
Also **EVANGELINE McGOWAN**
Who died 2nd December 1966

- *Gilbert T. McGowan (recorded age 52, labourer) and Evangeline (single, age 82, nurse): Ballykeel, Islandmagee*

D57

In loving memory of
**WILLIAM HOLMES**
Who died 24th April 1945
Also his wife **ESTHER**
Died 13th February 1983
Aged 87 years

* *Esther (recorded age 86):*
  *27, Langdale Lane, Islandmagee*

D58

**PULLIN**
In loving memory of
My dear husband
**ALEXANDER**
Died 25th August 1940
Aged 74 years
Also
**ISABELLA**
His wife
Died 25th September 1953
Aged 83 years

* *Alexander: Station Road, Ballycarry*

D59

In loving memory of
**MARGARET A. WILSON**
Who died 9th December 1951
Also her Aunt **ELLEN WILSON**
Who died 27th April 1941

* *Ellen (single, age 74): Ballykeel,*
  *Islandmagee*

D60

In loving memory of our dear mother
**ELIZABETH JOHNSTON**
Who died on the 12th of July 1947
**GEORGINA,** daughter of above
Died 22nd November 1981
Also her daughter **BESSIE**
Died 18th December 1989
**JOHNSTON**

* *Georgina (age 74) and Bessie (single, age*
  *75): 81, Ravenhill Gardens, Belfast*

D61

* *Buried 9.3.1941*
  ***JAMES ERNEST PALMER*** *(sailor): Jubilee*
  *Cottage, Prince of Wales Ave. Whitehead*

* *Buried 4.4.1973* ***Mrs. SARAH PALMER,***
  *(age 78, home duties):*
  *12, Windsor Crescent, Whitehead*

D62

**BOYD**
In memory of
**WILLIAM BOYD,**
Master, S.S. Castlehill
Lost by enemy action
2nd March 1941
Also his wife **MARGARET**
Died 3rd July 1965

D63

**SWAN**

* *Buried 4.2.1950* ***Mrs. ANNIE W. SWAN,***
  *(housewife): 25, Rowan Street, Belfast*

D64

**HEGGAN**
In loving memory of my wife
**JENNIE**
Died 31st Oct. 1941
Also our sons
**WILLIAM**
Lost at sea, Jan. 1927
And **HERBERT,**
Died 3rd December 1941
Also **WILLIAM HEGGAN**
Died 31st May 1958

* *Jenny and Herbert: Ballystrudder,*
  *Islandmagee*

D65

**WILSON**
My dear husband
**JAMES**
Died 4th January 1967
And his dear wife
**SARAH**
Died 3rd October 1982

- *James Williamson Wilson (age 76, shipyard worker): Brookside cottage, Boghall, Islandmagee*
- *Sarah (age 87); The Beeches, Ballyclare*

D66

- *Buried 21.6.1943* ***JOHN FRACKLETON** (age 64): Windsor Ave. Whitehead*
- ***VIOLET FRACKELTON** and **IRENE PATRICIA FRACKELTON** (details not recorded)*

D67-D68

- *Buried 9.7.1944*
  ***Mrs. MARTHA DICK HOPKINS:** Upper Gransha, Islandmagee*

D69-D70

In loving memory of
**ROBERT AULD**
Who died 20th June 1944 and his wife
**CATHERINE AULD**
Who died 13th January 1949
**JAMES AULD** died 13th May 1976
**ROBERT AULD** died 29th Jan. 1977
Erected by their family James,
Donald, John and Robert

- *Robert (1944, age 93, farmer) and James (age 81): Port Davey, Whitehead*

D71-D72

- *Buried 22.3.1935*
  ***MARGARET AGNES MORTON** (age 57, married): Craigailsa, Victoria Ave. Whitehead*

D73

Loving memories of
**SARA HAWTHORNE**
Died 9th December 1971
Also
**JOHN BOYD**
Died 29th September 1992

- *Sarah Nelson Hawthorne (age 69, home duties): Ballystrudder Gardens, Islandmagee*
- *John Ross Fleck Boyd (age 73): 43, Ballystrudder Gardens, Islandmagee*
- *Buried 23.3.1931*
  ***Mrs. ELLEN HAWTHORNE:** Ballymoney, Islandmagee*
- *Buried 19.2.1940* ***JAMES HAWTHORNE** (age 71): Ballymuldrough, Islandmagee*

D74

- *Buried 22.4.1928*
  ***ISABELLA DAVEY** (age 29, married): Ballymoney, Islandmagee*

D75-D76

**MARTIN**
Sacred to the memory of
Our dear daughter **DOROTHY JEAN**
Who was called home
28th February 1930
and my dear wife **JEAN** who died
20th April 1953
Safe in the arms of Jesus

- *Dorothy (age 12): Breezemount, Islandmagee*
- *Buried 19.9.1975*
  ***WILLIAM HOLMES MARTIN** (age 82): Ballycraigy, Ballymena*

D77

**SPROULE**
In
Loving memory of our dear parents
**ROBERT SPROULE**
Who died 10th July 1935
**ELIZABETH SPROULE**
Who died 8th November 1959

- *Robert (age 61, engineer): 7, Adelaide Ave. Whitehead*

D78-D79

In loving remembrance of
**SAMUEL HAYDOCK**
Died 6th March 1937
And his wife **MARY**
died 12th October 1939
Also their daughter **MARTHA**
died 15th November 1946
Their son **ROBERT**
died 26th June 1951
Interred at Danville Virginia U.S.A.
Their son **SAMUEL**
died 18th November 1952
On surround
Their daughter **MARY**
died 6th October 1966
Their son **WILLIAM JAMES**
died 5th March 1971
Their son **ALFRED** died 10th
January 1953 interred in this cemetery
Their son **JOHN** died 26th
December 1958 interred in Park
Lawn Cemetry Toronto

- *Samuel (age 76): Mayfield, Balfour Ave. Whitehead*
- *Martha (recorded as Mrs. Martha Haydock): Silverstream House, Greenisland*
- *Daughter Mary (age 68, single, company director): Silverstream House*
- *William (age 84, post office official): 78, Cable Road, Whitehead*

D80

- *Buried 3.7.1937*
  ***ELLEN McCONACHIE***
  *(age 76, housekeeper): Erection House, Islandmagee*
- *Buried 7.10.1937*
  ***CHARLES ST. CLAIR DAWSON:** same address*

D81-D82

**HANNA**
In loving memory of
A dear husband
father and grandfather
**HERBIE**
Died 28th May 1993
Also a dear wife
mother and grandmother
**OLIVE**
Died 15th December 2000

D81-D82

**GILLESPIE**
In loving memory of
our dear sister
**INEZ** died 25th June 1938
also our dear parents
**JAMES** died 21st July 1966
**ANNIE** died 3rd April 1978

- *Herbie Hanna (age 71), Jamesinez (age 10) and Annie Gillespie (age 79): 34, Brownsbay Road, Islandmagee*

D83

- *Buried 29.10.1938*
  ***Mr. FRANCIES McDOWELL BAILLIE***
  *(clerk of works): Portmuck, Islandmagee*
- *Buried 6.3.1983 **FRANK BAILLIE** (age 63): 6, Bank Quay, Larne*

D84-D85

In loving memory of
**GEORGE ALLEN**
Who died 11th Dec. 1940
And his wife **MADGE**
Who died 12th July 1954

- *George (solicitor): Treganna, Cable Road, Whitehead*

**D86**

Erected by Agnes Holmes
In Loving Memory
of her dear sister
**JANE H. LEWIS**
Who departed this life
11th April 1941
also her dear sister
**ISABELLA HOLMES**
died 18th December 1954
the above **AGNES HOLMES**
died 13th Feby. 1961 aged 84 years
Gone to be with Christ
which is far better

• *Jane (widow): Ballyharry, Islandmagee*

**D87**

• ***ROBERT LEMON:*** *Glenfaba, Ferris Bay, Islandmagee (no date recorded)*
• *Buried 16.12.1974*
***Mrs. MABEL LEMON*** *(age 72, housewife): 33A Islandmagee Road, Whitehead*

**D88**

In loving memory of
Our dear mother
**MARGARET N. BARNETT**
Who died 16th December 1943
And our dear father
**WILLIAM BARNETT**
Who died 3rd July 1948
Their daughter **ELIZABETH (LILY)**
Died 13th January 1976

• *Margaret N. McF. Barnett (Note – date of burial recorded as 17.3.1943) and William: Kimberlay Villas, Cable Road, Whitehead*
• *Lily: 23, Cable Road, Whitehead*

**D89**

In loving memory of
**SARAH FORSYTHE CRAIG**
Who died on the 6th March 1944
**JOHN CRAIG** died 17 May 1951

• *Sarah (married): Drumgurland, Islandmagee*

**D90**

• *Buried 9.3.1940* ***Mrs. ANNIE C. BOYD*** *(Estate agent): Islandvale, Chester Ave. Whitehead*
• *Buried 23.12.1996* ***C[lare] KIRK***

**D91**

• *Buried 16.4.1926*
***MARGARET JANE MILLAR***
*(age 21, single): Dundressan, Islandmagee*
• *Buried 13.7.1972* ***THOMAS J. COOK***
*(age 84): 96, Cornation Rd, Carrickfergus*

**D92**

On surround
**MACAULEY**
**MINNIE**
Died 14th February 1935 aged 41
**SAMUEL**
Died 13th April 1967 aged 79
**SAMUEL**
Died 2nd February 1929 aged 8

• *Samuel (farmer): Seaview, Mullaghdubh, Islandmagee*
• *Samuel (junior): Mullaghdubh, Islandmagee*

**D93**

• *Buried 7.11.1929* ***JOHN LEES*** *(age 75): Balmoral Ave. Whitehead*

**D94-D95**

**DICK**
In loving memory of
**THOMAS DICK**
Who died 26th March 1930
aged 70 years
Also his wife **SARAH DICK**
Who died 22nd February 1931
aged 71 years
Also their daughters **MARTHA DICK**
Died 17th December 1971 aged 77 years
**CATHERINE ELIZABETH DICK**
Died 20th June 1972 aged 80 years

• *Thomas (Master Mariner) and Sarah: 15, Newington Ave. Belfast*
• *Martha and Catherine: 167, Kings Road, Belfast*

D96-D97

**FLACK**
In loving memory of
**DAVID FLACK**
Died 30th Oct. 1915 aged 56 years,
buried at sea
Also his wife **MARGARET**
Died 20th February 1932 aged 75 years
and their elder son
**ROBERT ALEXANDER**
lost at sea 16th May 1932 aged 44 years
their daughter
**CATHERINE ELIZABETH**
died 20th July 1966 aged 74 years
On surround
Their daughter
**MARGARET JANE JONES**
Died 31st July 1957 aged 61 years
Their daughter **MARTHA SENIOR**
Died 23rd December 1959
aged 72 years

• Note – Surnames recorded as *FLECK*

• Margaret Flack and
Catherine (recorded age 73, single,
Presbyterian): 19, Alexandra Ave. Belfast

• Martha Pat Senior (housewife)

D98

**McCALMONT**
In loving memory of
**MARY**
beloved wife of Hugh McCalmont
Died 29th November 1950
And his mother **SARAH CAMPBELL**
Died 30th November 1935
Also his son
**HUGH R. McCALMONT**
Died 4th May 1931
The above **HUGH McCALMONT**
Died 13th January 1973
Also his son
**WILLIAM M. McCALMONT**
Died 5th September 1965
Interred Avonview Bristol

• Hugh Reginald (age 14):
Bognor, Knowehead, Islandmagee

• Hugh (age 84, seaman):
34, Gainsborough Drive, Belfast

D99

In loving memory of
**JANE WISNOM**
Who died on the 15th March 1934
And her husband
**WILLIAM WISNOM**
Who died on the 12th of January 1953

• Jane: Riverbrook, Cable Road, Whitehead

D100

The family burying ground
of
**JOHN FLECK**

• Buried 26.11.1939 **JOHN FLACK**
(age 28, mariner): The Hill, Islandmagee

• Buried 26.8.1967 **JOHN FLECK** (age 88):
The Hill, Islandmagee and then Carnduff,
Larne

D101 unused

D102

• Buried 16.11.1934 **WILLIAM POLLOCK**
(age 65, mariner): Mullaghboy,
Islandmagee

D103

• Buried 22.2.1953 **Miss MARY FLACK**:
Magheramorne House

• Buried 11.7.1978
**Mrs. MARY AGNES FLACK** (housewife):
Islandmagee Road, Whitehead

• Buried 20.3.1979 **ALEXANDER FLACK,**
(age 72): 67 Islandmagee Road,
Whitehead

D104

• Buried 28.12.1934 **ANDREW ROSS,**
(cattle dealer): 12, Ardenlee Parade,
Cregagh, Belfast

D105

• Buried 6.12.1946
**Mrs. ANNIE MULVENNA:**
Gransha, Islandmagee

D106 unused

**Grave Plots Plan**

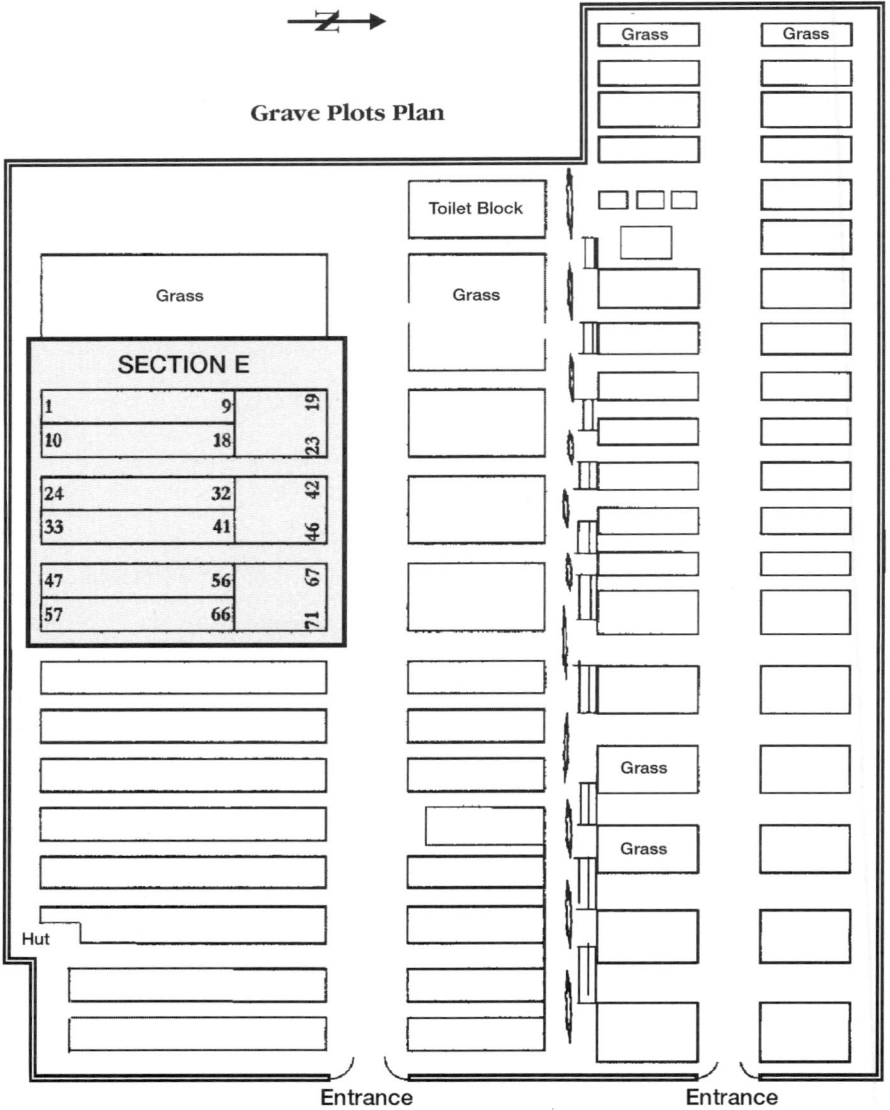

N →

| Grass | Grass |

Toilet Block

Grass

Grass

| SECTION E | | |
| 1 | 9 | 19 |
| 10 | 18 | 23 |
| 24 | 32 | 42 |
| 33 | 41 | 46 |
| 47 | 56 | 67 |
| 57 | 66 | 71 |

Hut

Grass

Grass

Entrance    Entrance

# ~ ISLANDMAGEE NEW CEMETERY ~

**Whitehead**    ~ **LOW ROAD** ~    **Ballylumford**

←    →

# SECTION E

| Name | Plot | Name | Plot | Name | Plot |
|---|---|---|---|---|---|
| Beattie | 29 | Higginson | 22 | Montgomery | 39 |
| Bell | 4 | Hill | 29 | Nash | 38 |
| Black | 59 | Hughes | 53 | Niblock | 8 |
| Blakely | 69 | Irvine | 70 | Niblock | 9 |
| Busby | 57 | Jones | 34 | Niblock | 67 |
| Cameron | 42 | Jones | 36 | Niblock | 68 |
| Clarke | 27 | Jones | 64 | Rea | 64 |
| Coleman | 63 | Kernaghan | 28 | Reid | 55 |
| Cooper | 71 | Macklin | 38 | Rowlatt | 45 |
| Crafter | 24 | Magill | 55 | Rowlatt | 46 |
| Dick | 17 | Martin | 7 | Rush | 5 |
| Dinsmore | 40 | Maxwell | 67 | Rush | 6 |
| Dinsmore | 41 | Maxwell | 68 | Sinclair | 14 |
| Dixon | 15 | McCallan | 37 | Smiley | 60 |
| Donaldson | 52 | McCluney | 50 | Stead | 51 |
| Egar | 54 | McCluskey | 65 | Stephenson | 21 |
| English | 17 | McComb | 32 | Taylor | 3 |
| English | 18 | McCorkell | 1 | Templeton | 60 |
| Gamble | 30 | McCorkell | 2 | Templeton | 61 |
| Gamble | 31 | McMaw | 19 | Thompson | 56 |
| Gillespie | 33 | McMaw | 20 | Toppon | 66 |
| Gillespie | 35 | McNally | 12 | Warwick | 63 |
| Grubba | 42 | McPherson | 23 | White | 16 |
| Hagan | 25 | Mitchell | 47 | Williamson | 10 |
| Hagan | 26 | Mitchell | 48 | Williamson | 11 |
| Hamilton | 35 | Mitchell | 49 | Wilson | 12 |
| Hamilton | 38 | Mitchell | 62 | Wilson | 13 |

## E1-E2

- *Buried 27.1.1981*
  **Mrs. JANE BELL McCORKELL**
  *(age 55, housewife):*
  *8, Islandmagee Road, Whitehead*

## E3

### TAYLOR
In loving remembrance of
**WILLIAM** who died 18th July 1959
And his wife **GEORGINA LINDSAY**
Died 2nd September 1983

- *William: Seabank, Promenade, Whitehead*
- *Georgina Taylor (age 84, homeduties):*
  *154, Main Street, Cloughey, Co. Down*

## E4

In fond memory of
**ELIZABETH LOUISA**
Loved wife of William John Bell
Died 13th July 1959
Also **WILLIAM J. BELL**
Died 20th April 1974
**WILLIAM JOHN BELL**
died 29th May 1995
Beloved husband of Greta
**BELL**

- *Elizabeth (housewife),*
  *William (age 87, railway official) and*
  *William John (age 75):*
  *5, Alexandra Ave. Whitehead*

## E5-E6

### RUSH
In loving memory of
**MARGARET INGRAM**
Dearly loved wife of
Thomas J. Rush
Who died 6th September 1973
The above **THOMAS J. RUSH**
Who died 24th April 1986
Also their son **T.P. INGRAM RUSH**
Who died 17th May 1990

- *Margaret (age 75):*
  *1, Locksley Park, Finaghy*
- *Thomas John (age 95):*
  *7, Gregg House, Lisburn*
- *Thomas Percival (age 56):*
  *196A, Ormeau Road, Belfast*

## E7

### MARTIN
In loving memory of
**JAMES DICK MARTIN**
Died 17th April 1971

- *James (age 72, supervisor):*
  *4, Glenbroome Park, Jordanstown*

## E8-E9

### NIBLOCK
In
Loving memory of
**ALEXANDER NIBLOCK,**
Master Mariner
Who died 4th July 1957 aged 60 years
His wife **ELIZA (LILY)**
Who died 31st January 1981
aged 79 years

- *Alexander: 32, Victoria Ave. Whitehead*
- *Lily: 24, Edward Road, Whitehead*

## E10-E11

In loving memory of
**MARY ANN**
Died 26th Dec. 1973 aged 85 years
Beloved wife of David
**WILLIAMSON**
Also the above named **DAVID**
Born 19th Sept. 1886
died 20th July 1977

- *Mary (recorded age 86, housewife):*
  *120 Disraeli Street, Belfast*
- *David (age 91):*
  *35 Woodburn Road, Carrickfergus*

E12-E13

**WILSON**
In loving memory of our dear son
**DAVID**
Who died 12th June 1959,
result of an accident
Aged 21 years
Also **ELIZABETH WILSON**
mother of the above named
Who died 10th July 1972
Also her husband **ALFRED E.**
Died 10th February 1973

- *David (recorded age 22),
  Elizabeth (age 59, housewife) and
  Alfred (age 61, green keeper):
  45, Islandmagee Road, Whitehead*
- *Buried 1.3.1973* **BRIAN McNALLY**
  *(age 35, wages clerk): Westland Park,
  Cookstown*

E14

In loving memory of
Our mother
**MARY SINCLAIR**
1908-1998

- *Mary (buried 19th October, age 90):
  Carnlough Nursing Home*

E15

- *Buried 16.8.1958*
  **SAMUEL JOHN DIXON:**
  *51, Windsor Ave. Whitehead*
- *Buried 7.1.1976* **Mrs. AGNES DIXON**
  *(housewife): 51 Windsor Ave.*
- *Buried 25.5.1983*
  **SAMUEL JOHN DIXON** *(age 55):
  Muckamore Abbey Hospital*

E16

- *Buried 26.4.1958 surname* **WHITE:**
  *27, Adelaide Ave. Whitehead*

E17-E18

**ENGLISH**
In
Loving memory of
**ALEXANDER ENGLISH, M.B.E.**
Master Mariner
Who died 15th September 1958
aged 82 years
Also his beloved wife
**MINNIE nee DICK**
Died 11th October 1989 aged 95 years

- *Alexander (date of death recorded as 1956):
  38, Cable Road, Whitehead*
- *Minnie: 73, Windsor Ave. Whitehead*

E19-E20

**McMAW**
In loving memory of
**WILLIAM McMAW**
Died 14th June 1956 aged 64 years
Also his sister **ELIZA JANE**
died 3rd May 1971 aged 86 years
And his wife **ELIZA MARY MANN**
Died 27th April 1984 aged 86 years
Also their son **ROBERT**
Died 1st November 1995 aged 71 years

- *William (farmer) and Eliza Jane (single):
  Dundressan, Islandmagee*
- *Eliza Mary Mann McMaw and Robert:
  50, Brownsbay Road, Islandmagee*

E21

**STEPHENSON**
In loving memory of
**THOMAS EDWARD STEPHENSON**
Called to higher service on
20th July 1961
With Thee O Lord forever to abide
In that blessed land that hath
No eventide

E22

- *Buried 13.7.1956*
  **HERBERT HIGGINSON:**
  *Portmuck, Islandmagee*
- *Buried 11.12.1962*
  **Mrs. FRANCES HIGGINSON:**
  *Portmuck*

## E23

- *Buried 5.8.1954* **Mr. W.E. McPHERSON:** *31, Hartington Street, Belfast*
- *Buried 3.1.1992* **Mrs. MARGARET McPHERSON** *(age 86): Belfast City Hospital*
- *Buried 20.6.1994* **Mrs. MARTHA McPHERSON** *(age 84): Minnowburn House, Shawsbridge, Belfast*

## E24

In
Loving memory of
**WILLIAM C. CRAFTER**
Died 7th March 1959
And his dear wife
**NESSA** died 7th May 1978

- *William C. (recorded as G) and Agnes M. (age 73): Clanferran, Islandmagee*

## E25

In loving memory of
**Captain SAMUEL HAGAN**
Master Mariner
Born 2nd January 1921
Died 24th February 1989
**MARGARET L.D. HAGAN**
(nee **Macdonald**)
born 2nd March 1929
died 11th October 1997

- *Samuel and Margaret Leighton Duff: 85A, Belfast Road, Carrickfergus*

## E26

In loving memory of
**WILLIAM SAMUEL HAGAN**
Commander (E) R.N.R.
Died 9th April 1958 aged 76
Also his wife
**WILHELMINA**
Died 21st April 1974 aged 83
And their beloved daughter
**ISOBEL CAMERON HAGAN**
Died 19th Aug. 2001 aged 77

- *William: Castletown, Whitehead*
- *Wilhelmina and Isobel (single): 23, McCreas Brae, Whitehead*

## E27

- *Buried 8.12.1957* **Mrs. MARGARET CLARKE** *(housewife): Mullaghboy, Islandmagee*
- *Buried 12.1.1967* **Mrs. ELIZABETH CLARKE** *(age 76, housewife): Mullaghboy*
- *Buried 23.12.1968* **THOMAS CLARKE** *(age 73, woodturner): Mullaghboy*

## E28

- *Buried 9.12.1954* **Mrs. ISABEL KERNAGHAN** *(housewife): 17, Victoria Ave. Whitehead*
- *Buried 10.7.1996* **JAMES WHITE KERNAGHAN** *(age 80): Whitehead Private Nursing Home*

## E29

In memory of
**JEAN BEATTIE**
Sister-in-law of Thomas Hill
Died 27th June 1961 aged 68 years
And his wife **MARGARET**
Died 31st January 1972 aged 81 years
The above **THOMAS HILL**
Died 27th Sept. 1972 aged 86 years

- *Margaret and Thomas: 44 Alexandra Ave. Whitehead*

## E30-E31

**GAMBLE**
In loving memory of
Our father and mother
**JAMES G. GAMBLE F.R.I.B.A.**
Died 5th January 1956
Aged 95
And his loving wife
**SARAH E. GAMBLE**
Died 6th May 1969
Aged 95

- *James Gardiner Gamble (year recorded as 1955): 8, Prince of Wales Ave. Whitehead*
- *Sarah (year recorded as 1968, age 93): 47, Denorrton Park, Belfast*

**E32**

In loving memory of
**THOMAS McCOMB**
Who died on the 27th August 1953

- *T. J. A. McComb: Stalhuim, Balfour Ave. Whitehead*
- *Buried 10.3.1986*
  **Mrs. SUSAN LOWRY McCOMB** *(age 89): 8, Balfour Ave. Whitehead*
- *Buried 28.2.1987*
  **THOMAS JAMES ARTHUR McCOMB D. F. C.** *(age 63): 8, Balfour Ave. Whitehead*

**E33**

In fond memory of
**JAMES W.**
Loved husband of
**Maud GILLESPIE**
Died 17th Sept. 1967

- *James Woodside Gillespie (age 55, seaman): Millbay, Islandmagee*

**E34**

In loving memory of
**ISOBEL ELIZABETH JONES**
Who died 14th Feby. 1967
aged 61 years
Also beloved husband **ANDREW**
Who died 16th Aug. 1997
aged 89 years

- *Isobel (recorded age 59): Millbay, Islandmagee*
- *Andrew: 67, Ballystrudder Gardens, Islandmagee*

**E35**

**HAMILTON**
In loving memory of
A dear husband and father
**THOMAS**
Died 22nd August 1955 aged 27 years
Result of an accident
Also beloved wife and devoted mother
**MAUREEN** (nee **GILLESPIE**)
Died 27th December 1991 aged 62 years
Till in Heaven we take our place

- *Thomas Alfred (sailor): Millbay, Islandmagee*
- *Maureen: 68, Ballystrudder Gardens, Islandmagee*

**E36**

**JONES**
In loving memory of
A devoted wife and mother
**JEANNIE JONES**
Died 18th February 1963
Also a devoted husband and father
**THOMAS JONES**
Died 27th May 1967
Present with the Lord

- *Jeannie:*
  *5, Egeria Street, Belfast*
- *Thomas (age 75, seaman):*
  *Clifton House, Clifton Street, Belfast*

**E37**

- *Buried 25.8.1954*
  **Mrs. ANNIE McCALLAN:**
  *Lower Gransha, Islandmagee*

E38

In loving memory of
**MARY JANE MACKLIN**
Died 30th November 1970
aged 93 years
Her daughter
**MARGARET JANE NASH**
Died in South Africa
2nd May 1987 aged 78 years
**DOROTHY HAMILTON** 1904-1994

- *Mary Jane (Jean), (married, recorded age 92): Ivydene, Ferris Bay, Islandmagee*
- *Dorothy (single, age 91): 4, Alexandra Court, Whitehead*

E39

In loving memory of
**WILLIAM**
husband of **Alice MONTGOMERY**
Died 28th May 1954

- *William: Redhall, Ballycarry*
- *Buried 1.6.1990*
  ***Mrs. ALICE MONTGOMERY** (age 99): 62, Windsor Ave. Whitehead*

E40-E41

In loving memory of
**AILEEN MARION**
Died 4th January 1954 also her mother
**MARION GARDINER**
died 28th December 1958
Also her father
**HENRY DINSMORE**
Died 16th November 1968
Also **DENIS H.**
Son of Henry and Marion
Died 13th April 1983
**DINSMORE**

- *Aileen Dinsmore and Ephraim Henry (age 75, civil servant): 28, Victoria Ave. Whitehead*
- *Denis (age 52): 8, Donegall Drive, Whitehead*

E42

**CAMERON**
In memory of
Our dear parents
**THOMAS**
Died 26th September 1957
**MARY**
Died 29th June 1990
Also their son
**DANIEL GREER**
Died April 1992

- *Mary (age 92) and Daniel Greer Cameron (buried 10.4.1992, age 64, single): Ransevyn Gardens, Whitehead*
- *Buried 23.4.1952 **Mrs. E. GRUBBA**: 7, Windsor Parade, Whitehead*

E43 unused

E44 unused

E45-E46

- *Buried 9.5.1951*
  ***PATRICIA W. E. ROWLATT**: 34 Windsor Ave. Whitehead*

E47

**MITCHELL**
In loving memory of
**WILLIAM SAMUEL**
Died 30th January 1993 aged 64 years

E48-E49

In loving memory of
**FLORENCE**
wife of Hamilton B. Mitchell
Died 12th October 1956 aged 72 years
The above
**HAMILTON B. MITCHELL**
Died 20th June 1973 in his 93rd year
Also their son
**HAMILTON B. MITCHELL**
Died 12th March 1986 aged 66 years

- *Florence and the first Hamilton: 2, Fordville, Islandmagee*
- *Son Hamilton Buchanan Mitchell: 15, Lough Road, Islandmagee*

**E50**

### McCLUNEY
In loving memory of
**THOMAS McCLUNEY**
Died 10th July 1967
And his wife **MARY BEATRICE**
Died 9th February 1993

- *Thomas (age 68, sign writer):*
  *8, Ransevyn Drive, Whitehead*

**E51**

- *Buried 26.12.1954*
  ***Mrs. MARGARET STEAD** (housewife):*
  *27 Balfour Ave. Whitehead*

**E52**

### DONALDSON
In loving memory of
**ALEXANDER**
Died 30th November 1986
And infant daughters
Born June 1951 and May 1954

- *Alexander (age 80): 58, Islandmagee*
  *Road, Whitehead*
- *The baby who died in 1954:*
  *Clan Ferran, Islandmagee*

**E53**

- *Buried 13.4.1954*
  ***WILLIAM ED. HUGHES** (schoolboy):*
  *Whitehouse, Islandmagee*
- *Buried (no date) **WILLIAM HUGHES***
  *(labourer): Ballylumford, Islandmagee*
- *Buried 27.5.1995*
  ***Mrs. FRANCES AGNES HUGHES***
  *(age 93): 35, Torr Gardens, Larne*

**E54**

### EGAR
In loving memory of
My dear husband **JAMES E. EGAR**
Died 30th October 1951

- *James: Shore Road, Greenisland*
- *Buried 3.4. 1978 **SARAH E. EGAR***
  *(age 80): Shore Road, Greenisland*

**E55**

### MAGILL
In loving memory of
**WILLIAM REID**
Beloved husband of Bessie Magill
Died 8th December 1957
Also his loving wife **BESSIE**
Died 26th March 1984
Also their dear son **ROBERT REID**
Died 19th June 1981
Beloved husband of Annie

- *Robert (age 69): 52, Deacon Street, Belfast*
- *Buried 4.9.1994 **ANNIE MAGILL** (age 79):*
  *52 Deacon Street*

**E56**

- *Buried 10.11.1953 **Infant THOMPSON:***
  *Ballyharry, Islandmagee*

**E57**

- *Buried 29.10.1956 **ROBERT BUSBY***
  *(farmer): Lower Gransha, Islandmagee*
- *Buried 18.2.1968 **Mrs. JANE S. BUSBY***
  *(housekeeper): Grace Ave. Ballygally*

**E58** unused

**E59**

In memory of
**HILARY ANN**
Beloved infant daughter of
Joan and Desmond Black
Died 16th January 1954
The above **JOAN**
Beloved wife of **Desmond BLACK**
Died 9th May 1959

- *Hilary: The Manse Islandmagee*
- *Joan: The Manse, Blackrock*

E60-E61

In loving memory of
**WILLIAM TEMPLETON**
Died 18th August 1958
Aged 78 years
Also his wife
**JENNIE LOUISE** nee **SMILEY**
Died 25th April 1977
Aged 86 years

E62

Erected by
Charles A. Mitchell
In loving memory of his wife
**SHEILA JANE**
Who died 28th October 1953
Also **JOANNA RUTH**
Loved daughter of Charles and Jean
Died 7th September 1974 aged 8 years
(the result of an accident)
also
**CHARLES ALEXANDER MITCHELL**
Died 9th August 1975 aged 51 years
"Safe in the arms of Jesus"

- *Sheila: Jesmond, Islandmagee*
- *Joanna and Charles (foreman fitter): 86, Brownsbay Road, Islandmagee*

E63

- *Buried 19.10.1953*
  *Miss JEAN WARWICK: Westview, Ballystrudder, Islandmagee*
- *Buried 24.4.1954*
  *Mrs. MARGARET WARWICK: Westview*
- *Buried 27.10.1987*
  *Miss ISOBEL COLEMAN (age 94): 26, Ballystrudder Road, Islandmagee*
- *Buried 15.1.1988*
  *Miss ELIZABETH WARWICK (age 88): 26 Ballystrudder Road*

E64

Flower holder
**JONES**
**SAMUEL**
13-9-1978
**ANNIE MARIE**
Died 6-1-1993
In loving memory of
**SAMUEL E. JONES**
died
13th September 1978
from
his son Brian
dtr.-in-law Anna
and family

Plaque
**JANE REA**
Died 13th Dec. 1956
**SAMUEL JONES**
Died 13th September 1978
**ANNIE MARIE JONES**
Died 6th Jan. 1993

- *Mrs. Jane Rea (housewife): 22, Shore Road, Magheramorne*
- *Annie (age 76, married): 5, Glenvale Park, Glynn*

E65

**McCLUSKEY**
In
Loving memory of my dear husband
**WALTER**
Who died 23rd October 1952
**JEANIE** wife of the above
Died 21st October 1981

(on surround)
In loving memory of **BRIAN**
a dear husband and father,
died 5th August 1992

- *Walter and Jeannie Alexandra Burns McCluskey (age 77, housewife): 17, Ballytober Lane, Islandmagee*
- *WALTER BRIAN McCLUSKEY (age 49, N.I.E. employee): 16, Loughview Bungalows, Islandmagee*

E66

- *Buried 2.10.1951*
  **JOSEPH GEORGE TOPPON:**
  *Ballytober, Islandmagee*

E67-E68

In loving memory of
**ANDREW NIBLOCK**
Died 31st March 1951 aged 64 years
His wife **AGNES**
Died 7th March 1907 aged 31 years
And was interred in
Old Church Burying Ground
And their son-in-law
**SAMUEL MAXWELL**
Died 21st Nov. 1959 aged 65 years
And **MARY** wife of the above
Samuel Maxwell
Died 24th May 1976 in her 82nd year

- *Andrew: Mullaghdubh*
- *Mary: 54 Ballystrudder Gardens,
  Islandmagee*

E69

In loving memory of
Our darling daughter
**MARGARET ANNE BLAKELY**
Who passed to the higher life
15th February 1951 in her 21st year
also her father **DAVID**
died 14th November 1985
aged 90 years
also her mother **SARAH**
died 15th October 1988 aged 90 years
**BLAKELY**

- *Margaret: Blackhead Lighthouse,
  Whitehead*
- *David Thomas McCullough Blakely and
  Sarah: 392 Antrim Road, Glengormley*

E70

In fond remembrance of
**JOHN IRVINE**
Beloved husband of
**ANNIE B. IRVINE**
Died 14th February 1951 aged 48 years
And his wife **ANNIE**
Died 28th February 1979 aged 67 years

- *John (turbine driver): Ballymuldrough,
  Islandmagee*
- *Annie Bryson Irvine:
  2, Queensway, Carrickfergus*

E71

In loving memory
of
**JOHN BUCKNALL COOPER**
Who died 7th February 1951
Aged 88 years

- *John: Tara, Cloughfin, Islandmagee*
- *Buried 6.4.1959* **Miss E. M. COOPER:**
  *Whitehead*

# Grave Plots Plan

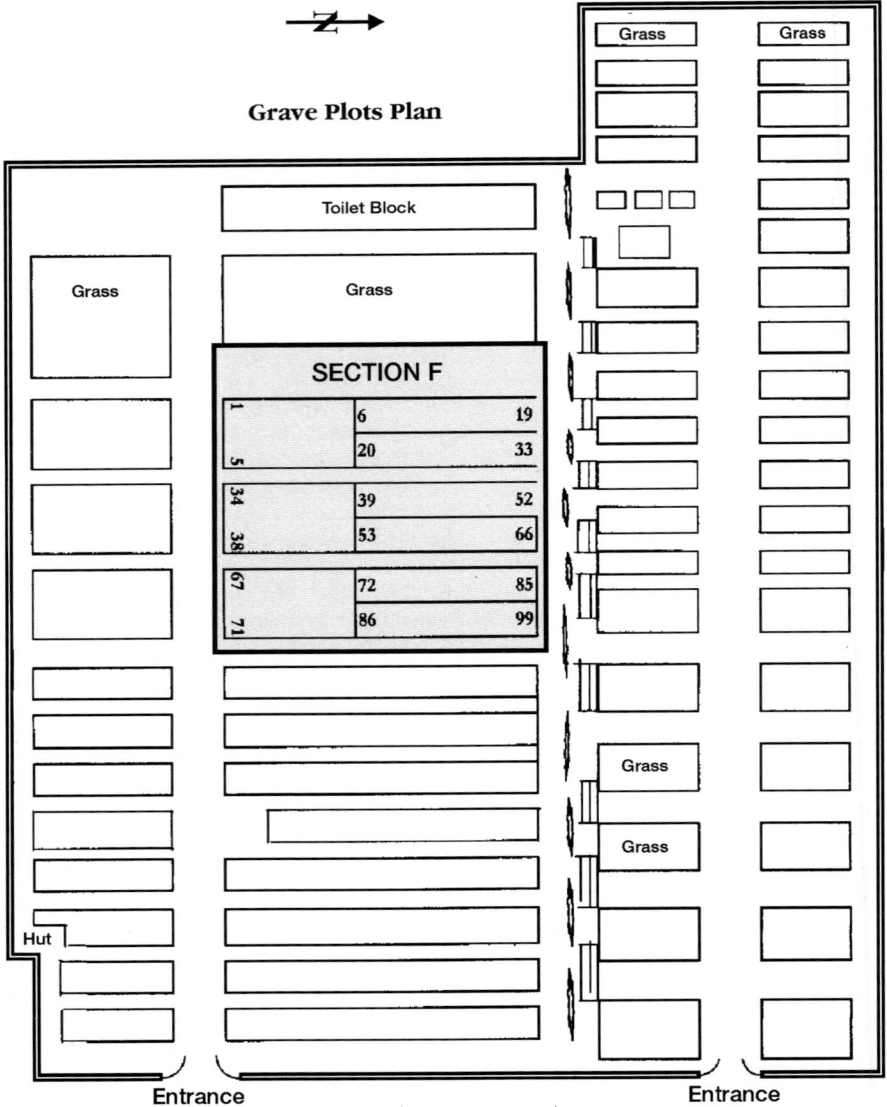

Toilet Block

Grass

Grass

## SECTION F

| | | |
|---|---|---|
| 1 | 6 | 19 |
| 5 | 20 | 33 |
| 34 | 39 | 52 |
| 38 | 53 | 66 |
| 67 | 72 | 85 |
| 71 | 86 | 99 |

Grass

Grass

Grass

Grass

Grass

Grass

Hut

Entrance

Entrance

## ~ ISLANDMAGEE NEW CEMETERY ~

**Whitehead**

~ LOW ROAD ~

**Ballylumford**

# SECTION F

| Name | Plot | Name | Plot | Name | Plot |
|------|------|------|------|------|------|
| Acheson | 77 | Donnelly | 95 | McCafferty | 67 |
| Adair | 22 | Duncan | 6 | McCalmont | 80 |
| Adair | 23 | Duncan | 7 | McClure | 21 |
| Adams | 98 | Esler | 77 | McDowell | 26 |
| Adamson | 17 | Forsythe | 97 | McGowan | 13 |
| Adamson | 18 | Fulton | 34 | McKinstry | 96 |
| Agnew | 29 | Gallimore | 39 | McMaster | 11 |
| Bashford | 15 | Gamble | 14 | McNeill | 1 |
| Bingham | 48 | Gillespie | 59 | Meeke | 32 |
| Blyth | 90 | Gordon | 50 | Meeke | 33 |
| Blyth | 91 | Gordon | 60 | Morgan | 10 |
| Boucher | 40 | Gordon | 61 | Murdock | 32 |
| Boyd | 20 | Gray | 16 | Murdock | 33 |
| Branagh | 88 | Greaves | 93 | O'Connell | 45 |
| Branagh | 89 | Hall | 82 | Osborne | 56 |
| Brooks | 68 | Hanvey | 81 | Osborne | 57 |
| Browne | 56 | Hay | 68 | Reid | 49 |
| Browne | 57 | Hay | 69 | Ross | 38 |
| Budd | 92 | Haydock | 76 | Semple | 36 |
| Busby | 58 | Hill | 71 | Semple | 37 |
| Campbell | 46 | Hinton | 62 | Sheppard | 12 |
| Campbell | 47 | Houston | 41 | Simpson | 40 |
| Casey | 73 | Irwin | 78 | Sims | 9 |
| Casey | 74 | Irwin | 82 | Smyth | 27 |
| Casey | 87 | Johnston | 95 | Smyth | 54 |
| Connelly | 6 | Jones | 63 | Smyth | 55 |
| Connelly | 7 | Kane | 5 | Speirs | 72 |
| Crabbe | 58 | Kane | 53 | Stevenson | 79 |
| Craig | 73 | Kell | 75 | Templeton | 86 |
| Craig | 74 | Knox | 85 | Todd | 19 |
| Cummings | 70 | Long | 64 | Whatley | 88 |
| Dallas | 45 | Long | 65 | Whatley | 89 |
| Dick | 3 | Macdonald | 30 | Wilson | 83 |
| Dick | 24 | Macdonald | 31 | Wilson | 84 |
| Dick | 25 | Magee | 8 | Witherspoon | 42 |
| Dick | 43 | Magowan | 35 | Wotherspoon | 42 |
| Dick | 44 | Martin | 28 | Young | 50 |
| Dick | 4 | Martin | 72 | | |
| Donaldson | 62 | Mawhinney | 4 | | |

## F1

Black metal cross
**G & R McNEILL**

- *Buried 16.11.1973 **GEORGE McNEILL**
  (age 83: 33 Mervue St. Belfast*
- *Buried 8.1.1982
  **Mrs. RACHAEL McNEILL** (age 91):
  Masserene Hospital*

## F2 unused

## F3

In loving memory of
**HUGH** eldest son of
Thomas A. and Margaret **DICK**
Died 10th March 1974 aged 52 years

- *Hugh (railway worker): 21 Edward Road,
  Whitehead*

## F4

**DICK**
In loving memory of
**THOMAS AUGUSTUS**
Died 12th April 1972 aged 81 years
And his wife
**MARGARET** nee **Mawhinney**
Died 24th June 1981 aged 81 years
Also my dear parents
**WILLIAM** and **ABBY MAWHINNEY**
And their sons
**ANDREW and JAMES**
Killed in action
The Lord is my shepherd

- *Thomas and Margaret: 21 Edward Road,
  Whitehead*
- *Abby (buried 10.9.1954): Ballystrudder,
  Islandmagee*

## F5

In loving memory of
Our dear parents
**JOHN** died 5th May 1954
**MARTHA JANE** died 30th Nov. 1973
**KANE**

- *John (farmer) and Martha (age 70,
  housewife): Mullaghboy, Islandmagee*

## F6-F7

In
Loving memory of
**JOHN RENNIE CONNELLY**
Died 21st February 1957 aged 68 years
And his brother
**JAMES R. CONNELLY**
Died 5th June 1962 aged 67 years
Also **MARY ELLEN DUNCAN**
Died 16th December 1965
Beloved wife of Samuel D. Duncan

- *Buried 29.10.1974
  **SAMUEL DAVIDSON DUNCAN** (age 86):
  Clifton House, Belfast*

## F8

- *Buried 12.4.1957
  **Mrs. JANET P. MAGEE** (housewife):
  Kenbaan, Bentra, Ballycarry*

## F9

- *Buried 5.6.1959 **Mrs. MARION SIMS:**
  1, Sandymount, Comber Road,
  Dundonald*

## F10

**MORGAN**
In loving memory
Of my dear husband
**WILLIAM EWING MORGAN**
Died 12th March 1957
Also his dear wife
**MAUD**
Died 29th April 1977

- *Maud (age 81, housewife):
  12, Chester Ave. Whitehead*

## F11

In loving memory of
**WILLIAM McMASTER**
Master Mariner
Lost at sea 18th September 1944
Deeply missed
And his wife **ANNIE A.**
Died 15th December 1995
Beloved mother and grandmother

- *Annie Agnes (age 93):
  26, Sunningdale Park, Belfast*

F12

In fond memory of
**MARY ISOBEL**
Loved wife of Thomas Sheppard
Died 12th September 1957
Also her loved husband **THOMAS**
Died 18th October 1981
**SHEPPARD**

- *Mary: 5, Windsor Ave. Whitehead*
- *Thomas (age 76): 4, Church Ave. Bangor*

F13

- *Buried 18.8.1959 **TREVOR McGOWAN**
  (labourer): Seaview, Cloughfin Islandmagee*
- *Buried 25.6.1971
  **Mrs. UNA KATHLEEN McGOWAN:**
  (age 76): Seaview*
- *Buried 26.9.1997
  **TREVOR HOUSTON McGOWAN**
  (age 65): 35, Port Road, Islandmagee*

F14

**GAMBLE**
In loving memory of
Our devoted parents
**JAMES**
Died 17th May 1959
Aged 64 years
**MARGARET**
Died 17th February 1978
Aged 86 years

- *James and Margaret (recorded age 85):
  19, Portland Place, Magheramorne*

F15

On surround
In memory of **WILLIAM BASHFORD**
Died 13th July 1958
**JEAN BASHFORD**
Died 15th September 1976

- *William (painter) and Jean (age 69,
  factory worker): Windsor Ave. Whitehead*

F16

In loving memory of
**WILLIAM JOHN GRAY O.B.E.**
Master Mariner
Died 7th April 1958 aged 73 years
Also his wife **ELIZABETH AGNES**
Died 2nd May 1971 aged 81 years

- *William and Elizabeth (recorded age 80):
  Cloneen, Islandmagee*

F17-F18

**ADAMSON**
**IRIS LOUISE ADAMSON**
Died 14th March 1957
Also
**ROSSELL SHANNON ADAMSON**
Died 2nd May 1977

- *Iris: 2, Sandown Park, Belfast*
- *Rossell (age 72): Ashling, Station Road,
  Craigavad*

F19

**TODD**
**ALFRED ORSON TODD**
Beloved husband of Frances
Died 7th October 1957
Also his wife
**FRANCES**
Died 7th January 1965

- *Alfred: Erection Villa, Islandmagee*

F20

In loving memory of
**THOMAS BOYD** Master Mariner
Who died 4th May 1956
Also his son **JAMES**
Died 18th February 1970
Dearly loved husband of Rita Boyd
And
**MARTHA WILHELMINA (MINA)**
wife of the above Thomas
Died 19th March 1985

- *Thomas: Alloway, Shore Road, Greenisland*
- *James (age 46, clerk): 42 Benview Park,
  Belfast*
- *Mina (age 85): Greenisland Hospital*

## F21

**McCLURE**
**ISOBEL** loved wife of
**Rev. Henry H. McClure**
Died 14th May 1977
**Rev. HENRY H. McCLURE**
died 2nd May 1990

- *Isobel (age 65): 26, Sinclair Road, Bangor*
- *Rev. McClure (age 75):*
  *69, Sydenham Ave. Belfast*

## F22-F23

Here lies all that can die
**ADAIR**
**COLIN**
Died 28th July 1956
Aged 1 year
His mother
**MARY AGNES**
Died 19th Feby. 1982
Aged 61 years
**ROBERT**
died 21st January 1958
aged 76 years
his wife
**MARY CLARKE**
died 2nd September 1960
aged 84 years

In loving memory of
**W.T. CLARKE ADAIR**
Lost at sea 16th February 1942
aged 31 years

- *Colin: 1, Loughview Bungalows,*
  *Islandmagee*
- *Mary Agnes: 91 Woodburn Ave.*
  *Carrickfergus*
- *Mary Clarke (year recorded as 1966,*
  *housewife): Ballycarry Station*
- *Buried 20.9.2001 J. H. JACKSON ADAIR*
  *(age 84): Jordanstown Private Nursing*
  *Home*

## F24-F25

In memory of
**ANNIE GERTRUDE**
wife of **John Wesley DICK**
died 8th May 1968
Also his mother **ABBIE DICK**
died 6th June 1956
And his father **ROBERT DICK**
died 15th Feby. 1957
The memory of the just is blessed

- *Annie (age 67): Town Lane, Islandmagee*
- *Abbie: Cloughfin, Islandmagee*
- *Buried 28.1.1979 JOHN WESLEY DICK*
  *(age 76): Town Lane, Islandmagee*

## F26

**McDOWELL**
In
Loving memory of
**WILLIAM**
Died 10th December 1958
Beloved husband of
**CATHERINE McDOWELL**
Who died 8th June 1965

- *William (stationmaster):*
  *26, Chester Ave. Whitehead*

## F27

- *Buried 16.12.1967 PATRICK SMYTH*
  *(age 72, labourer): Ballystrudder Gardens,*
  *Islandmagee*
- *Buried 11.5.1969 Mrs. MARY SMYTH*
  *(age 70, home duties): 53, Ballystrudder*
  *Gardens*

## F28

**MARTIN**
In memory of
**FREDERICK JOSEPH**
1877-1959
his wife **ALICE JANE**
died 1958
their daughter
**"B" NOEL**
1904-1983

- *Alice (date recorded 24.2.1957):*
  *24, Marine Parade, Whitehead*

F29

In loving memory of
**SAMUEL AGNEW**
Who died 30th October 1918
And his son **JOHN**
died 13th January 1962
Also his daughter **INA**
died 14th April 1963
**SARAH** wife of Samuel
Died 18th May 1979 in her 98th year
Also their daughter **ELMA**
Died 20th February 1995

- *Sarah: 105, Ballystrudder Road, Whitehead*

F30-F31

**MACDONALD**
In
Loving memory of our dear mother
**JEMIMA MACDONALD**
Who died 27th December 1957
Also our dear father
**JOHN MACDONALD**
Who died 12th December 1958
Also beloved wife of Captain Angus
**HELEN**
Died 9th May 1997

- *Jemima: Mullaghboy, Islandmagee*
- *Mrs. Helen Macdonald (age 74): Town Lane, Islandmagee*

F32-F33

In loving memory
Of
**ANNA MARGARET MURDOCH**
31st January 1960
also her nieces
**JESSICA F. MEEKE**
22nd September 1968
**ANNA ZELIE MEEKE**
30th July 1978
**YVETTE SEARLE MEEKE**
13th August 1981

- *Jessica (age 75, single, cashier) and Yvette (age 82, single): 35, Marine Parade, Whitehead*

F34

In
Loving memory of
**MARY ELIZABETH FULTON**
Died 28th August 1952
And her son
**KENNETH FULTON**
Died 13th March 2001
Dear husband of Doreen

- *Kenneth (age 78): 11, Marine Parade, Whitehead*

F35

**MAGOWAN**
In loving memory of
**ARTHUR**
Beloved husband of Mary Magowan
Who died 2nd January 1958
aged 66 years
Also our dear sons
**CECIL** who died 15th July 1954
aged 33 years
**JOHN BRENNAN**
who died in infancy
Also **MARY AGNES**
wife of above Arthur
Died 27th February 1983
aged 87 years

- *Arthur (farmer): Blackhead, Islandmagee*
- *Cecil: 6, Windsor Parade, Whitehead*
- *Mary (recorded age 86): 39, McCreas Brae, Whitehead*

F36-F37

**SEMPLE**
Erected in memory of
**JAMES HARRISON**
Died 3rd Aug. 1952
His brothers **ROBERT**
Died 11th May 1953
**JOHN ALFRED**
Died 13th Feb. 1963
Their sister **VIOLET MARY**
Died 8th Jan. 1990

- *James and Robert: Bentra, Ballycarry*
- *Violet (age 88, single): 34, Larne Road, Whitehead*

## F38

- Buried 10.3.1952 **Mrs. ROSS:**
  Pebble Cottages, Islandmagee

## F39

**GALLIMORE**
In loving memory of
**GEORGE**
Died 6th February 1955
And his wife **EVELYN**
Died 26th June 1991

- George: 10, Adelaide Ave. Whitehead
- Evelyn (age 80): 8, Malone Ave.
  Whitehead

## F40

**SIMPSON**
In
Loving memory of
**Captain ALEXANDER SIMPSON**
Who died 12th August 1954

On surround
**GEORGE JAMES BOUCHER B.D.**
born 1907 died 1980

- Captain Simpson and George (age 70):
  Brownsbay, Islandmagee
- Buried 5.1.2001, died 29.12.2000
  **Mrs. EVELEEN BOUCHER:**
  Seabank Residential Home, Portrush

## F41

In loving memory of
**JEAN**
Died 19th June 1955
Beloved wife of
**Herbert HOUSTON**
Love

- Jean (housewife): 35, Alexandra Ave.
  Whitehead

## F42

- Buried 2.9.1954
  **NORMAN F. WOTHERSPOON:**
  8, Chester Ave. Whitehead
- Buried 6.4.1995
  **JOAN MARY WOTHERSPOON** (infant):
  19, Willowvale Drive, Islandmagee

## F43-F44

**DICK**
In loving memory of
A devoted wife and mother
**JANE ELIZABETH (BETTY)**
Who died 5th March 1956
Also a devoted husband and father
**THOMAS**
Who died 3rd April 1982

- Betty: Bayview, Drumgurland,
  Islandmagee
- Thomas: 68, Brownsbay Road,
  Islandmagee

## F45

- Buried 27.2.1954
  **Mrs. RACHAEL O'CONNELL**
  (housewife): 61, Windsor Ave. Whitehead
- Surround has name **DALLAS**

## F46

**CAMPBELL**
In
Loving memory of
Our only darling daughter
**JEAN ELIZABETH (SHEINA)**
Who died 4th July 1955 aged 25 years
Also **WILLIAM**
father of the above
Died 20th Feb. 1974
And his wife **JEAN** died 22nd Jan. 1985

- Sheina and William Geoff (age 86,
  accountant/auditor): 6, Chester Ave.
  Whitehead
- Jean (age 89): Joymount House,
  Carrickfergus

## F47

- Buried 23.9.1957
  **Mrs. SARAH CATHERINE CAMPBELL**
  (housewife): 38, Lawnbrook Ave. Belfast

F48

**BINGHAM**
In loving memory of
**ANNIE**
beloved wife of William P. Bingham
Died 24th August 1955
Also
**CATHERINE McARTHUR**
**BINGHAM**
died 19th October 1958
The above **WILLIAM P. BINGHAM**
died 4th April 1966

- *Annie: 29, Balfour Ave. Whitehead*

F49

- *Buried 13.6.1958 **Mr. B. S. REID,**
(tobacconist): 14, Cable Road, Whitehead*

F50

- *Buried 9.4.1956 **Mrs. MINNIE GORDON:**
100 Garden Village, Whitehead*
- *Buried 17.12.1969 **Miss ELLEN YOUNG**
(age 74): 39, Lestannon Ave. Whitehead*
- *Buried 9.8.1971 **Miss MATILDA YOUNG**
(age 71): 39 Lestannon Av.*

F51  unused

F52  unused

F53

In loving memory of
**DANIEL KANE M.B.E.**
Who died 24th October 1952
Also his daughter **NORAH**
who died 20th July 1929
Also his wife **ANNIE**
who died 30th Nov. 1968
Also their daughter **BERTHA**
died 19th Feb. 1983

- *Daniel (sailor): Mullaghboy, Islandmagee*
- *Annie (age 83):
6, Mullaghboy Bungalows, Islandmagee*
- *Bertha Kathleen (age 73, single):
32, Mullaghboy Road, Islandmagee*

F54-F55

In fond memory of
**WILLIAM**
Beloved husband of Isabella B. Smyth
Died 6th December 1953 aged 78 years
Also his beloved wife
**ISABELLA B. SMYTH (ISA)**
Died 8th January 1956 aged 78 years
**GLADYS SMYTH**
Died 19th November 1988
Ever in our thoughts
a darling wife and mother
**HERBERT JAMES SMYTH**
died 16th October 1998
Beloved husband and father
**SMYTH**

- *William (linen merchant):
Norwood Tower, Whitehead*
- *Gladys McCartney Smyth (age 85);
1, Windsor Ave. Whitehead*
- *Herbert (age 95): Chester Park Nursing
Home, Whitehead*

F56-F57

In loving memory of
**JAMES OSBORNE,** Sligo
Who died 15th January 1958
aged 83 years
And his wife **SARA ELIZABETH**
Who died 19th March 1958
aged 83 years
And their son-in-law
**WILLIAM T. BROWNE**
Who died 26th November 1962

- *James: Donegal House, Whitehead*

F58

In loving memory of
**JOHN BERTRAM CRABBE**
Died 23rd March 1987
Master Mariner
And
**INA CRABBE** nee **BUSBY**
Died 2nd February 1994
**MARGARET CRABBE**
18th June 1954
**ERNEST RICHARD CRABBE**
12th February 1960

- *John (age 71): 47, Houston Park, Belfast*
- *Margaret (married): Portmuck, Islandmagee*

**F59**

### GILLESPIE
In loving memory of
My dear parents
**ROBERT FEE**
died 23rd February 1956
**MARY KATHLEEN**
died 23rd October 1971

- *Robert: Castletown, Whitehead*
- *Mary (age 80, housewife):*
  *4, Fairview Terrace, Woodburn,*
  *Carrickfergus*

**F60** unused

**F61**

- *Buried 23.3.1967*
  ***Mrs. SUSANAH GORDON** (age 68,*
  *housewife): Port Davey, Whitehead*

**F62**

### DONALDSON
In
Loving memory of my dear husband
**WILLIAM**
Who died 2nd April 1956
And his dear wife **MAUD L.**
Who died 23rd February 1986
Also their son **JOHN**
Who died 17th October 1990
**FRANCES E. F. HINTON**
Who died 10th March 1986
Much loved by the above

- *William: Inglenook, Marine Lane,*
  *Whitehead*
- *Maud Lewis (age 91), John (age 69) and*
  *Mrs. Frances Elizabeth Frazer Hinton (this*
  *is surname, age 60): 5, Marine Lane,*
  *Whitehead*

**F63**

In
Fond and loving remembrance of
**ALFRED M. JONES**
Died 4th December 1956 aged 43 years
And his wife **ALEXANDRA**
Died 1st May 1974 aged 53 years

- *Captain Jones and Alexandra W:*
  *Upper Gransha, Islandmagee*

**F64-F65**

### CATHERINE LONG
Died 20-6-67
### ROBERT LONG
Died 14-11-59

- *Robert (buried 16.12.1959, farmer) and*
  *Catherine (buried 22.6.1967, married):*
  *Forthill, Ballycarry*
- *Buried November 1964 Miss Kathleen Long:*
  *Forthill, Ballycarry*

**F66** unused

**F67**

In loving memory of
**THOMAS McCAFFERTY**
Who died 12th December 1952
and his mother
**SARAH JANE McCAFFERTY**
Who died 18th June 1955

- *Thomas: 11, Edward Ave. Whitehead*

**F68-F69**

In memory of
**HELENA**
The beloved wife of John Hay
Died 26th June 1952
Their son **WILLIAM JAMES HAY**
Lost at sea 16th November 1917
The above **J. HAY** died 30th June 1958
Their son **F. HAY** died 3rd March 1972
**LETITA HAY** (nee **BROOKS**)
died 30th Aug. 1974
Beloved mother of J.S.Hay

On marble slab
Cherished memories
**MARY DAVIDSON HAY (MOLLY)**
Died 23rd March 1997
Dearly loved wife of Studley,
devoted mother
Of Cindy, Barbara, Kerry and John
Were there nothing else but our
love for each other
We would still have all we need

- *Helena: Studley, Balfour Ave. Whitehead*
- *Frederick (age 70): 11, Ransevyn Drive,*
  *Whitehead*
- *Letitia and Molly: 16, Balfour Ave. Whitehead*

F70

In
Loving memory of
Our dear sons
**JOSEPH CUMMINGS**
died 8th November 1951
Aged 25 years
**HERBERT** beloved father of Joseph
Died 16th January 1981
**JANE G.** a beloved wife and mother
Died 8th October 1982
Thy will be done

- *Joseph, Herbert (age 82) and*
  *Jane Gordon Cummings (age 86):*
  *12, Ebor Street, Belfast*

F71

In memory of
**JAMES HILL**
Died 28th October 1951
And his wife **JANE S. HILL**
Died 23rd January 1955

- *James (farmer) and Jane Shaw Hill:*
  *Mullaghboy, Islandmagee*

F72

In loving memory of
**WILLIAM HUGH MARTIN**
20th May 1875 - 20th March 1951
and of his wife
**ROSINA WATTERS MARTIN**
26th February 1877 - 4th October 1958
their daughter
**MARIE DENNISON SPEIRS**
15th March 1903 - 23rd August 1985

- *William (school teacher): Mount Oriel,*
  *Whitehead*

F73-F74

- *Buried 6.2.1953* ***Dr. JOHN F. CRAIG:***
  *Seaband, Ferris Bay, Islandmagee*

F75

- *Buried 2.9.1952* ***Mrs. ANNIE KELL:***
  *Quarry Cottages, Whitehead*

F76

In loving remembrance of
**ALFRED**
Beloved husband of
**Mary HAYDOCK**
Died 10th January 1953

- *Alfred: Woodhill, Shore Road, Greenisland*
- *Buried 25.3.1975*
  ***Mrs. MARY HAYDOCK** (housewife):*
  *36, Chester Ave. Whitehead*

F77

**ESLER**
In loving memory of
Our dear parents
**ROBERT BALFOUR**
Died 1st April 1946 aged 56 years
Interred in New York
**ELIZABETH** nee **Acheson**
Died 4th August 1971 aged 78 years

- *Elizabeth (date recorded as 1970):*
  *1, Alexandra Ave. Whitehead*

F78

**IRWIN**
In loving memory of
**JOHN IRWIN**
Who died 1st December 1966
Also his wife **AGNES**
Who died 24th March 1985

- *John (age 80, clerk): Dillons Ave.*
  *Whiteabbey*
- *Agnes (age 85): 146 Shore Road,*
  *Greenisland*

F79

- *Buried 21.1.1955*
  ***Mrs. MARGARET STEVENSON***
  *(housewife): Top View, New Road,*
  *Islandmagee*

F80

- *Buried 9.12.1955* ***Baby McCALMONT:***
  *Iverna, Mullaghboy, Islandmagee*
- *Died 1.6.2002, buried 5.6.2002*
  ***Mrs. MARY McCALMONT** (age 73):*
  *22, Lunnon Road, Islandmagee*

F81
## HANVEY
In loving memory of
Our baby daughter **SHIRLEY**
Died 5th April 1958 aged 8 months
Also a loving husband
**JAMES McNEIL (NEIL)**
Died 25th October 1986 aged 56 years

- *Shirley: Mullaghboy, Islandmagee*
- *Neil: 36, Ashvale Park, Islandmagee*
- *Flower holder says: Neil love Elsie*

F82
In loving memory
Of
## BEATRICE BERTHA IRWIN
Who spent her life making others happy
Entered into rest 4th May 1962
Also her devoted sister
**MARTHA HELENA**
Passed away 13th February 1964
Beloved wife of
**JOSEPH N. HALL** Whitehead
Who died 11th December 1976

- *Joseph (age 89, school teacher):*
  *6, York Ave. Whitehead*

F83-F84
In fond memory of
## WILLIAM
Beloved husband of Annie Wilson
Died 3rd March 1957 aged 77 years
Also their twin daughters
who died in infancy
The above named **ANNIE WILSON**
Died 14th May 1962 aged 79 years
Also their son **WILLIAM**
Died 2nd May 1979 aged 57 years
And his wife **SARA JANE**
Died 18th September 1979
aged 59 years

- *William (sailor), son William (farmer)*
  *and Sara (school teacher): Holmesyde,*
  *Islandmagee*

F85
## KNOX
In loving memory
Of my dear husband
**WILLIAM A.**
Who died 17th January 1957

- *William: Sunningdale, Cloughfin,*
  *Islandmagee*
- *Buried 21.6.1979* **Mrs. REBECCA KNOX**
  *(age 66, housewife):*
  *2, Chichester Gardens, Whitehead*

F86
In fond memory of
**JOHN M. TEMPLETON M.N.**
Who died 16th June 1951
Aged 35 years
Also his father
**THOMAS TEMPLETON**
Who died 16th April 1959
Aged 75 years
And his mother
**ANNA MARY TEMPLETON**
Who died 8th December 1966
Aged 75 years
And his brother
**ROBERT THOMAS**
Who died 12th January 1996
Aged 78 years

- *John (insurance agent): Breezemount,*
  *Islandmagee*
- *Captain Thomas and Anna (recorded age*
  *74): Bogside, Islandmagee*
- *Robert: Ben Madigan Nursing Home,*
  *Newtownabbey*

F87
Flower holder
## CASEY

- *Buried 25.2.1952* **LAURENCE V. CASEY:**
  *130, Garden Village, Whitehead*

F88-F89

- *Buried 14.6.1952* **Mrs. ELLA BRANAGH:**
  *7, Marine Parade, Whitehead*
- *Buried 1.4.1957* **WALTER BRANAGH:**
  *7, Marine Parade*

- *Buried 28.9.2001*
  **Mrs. SHEILA EDWINA SALLY WHATLEY**
  *(age 86): 7, Marine Parade*

## F90-F91

- *Buried 15.4.1962*
  **Mrs. MARGARET BLYTH** *(housewife):*
  *16, Chester Ave. Whitehead*
- *Buried 1.7.1969* **HERBERT BLYTH**
  *(age 74): 16, Chester Av.*

## F92

- *Buried 4.2.1953* **DAVID BUDD:**
  *60 Alexandra Ave. Whitehead*

## F93

Remembrance
**PERCIVAL THOMAS GREAVES
(PETER)**
died 26th March 1953 aged 52 years

- *Last known residence; Whitehead*

## F94 unused

## F95

Treasured memories of
**KATE DONNELLY**
Died 30.3.1954
Her daughter
**TILLY JOHNSTON**
Died 27.9.1986
Her husband
**JOE JOHNSTON**
Died 9.3.1988

- *Mrs. Catherine J. (housewife):*
  *Ballymuldrough, Islandmagee*
- *Mrs. Matilda Johnson (age 73, housewife):*
  *30, Hawthorn Grove, Glynn*
- *Joseph McCalmont Johnson (age 82):*
  *122, Glenarm Road, Larne*

## F96

**McKINSTRY**
In loving memory of our dear parents
**THOMAS**
1.9.1887 - 5.4.1954
**WILHELMINA**
7.8.1895 - 8.9.1960
their son **JAMES JACKSON**
26.7.1923 - 2.10.1996
loved husband of Allison
also **JOHN**
26.10.1925 - 24.5.2000
Sadly missed

- *Thomas (carpenter): Lower Gransha,*
  *Islandmagee*
- *James (age 73): 110, Low Rd, Islandmagee*
- *John (age 74): Cherrytree Private Nursing*
  *Home, Carrickfergus*

## F97

In fond memory of
**ELEANOR**
Beloved wife of Capt. Samuel Forsythe
Died 6th April 1955 aged 55 years
The above
**Capt. SAMUEL FORSYTHE**
Died 11th July 1967 aged 85 years
Also their beloved daughter **NANCY**
Died 22nd March 1966

- *Eleanor and Captain Forsythe (recorded age*
  *86): Laurington, Cloughfin, Islandmagee*
- *Agnes McMaster Forsythe (Nancy, age 71,*
  *single): Orlington, Upper Rd, Greenisland*

## F98

**ADAMS**
In loving memory of
**THOMPSON**
Who died 16th October 1972
And his wife
**ELLEN ELIZABETH (EILEEN)**
Who died 16th February 1994
The day thou gavest Lord is ended

- *Thompson (age 63, garage employee):*
  *Coastguard Road, Larne Harbour*
- *Eileen (age 86): Whitehead Private*
  *Nursing Home*

## F99 unused

FLACK

IN LOVING MEMORY OF
DAVID FLACK,
DIED 30TH OCT. 1915, AGED 56 YEARS, BURIED AT SEA.
ALSO HIS WIFE MARGARET,
DIED 20TH FEBRUARY 1932, AGED 75 YEARS.
AND THEIR ELDER SON ROBERT ALEXANDER,
LOST AT SEA 16TH MAY 1932, AGED 44 YEARS.
THEIR DAUGHTER CATHERINE ELIZABETH
DIED 28TH JULY 1966, AGED 74 YEARS.

IN LOVING MEMORY OF
MARY AMELIA, BELOVED WIFE OF F.C. DICK,
DIED 16TH SEPTEMBER 1946.
ALSO FRANCIS CHALMERS DICK (MASTER MARINER)
DIED 30TH JULY 1960
THEIR SON WILLIAM FRANCIS
DIED 4TH NOVEMBER 1985
AND HIS LOVING WIFE MARY JANE (MOLLIE)
DIED 2ND OCTOBER 1990.

DICK

## POLLIN

In Loving Memory Of

NATHANIEL JAMES (NAT)

A DEARLY LOVED HUSBAND

FATHER AND GRANDFATHER

DIED 3rd APRIL 1992

Loved and Remembered Always.

PICKEN
IN LOVING MEMORY OF
JOHN, MASTER MARINER
DIED 22ND APRIL 1966
HIS SON MAURICE
DIED 18TH AUGUST 1969

JAMES B. PICKEN, MASTER MARINER
DIED 5TH JANUARY 1982, AGED 88 YRS.
HIS BELOVED WIFE SOPHIA WILHELMINA
DIED 12TH JANUARY 1985, AGED 84 YRS.

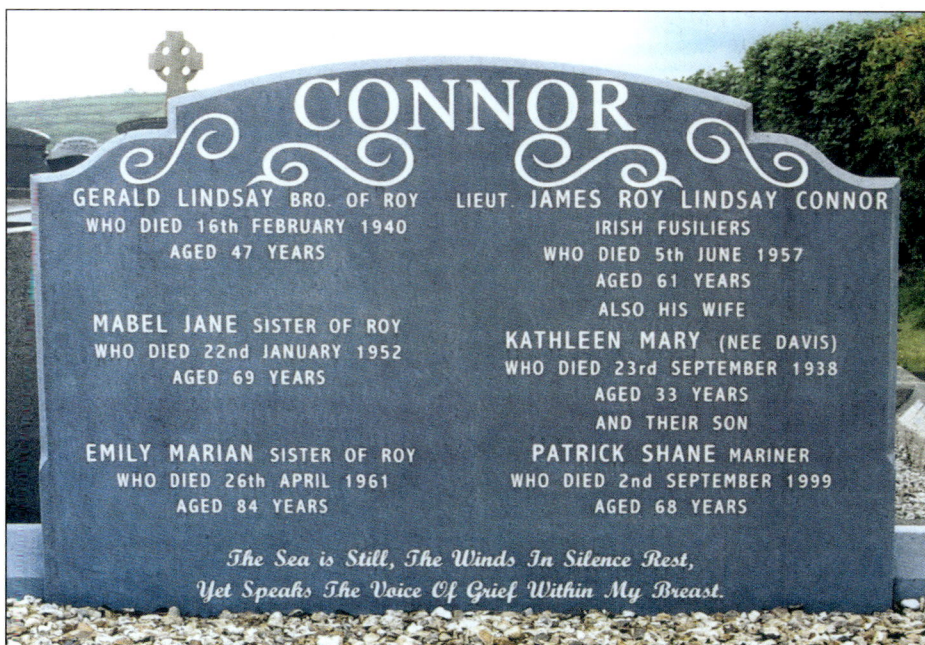

CONNOR

GERALD LINDSAY BRO. OF ROY
WHO DIED 16th FEBRUARY 1940
AGED 47 YEARS

MABEL JANE SISTER OF ROY
WHO DIED 22nd JANUARY 1952
AGED 69 YEARS

EMILY MARIAN SISTER OF ROY
WHO DIED 26th APRIL 1961
AGED 84 YEARS

LIEUT. JAMES ROY LINDSAY CONNOR
IRISH FUSILIERS
WHO DIED 5th JUNE 1957
AGED 61 YEARS
ALSO HIS WIFE

KATHLEEN MARY (NEE DAVIS)
WHO DIED 23rd SEPTEMBER 1938
AGED 33 YEARS
AND THEIR SON

PATRICK SHANE MARINER
WHO DIED 2nd SEPTEMBER 1999
AGED 68 YEARS

The Sea is Still, The Winds In Silence Rest,
Yet Speaks The Voice Of Grief Within My Breast.

IN LOVING MEMORY OF
STAFFORD THOMPSON,
WHO DIED ON THE 15TH JULY 1942.
HIS WIFE SUSAN MAUDE
DIED 20TH SEPT 1968
HELEN BONUGLI 1918 – 1993.
GIUSEPPE BONUGLI
BORN 8TH APRIL 1915 – DIED 5TH AUG. 1996.

In Loving Memory Of
JOSEPH
Beloved Husband Of ELIZABETH MANN.
Who Lost His Life When M.V."INVERILEN" Was
Torpedoed In The Atlantic 3RD February 1945.
Aged 46 Years.

1929

In
Loving Memory
of
Eleanor Margaret Auld,
(Peggy)
Died 25th February 1927,
Aged 21 Years.
Agnes M. Niblock,
Died 11th June 1951,
Aged 74 Years.
William Niblock,
Master Mariner.
Died 18th August 1953,
Aged 77 Years.
Wm. Laurence Niblock
Died 5th Sept. ____,
Aged 78 Years.
Mary (Maisie) Niblock
Died 25th Feb. 1999
Aged 83 Years

NIBLOCK

In Fond Remembrance Of
SAMUEL MILLIKEN KANE,
DEARLY LOVED HUSBAND OF
ISOBEL KANE,
WHO WAS LOST AT SEA OWING TO
ENEMY ACTION ON THE 16TH FEB. 1942,
AGED 28 YEARS.
ALSO HIS COUSIN
JOHN MANN KANE,
MASTER MARINER,
DIED 11TH JUNE 1991.

In Memory Of

· ELSIE ·

THE BELOVED WIFE OF

THE REV. SAMUEL GILMORE

WHO DIED 8TH FEBRUARY 1933.

ALSO

THE REV. SAMUEL GILMORE

WHO DIED 13TH FEBRUARY 1950

ALSO HIS 2ND WIFE JESSIE ELIZ. DIED 18-1-98.

In Thy light shall we see light

GILMORE

**Grave Plots Plan**

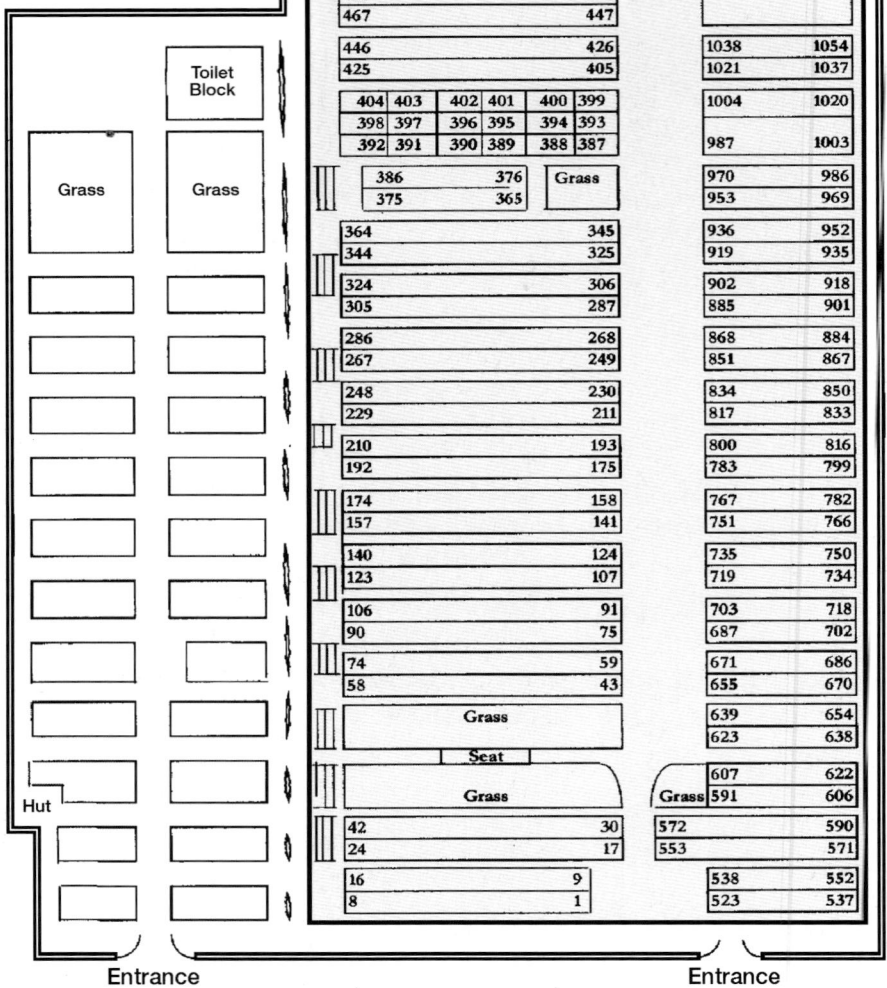

| Grass | Grass |
| --- | --- |

**South**     **SECTION X**     **North**

| 522 | 506 |
| 505 | 489 |

| 488 | 468 |
| 467 | 447 |

| 446 | 426 | | |
| 425 | 405 | | |

| | | | | | | 1038 | 1054 |
| | | | | | | 1021 | 1037 |

| 404 | 403 | 402 | 401 | 400 | 399 | 1004 | 1020 |
| 398 | 397 | 396 | 395 | 394 | 393 | | |
| 392 | 391 | 390 | 389 | 388 | 387 | 987 | 1003 |

| 386 | 376 | Grass | 970 | 986 |
| 375 | 365 | | 953 | 969 |

| 364 | 345 | 936 | 952 |
| 344 | 325 | 919 | 935 |

| 324 | 306 | 902 | 918 |
| 305 | 287 | 885 | 901 |

| 286 | 268 | 868 | 884 |
| 267 | 249 | 851 | 867 |

| 248 | 230 | 834 | 850 |
| 229 | 211 | 817 | 833 |

| 210 | 193 | 800 | 816 |
| 192 | 175 | 783 | 799 |

| 174 | 158 | 767 | 782 |
| 157 | 141 | 751 | 766 |

| 140 | 124 | 735 | 750 |
| 123 | 107 | 719 | 734 |

| 106 | 91 | 703 | 718 |
| 90 | 75 | 687 | 702 |

| 74 | 59 | 671 | 686 |
| 58 | 43 | 655 | 670 |

| Grass | 639 | 654 |
| | 623 | 638 |

**Seat**

| Grass | 607 | 622 |
| | Grass | 591 | 606 |

| 42 | 30 | 572 | 590 |
| 24 | 17 | 553 | 571 |

| 16 | 9 | 538 | 552 |
| 8 | 1 | 523 | 537 |

**Toilet Block**

**Grass**     **Grass**

**Hut**

Entrance               Entrance

# ~ ISLANDMAGEE NEW CEMETERY ~

**Whitehead**          **~ LOW ROAD ~**          **Ballylumford**

# SECTION X
## (SOUTH)

| Name | Plot | Name | Plot | Name | Plot |
|------|------|------|------|------|------|
| Adams | 325 | Campbell | 226 | Cuthbert | 10 |
| Aiken | 115 | Campbell | 291 | Dallas | 130 |
| Allen | 245 | Campbell | 300 | Davidson | 194 |
| Anderson | 99 | Canning | 70 | Davis | 273 |
| Anderson | 257 | Cathcart | 161 | Davison | 342 |
| Armour | 15 | Chambers | 107 | Dawson | 208 |
| Armstrong | 5 | Chambers | 108 | Devine | 426 |
| Armstrong | 78 | Clarke | 295 | Devon | 247 |
| Arnold | 388 | Cleary | 447 | Dick | 140 |
| Arnold | 394 | Clements | 21 | Donaghy | 440 |
| Bannon | 414 | Clifford | 101 | Donald | 1 |
| Barbour | 42 | Clugston | 120 | Donald | 354 |
| Barclay | 266 | Coburn | 381 | Donnan | 139 |
| Bashford | 184 | Coburn | 382 | Dorrans | 181 |
| Bell | 68 | Coburn | 383 | Drysdale | 355 |
| Bell | 379 | Collier | 7 | Duff | 193 |
| Bennett | 128 | Conlon | 498 | Duncan | 146 |
| Blake | 272 | Connor | 41 | Dunn | 40 |
| Boal | 293 | Connor | 156 | Edens | 119 |
| Bosomworth | 200 | Connor | 283 | Edens | 157 |
| Bowman | 125 | Connor | 284 | Evans | 401 |
| Boyd | 176 | Cooke | 219 | Fee | 30 |
| Boyd | 259 | Cooke | 302 | Fee | 34 |
| Boyd | 304 | Cooke | 405 | Ferguson | 127 |
| Boyles | 282 | Corr | 177 | Ferguson | 326 |
| Bradford | 371 | Coulter | 337 | Ferris | 199 |
| Brady | 437 | Coulter | 338 | Forbes | 84 |
| Brennan | 131 | Cowan | 137 | Forsythe | 159 |
| Brennan | 242 | Coyle | 36 | Forsythe | 160 |
| Brennan | 243 | Coyle | 37 | Foster | 210 |
| Briggs | 334 | Coyle | 198 | Fox | 512 |
| Brookes | 330 | Coyle | 217 | Foy | 93 |
| Brown | 268 | Craig | 236 | Frackleton | 351 |
| Brownlee | 307 | Crawford | 28 | Fullerton | 239 |
| Buckle | 186 | Crawford | 29 | Fulton | 425 |
| Buckle | 188 | Crawford | 74 | Garrett | 339 |
| Burrows | 398 | Crawford | 345 | Gibson | 4 |
| Cairns | 175 | Crawford | 346 | Gibson | 328 |
| Cameron | 79 | Crooks | 52 | Gibson | 366 |
| Campbell | 116 | Crossan | 145 | Gilmour | 236 |
| Campbell | 117 | Crowhurst | 264 | Girvin | 86 |
| Campbell | 134 | Crozier | 109 | Gordon | 267 |

| Name | Plot | Name | Plot | Name | Plot |
|------|------|------|------|------|------|
| Gourley | 185 | Houston | 205 | Lowry | 305 |
| Graham | 60 | Houston | 370 | Lucas | 47 |
| Graham | 124 | Hughes | 258 | Lydon | 413 |
| Graham | 129 | Hunter | 53 | Lynagh | 96 |
| Graham | 163 | Hunter | 101 | Lynagh | 97 |
| Grainger | 358 | Hunter | 348 | Lynn | 399 |
| Grant | 271 | Irvine | 218 | Lyttle | 57 |
| Gray | 24 | Irvine | 359 | Macauley | 38 |
| Gray | 25 | Jackett | 70 | Macauley | 39 |
| Gray | 35 | Jackson | 16 | Macauley | 58 |
| Gray | 92 | Jackson | 83 | Macauley | 180 |
| Gray | 102 | Jeffrey | 72 | Magowan | 225 |
| Gregg | 23 | Johnson | 220 | Mair | 91 |
| Gregg | 122 | Johnson | 221 | Mann | 134 |
| Gregg | 228 | Johnson | 360 | Mann | 174 |
| Gupta | 397 | Johnston | 204 | Mann | 269 |
| Hall | 98 | Johnston | 211 | Martin | 331 |
| Hall | 235 | Johnston | 251 | Martin | 387 |
| Hamilton | 167 | Johnston | 393 | Mateer | 309 |
| Hamilton | 187 | Jones | 22 | Matson | 391 |
| Hanna | 303 | Jones | 125 | Mawhinney | 95 |
| Hannah | 306 | Jones | 336 | Mawhinney | 209 |
| Hanvey | 278 | Kane | 63 | Maxwell | 100 |
| Hanvey | 392 | Kane | 71 | Maxwell | 142 |
| Harkness | 390 | Kane | 168 | Mayberry | 110 |
| Harper | 271 | Kane | 202 | McAllister | 409 |
| Haveron | 485 | Kane | 229 | McAloney | 11 |
| Haveron | 486 | Kane | 395 | McAuley | 478 |
| Heddles | 54 | Kealey | 61 | McBride | 149 |
| Heddles | 152 | Keenan | 203 | McBride | 427 |
| Heggan | 195 | Kerby | 372 | McCalmont | 20 |
| Henderson | 402 | Kerr | 14 | McCalmont | 46 |
| Heron | 222 | Kerr | 56 | McCalmont | 66 |
| Hewitt | 45 | Kerr | 64 | McCalmont | 67 |
| Higginson | 17 | Kerr | 114 | McCalmont | 276 |
| Hilditch | 184 | Kielty | 260 | McCalmont | 277 |
| Hilditch | 275 | Kilpatrick | 76 | McCartney | 136 |
| Hill | 13 | Kilpatrick | 77 | McCaskey | 311 |
| Hill | 24 | Kyle | 335 | McClean | 356 |
| Hill | 25 | Laird | 256 | McClure | 215 |
| Hill | 33 | Lamont | 113 | McClurkin | 27 |
| Hill | 43 | Lancaster | 281 | McCormick | 75 |
| Hill | 138 | Laverty | 18 | McCosh | 321 |
| Hockings | 141 | Leslie | 51 | McCoy | 133 |
| Hogg | 6 | Leslie | 166 | McCreal | 386 |
| Hood | 171 | Logan | 218 | McCullough | 357 |
| Hood | 324 | Logan | 368 | McDonald | 365 |

| Name | Plot | Name | Plot | Name | Plot |
|------|------|------|------|------|------|
| McDowell | 396 | Nimick | 164 | Slater | 406 |
| McFall | 329 | Nixon | 233 | Sloan | 132 |
| McFarlane | 88 | Nolan | 376 | Stainer | 389 |
| McGee | 20 | Noonan | 298 | Steele | 262 |
| McGuigan | 369 | Nuttall | 154 | Steele | 263 |
| McIlwaine | 178 | O'Neill | 384 | Stewart | 82 |
| McKay | 214 | Orr-McAuley | 118 | Stewart | 378 |
| McKay | 248 | Patterson | 20 | Stitt | 147 |
| McKee | 50 | Patterson | 291 | Stitt | 165 |
| McKee | 89 | Patton | 179 | Stitt | 377 |
| McKelvey | 2 | Paxton | 48 | Stronge | 307 |
| McKelvey | 3 | Perry | 158 | Stuart | 224 |
| McKenzie | 212 | Phillips | 227 | Surgenor | 294 |
| McKibben | 26 | Picken | 31 | Sweetnam | 191 |
| McKinstry | 292 | Picken | 32 | Sweetnam | 192 |
| McLeer | 373 | Pink | 162 | Thomas | 19 |
| McLeod | 266 | Pink | 280 | Thompson | 215 |
| McLernon | 9 | Pitcaithley | 105 | Thompson | 363 |
| McMaster | 44 | Pitcaithley | 106 | Tierney | 353 |
| McMaster | 313 | Poag | 104 | Tumelty | 253 |
| McMaster | 314 | Preston | 12 | Tyrie | 224 |
| McMaster | 315 | Rankin | 387 | Upton | 49 |
| McMaw | 349 | Rankin | 81 | Walker | 170 |
| McMillan | 352 | Rea | 196 | Warren | 53 |
| McMullan | 261 | Reid | 94 | Warren | 101 |
| McMurtry | 181 | Reynolds | 244 | Warwick | 312 |
| McMurtry | 399 | Reynolds | 299 | Watson | 430 |
| McNeill | 126 | Richardson | 385 | Welch | 212 |
| Mercer | 333 | Richardson | 404 | Whittingham | 274 |
| Monteith | 319 | Riley | 213 | Wilson | 59 |
| Montgomery | 85 | Robinson | 283 | Wilson | 87 |
| Montgomery | 182 | Robinson | 284 | Wilson | 135 |
| Montgomery | 216 | Rodgers | 62 | Wilson | 230 |
| Montgomery | 308 | Ross | 240 | Wilson | 231 |
| Montgomery | 344 | Ross | 241 | Wilson | 232 |
| Montgomery | 347 | Ross | 310 | Wilson | 296 |
| Moore | 289 | Rossborough | 234 | Wilson | 297 |
| Moore | 327 | Rowe | 316 | Wilson | 301 |
| Moorhead | 121 | Rowe | 317 | Wood | 318 |
| Mowat | 249 | Rutherford | 279 | Woods | 350 |
| Mulholland | 111 | Sampson | 290 | Wright | 250 |
| Neill | 155 | Service | 201 | Wright | 287 |
| Neill | 323 | Shanks | 80 | | |
| Nelson | 112 | Sheriff | 285 | | |
| Nelson | 254 | Simms | 153 | | |
| Niblock | 320 | Simms | 322 | | |
| Niblock | 362 | Sinclair | 65 | | |

# SECTION X
## (NORTH)

| Name | Plot | Name | Plot | Name | Plot |
|---|---|---|---|---|---|
| Abbott | 776 | Campbell | 834 | Glass | 819 |
| Adams | 764 | Carson | 700 | Gracey | 739 |
| Adams | 799 | Chambers | 788 | Graham | 526 |
| Alexander | 904 | Clarke | 730 | Graham | 527 |
| Armour | 568 | Cleland | 619 | Graham | 717 |
| Armour | 569 | Cowell | 769 | Graham | 718 |
| Armstrong | 557 | Craig | 610 | Graham | 737 |
| Arthurs | 791 | Craig | 898 | Graham | 738 |
| Arthurs | 792 | Crampton | 545 | Gray | 972 |
| Arthurs | 793 | Cunningham | 558 | Hall | 597 |
| Atkinson | 542 | Davey | 666 | Hall | 598 |
| Atkinson | 623 | Deane | 591 | Hall | 599 |
| Baillio | 651 | Dempster | 532 | Hamilton | 575 |
| Baird | 746 | Dick | 539 | Hamilton | 804 |
| Baird | 748 | Dick | 637 | Hanna | 862 |
| Beattie | 626 | Dick | 672 | Hanna | 863 |
| Beggs | 853 | Ditty | 970 | Hawkins | 537 |
| Bell | 708 | Dobbin | 826 | Hawkins | 835 |
| Bell | 709 | Donald | 939 | Hawkins | 852 |
| Bell | 737 | Drillingcourt | 646 | Heddles | 627 |
| Black | 928 | Earls | 703 | Heggen | 885 |
| Boles | 576 | Elliott | 910 | Henderson | 649 |
| Bonar | 632 | Finlay | 752 | Heyburn | 954 |
| Bonar | 660 | Flack | 669 | Higginson | 547 |
| Bonar | 661 | Ford | 561 | Higginson | 551 |
| Bonar | 664 | Ford | 644 | Higginson | 856 |
| Bonar | 665 | Ford | 658 | Hill | 538 |
| Boyd | 1032 | Forsythe | 657 | Hill | 690 |
| Boyle | 820 | Forsythe | 832 | Hope | 937 |
| Boyles | 876 | Foster | 580 | Houston | 607 |
| Brown | 571 | Foster | 634 | Houston | 617 |
| Brown | 624 | Foster | 635 | Houston | 827 |
| Brown | 868 | Foster | 636 | Howlin | 722 |
| Brunt | 987 | Freil | 540 | Hughes | 596 |
| Brunt | 988 | Gibson | 853 | Jones | 533 |
| Burns | 577 | Gilbert | 612 | Jones | 743 |
| Busby | 845 | Gillespie | 791 | Jones | 744 |
| Busby | 846 | Gilliland | 736 | Kane | 753 |
| Calwell | 703 | Gilmour | 864 | Keatley | 771 |
| Calwell | 874 | Gilmour | 878 | Keatley | 772 |
| Calwell | 875 | Gilroy | 609 | Kerr | 539 |
| Campbell | 803 | Glass | 818 | Kerr | 627 |

| Name | Plot | Name | Plot | Name | Plot |
|------|------|------|------|------|------|
| Kiley | 697 | McKeown | 858 | Ross | 630 |
| Kiley | 698 | McKinty | 525 | Ross | 690 |
| Knox | 728 | McKinty | 554 | Ross | 694 |
| Laing | 723 | McKinty | 556 | Ross | 695 |
| Lappin | 767 | McKnight | 652 | Rossborough | 655 |
| Lawler | 528 | McLaughlin | 978 | Running | 942 |
| Leckie | 704 | McMaster | 544 | Ryan | 755 |
| Leckie | 705 | McMaw | 608 | Scholey | 670 |
| Leckie | 706 | McMaw | 685 | Skelton | 548 |
| Leitch | 1025 | McMaw | 686 | Skelton | 549 |
| Linton | 825 | McNeice | 696 | Sloan | 683 |
| Logan | 717 | McNeill | 851 | Sloss | 582 |
| Long | 811 | McSpadden | 816 | Smith | 711 |
| Long | 812 | McWilliam | 762 | Smyth | 879 |
| Long | 813 | Meek | 631 | Smyth | 1006 |
| Lorimer | 687 | Millar | 775 | Stephens | 684 |
| Lowry | 974 | Montgomery | 590 | Stewart | 802 |
| Lucas | 758 | Montgomery | 1072 | Taggart | 668 |
| Lyle | 765 | Montgomery | 1073 | Telford | 650 |
| Macaulay | 800 | Montgomery | 1074 | Templeton | 688 |
| MacDonald | 620 | Moody | 751 | Tomasso | 774 |
| MacKenzie | 794 | Moore | 529 | Topping | 783 |
| Maguire | 1103 | Moore | 530 | Urquart | 1004 |
| Mann | 786 | Morrow | 534 | Urquart | 1005 |
| Martin | 654 | Neill | 1055 | Waring | 680 |
| Martin | 902 | Nesbitt | 1077 | Watson | 1072 |
| Martin | 903 | Newbold | 860 | Watson | 1073 |
| McAllister | 814 | Niblock | 555 | Watson | 1074 |
| McCalmont | 671 | Niblock | 761 | Wells | 581 |
| McCammon | 756 | Orr | 640 | Wells | 1056 |
| McCammon | 757 | Picken | 642 | Welsh | 523 |
| McClung | 801 | Picken | 643 | Welsh | 524 |
| McConnell | 724 | Picken | 663 | Welsh | 754 |
| McCormick | 936 | Pollin | 691 | Whitall | 633 |
| McCune | 887 | Pollock | 720 | White | 638 |
| McDevitte | 798 | Prenter | 618 | Wilson | 586 |
| McDowell | 579 | Ramsey | 707 | Wilson | 615 |
| McDowell | 584 | Redford | 726 | Wilson | 721 |
| McFarlane | 890 | Redford | 727 | Wilson | 725 |
| McFarlane | 891 | Reid | 600 | Wilson | 851 |
| McGookin | 653 | Reid | 713 | Wilson | 895 |
| McGowan | 731 | Renwick | 674 | Wolfe | 940 |
| McHugh | 737 | Reynolds | 971 | Woodside | 840 |
| McHugh | 738 | Riddle | 667 | Woodside | 841 |
| McIlreavy | 541 | Rides | 809 | Woodside | 842 |
| McIlroy | 570 | Rodgers | 590 | Woodside | 843 |
| McKechnie | 1038 | Ross | 626 | Young | 625 |

**X1**

In fond memory of
**SARAH ANN (CIS)**
Beloved wife of **Thomas DONALD**
Died 16th March 1964

- *Sarah: 15, Moyola St. Belfast*

**X2-X3**

In loving memory of
**JOHN DAVISON McKELVEY**
Dearly loved husband of Doreen
Died 3rd October 1965
And his father
**JOHN DAVISON McKELVEY**
Dearly loved husband of Mina
Died 17th February 1972
The above **MINA** devoted wife and
mother died 9th Feby. 1976

- *John (accountant): 12, Lansdowne Cres. Larne*
- *John (father, age 73) and Wilhelmina (age 75, home duties): 3, Causeway Villas, Ballycarry*

**X4**

In memory of
**JOSEPH**
Died 12th Oct. 1965
His wife **MARIE**
Died 23rd March 1967
**GIBSON**

- *Joseph and Maria (age 67): 141, Islandmagee Road, Whitehead*

**X5**

- *Buried 26.1.1967*
  ***THOMAS ALFRED ARMSTRONG***
  *(married, school teacher, Church of Ireland): Uplands, Islandmagee*
- *Buried 29.6.1967*
  ***JUANITA ARMSTRONG***
  *(widow, age 70, Church of Ireland): Uplands, Islandmagee*

**X6**

**HOGG**
In loving memory of
A devoted husband and father
**FREDERICK JAMES HOGG**
Who died 27th July 1970
Also a dear wife and mother
**JEAN BRADLEY HOGG**
Who died 21st January 1987

- *Frederick (age 72, Presbyterian, building contractor): 100, Downview Park West, Belfast 15*
- *Jane (age 82, Presbyterian): 5, Glengarry Park, Jordanstown*

**X7**

In loving memory of
**ELLEN CHRISTINA COLLIER**
Who died 19th December 1971

- *Ellen (age 63, widow, Presbyterian): 132, Middle Road, Islandmagee*

**X8** unused

**X9**

- *Buried 13.11.1965* ***ROBERT McLERNON:*** *Cloughfin, Islandmagee*

**X10**

- *Buried 13.5.1972* ***Infant CUTHBERT*** *(Presbyterian)*

**X11**

- *Buried 6.2.1966*
  ***ROBERT SWANN McALONEY***
  *(garage proprietor): Braeside, Raw Brae, Whitehead*
- *Buried 16.1.1992*
  ***Mrs. MATILDA McALONEY*** *(age 92): 6, Larne Road, Whitehead*

**X12**

**PRESTON**
**WALTER** 13-11-67
**JEANETTE** 3-3-87

- *Walter (age 55, married, Presbyterian, civil servant) and Jeanette (age 78, widow): 61, Islandmagee Road, Whitehead*

## X13

**HILL**
In loving memory of
**Captain JOHN HILL M.N.**
Died 3rd March 1960 buried at sea
Also his wife
**HERBRETTA (BERTIE)**
Died 13th May 1974

- *Herbretta (age 58, Presbyterian, housewife): 33, Carnvue Road, Carnmoney*

## X14

**KERR**
In loving memory of
**TOMMY**
Died 18th March 1972

- *Tommy (age 38, Presbyterian, married, manager): 19, Manse Road, Carnmoney*

## X15

In fond memory of
**JOHN ARMOUR**
Beloved husband of Mary Jane
Died 30th January 1975
The above **MARY JANE**
Died 19th September 1979

- *John (age 74, Presbyterian, retired seaman, and Mary (age 78): Ashvale, Mullaghboy, Islandmagee*

## X16

Sacred to the memory of
**HUGH KERR JACKSON**
Master Mariner
Beloved husband of Eva
Died September 10th 1965
Also the above named **EVA**
Died August 27th 1982

Dear parents of Terence

- *Hugh: Hilltop House, Portmuck, Islandmagee*
- *Mrs. Annie E. (age 85): 36, Hopefield Ave. Belfast*

## X17

- *Buried 24.3.1972* ***ANNA C. HIGGINSON*** *(age 77, single, Presbyterian): Mullaghboy, Islandmagee*

## X18

- *Buried 14.12.1964* ***Mrs. JANIE LAVERTY*** *(housewife): Northern Bank House, Larne*
- *Buried 24.1.1991* ***JAMES LAVERTY*** *(age 87): 29 Balfour Ave. Whitehead*

## X19

- *Buried 26.9.1965* ***KEITH NICHOLAS THOMAS*** *(age 2½): 51 Islandmagee Road, Whitehead*
- *Buried 19.3.1986* ***Mrs. ELLEN JANE THOMAS*** *(age 59): same address*
- *Buried 8.1.01* ***GEORGE ALEXANDER THOMAS*** *(age 77): same address*

## X20

In loving memory of
**THOMAS JOSEPH McGEE**
9.1.1901 - 24.7.1977
His wife
**ANNIE CATHERINE**
30.4.1900 - 10.10.1973
Their daughters
**PATRICIA** 11.11.1930 - 26.6.1948
**CATHERINE** (stillborn) 18.11.1936
Their grandsons
**CHRISTOPHER PATTERSON**
17.3.1965 - 8.7.1985
Beloved son of Philomena and George
**PAUL McCALMONT**
3.4.1963 - 19.3.1966
Beloved son of Lelia and Leslie
Loves last gift remembrance

- *Thomas: 28, Adelaide Ave. Whitehead*
- *Annie Kathleen McGee (housewife): Windsor Ave. Whitehead*
- *Christopher (police constable): Balfour Ave. Whitehead*
- *Christopher Paul McCalmont: 67, Islandmagee Road, Whitehead*

### X21

**CLEMENTS**
In loving memory of a
Devoted husband and father
**JAMES**
Died 3rd February 1967
Also his beloved wife
And our dear mother
**ELIZABETH**
Died 7th June 1989
Safe in the arms of Jesus
Also their son **DAVID**
died 7th May 1994

- *James (age 75, C of I, house painter):*
  *Quarry Cottages, Whitehead*
- *Elizabeth (age 94, C of I):*
  *14 Longfield Gardens, Greenisland*
- ***DAVID CLEMENTS***
  *(cremated remains buried 31.3.1995):*
  *c.o. 45, Edward Road, Whitehead*

### X22

Flower holder
**JONES**

- *Buried 2.5.1967*
  ***MATILDA BOYLE JONES***
  *(age 25, Presbyterian, married):*
  *Millbay Islandmagee*

### X23

**GREGG**
Sacred
To the memory of
**GEORGE ALEXANDER GREGG**
Loved husband of Margaret
Called home June 25th 1968
**MARGARET** died Jan. 3rd 1979

- *George (age 74, Presbyterian, retired*
  *company director) and Margaret (age 86,*
  *Presbyterian): 7, Donegall Ave. Whitehead*

### X24-X25

**GRAY**
In loving memory of our dear mother
**NORAH**
Who died 5th January 1971

- *Norah (age 48, married, Presbyterian):*
  *The Moat, Ballydown, Islandmagee*
- *Buried 8.7.1988* ***Baby HILL***
  *(female, Presbyterian):*
  *5, Castleburn, Carrickfergus*

### X26

In
Fond memory of
**SAMUEL**
Loved husband of **Lucy McKIBBEN**
Died 2nd May 1967
Also the above named **LUCY**
Died 21st June 1983

- *Samuel (age 61, Presbyterian, crane driver):*
  *The Hill, Ballylumford, Islandmagee*
- *Elizabeth (Lucy, age 75, Presbyterian):*
  *79, Ballylumford Road, Islandmagee*

### X27

**McCLURKIN**
In loving memory of
My dear husband
**JAMES**
Died 7th January 1967
Also his beloved wife **JEANNIE**
Died 3rd October 1988

- *James (age 61, Presbyterian, retired clerk)*
  *and Jeannie (age 76, Presbyterian):*
  *31 Portmuck Road, Islandmagee*

### X28-X29

**CRAWFORD**
In fond memory of **MARY AGNES**
dearly loved
wife of William Stewart
died 5th March 1965
Also the above **WILLIAM STEWART**
Died 29th August 1987

- *Mary (housewife) and*
  *William Stewart Crawford (age 92):*
  *69, Portmuck Road. Islandmagee*

X30

### FEE
In loving memory of
**WILLIAM FEE**
Died 21st October 1964
And his wife **ESTHER**
Died 13th July 1973
The Lord is my Shepherd

- *William and Esther (age 82): Portmuck, Islandmagee*
- *Buried 5.3.1974* **Miss MARY BLAIR FEE** *(age 74, home duties): 168 Shore Road, Greenisland*

X31-X32

### PICKEN
In loving memory of
**JOHN** Master Mariner
Died 22nd April 1966
His son **MAURICE**
Died 18th August 1969
**JAMES B. PICKEN** Master Mariner
Died 5th January 1982 aged 88 years
His beloved wife
**SOPHIA WILHELMINA**
Died 12th January 1985 aged 84 years

- *John: Fiona, Mullaghboy, Islandmagee*
- *Maurice John (age 4 years 10 months): Bay Road, Larne*
- *James Busby Picken (recorded age 87) and Sophia: 50, Mullaghboy Road, Islandmagee*

X33

### HILL
In loving memory of
My dear wife
**OLIVE ELIZABETH**
Died 14th September 1979
aged 65 years

- *Olive: 34, Cable Road, Whitehead*
- *Buried 12.4.1988* **Captain JAMES HILL** *(age 76): Rapax Road, Hale, Cheshire*

X34

In remembrance of
**ANDREW FEE** Master Mariner
Loved husband of
Maureen died 30th Decr. 1968
And the above named **MAUREEN**
died 13th Novr. 1995
Dearly loved parents of
Leonard, Patricia and Janet

- *Andrew (age 52, Merchant Navy Captain, Presbyterian): Beach House, Portmuck, Islandmagee*
- *Maureen Agnes Fee (Brethren): 12, Larne Road, Carrickfergus*

X35

### GRAY
In loving memory of my dear husband
**MAURICE LESLIE**
Who died 10th January 1971

- *Maurice (age 50, Presbyterian, employee of Standard Cables): 185, Monkstown Road, Newtownabbey*

X36-X37

### COYLE
In loving memory of
Our dear daughter
**MARIE J. D.**
Who died 23rd June 1966
Also my dear husband
**JOHN McNEILLY**
Died 2nd June 1971
Also a devoted wife and mother
**MARTHA JEMIMA (META)**
Died 7th May 2001
In Heavenly Love Abiding

- *Marie (policewoman) and John Coyle (age 68): Rock Cottage, Ballymuldrough, Islandmagee*
- *Mrs. Martha Coyle (age 91): Chester Park Nursing Home, Whitehead*

## X38-X39
In loving memory of
**DOROTHY HAZEL MACAULEY**
Beloved wife of John
died 24th July 1966
Lead us Heavenly Father lead us

- *Dorothy (age 32, C of I, schoolteacher):*
  *8, Alexandra Ave. Whitehead*

## X40

- *Buried 4.4.1985* ***ROBERT THRUE DUNN***
  *(age 74, married, Presbyterian):*
  *8, Malone Ave. Whitehead*

- *Buried 8.1.1987* ***MARTHA JANE DUNN***
  *(age 80, widow, Presbyterian):*
  *Greenisland House, Carrickfergus*

## X41
In fond memory of
**FANNY**
Loved wife of Samuel Connor
Died 2nd January 1968
Also her husband
**SAMUEL CONNOR**
Died 26th Oct. 1987

- *Fanny (age 72, Presbyterian) and*
  *Samuel (age 93, Presbyterian):*
  *Ford Cottages, Whitehead*

## X42
Flower holder
**R. & L. BARBOUR**

- *Buried 30.10.1966*
  ***ROBERT JOHN BARBOUR*** *(age 65,*
  *Presbyterian, electrician, married):*
  *Boghall, Islandmagee*

- *Buried 31.1.1985*
  ***Mrs. LILIAN BARBOUR*** *(age 90, Church*
  *of God, widow): Inver House, Larne*

## X43

**HILL**
In loving memory of
**HUGH BOYLE**
Who died 19th November 1968
Beloved husband of Agnes Hill
**AGNES HILL**
Died 10th May 1986
Their beloved daughter **SHIRLEY**
Died 7th June 1985
Also their beloved daughter
**MABELLE**
Died 8th March 2002

- *Hugh (age 68, farmer): Chatswood,*
  *Kilcoan, Islandmagee*

- *Agnes (age 88) and Maybelle Mary*
  *Isabella Hill (age 74, single):*
  *164 Brownsbay Road Islandmagee*

## X44

**McMASTER**
In
Memory of our dear parents
**ANDREW C. J.**
died 21st February 1967
**AGNES**
died 28th September 1977
At rest

- *Andrew Campbell Jackson*
  *(age 59, joiner, Presbyterian):*
  *Lower Gransha, Islandmagee*

- *Agnes (age 66 ):*
  *57, Ballystrudder Gardens, Islandmagee*

## X45

- *Buried 12.12.1968*
  ***WILLIAM JOHN HEWITT*** *(age 66,*
  *married, company director, Presbyterian):*
  *28, Lumford Ave. Whitehead*

X46

### McCALMONT
In loving memory of
A devoted husband and father
**JAMES McCALMONT**
Who died 4th August 1969
Also a loving wife and mother
**LILY**
Who died 11th August 1993
Loves last gift Remembrance

- *James (age 68, yard foreman, Presbyterian)
  and Eliza (Lily) (age 89, Presbyterian):
  Millbay, Islandmagee*

X47

- *Buried 18.2.1970
  **ERNEST EDWARD LUCAS**
  (age 80, C of I, married):
  Langdale, Mullaghdubb, Islandmagee*

X48

- *Buried 3.4.1970 **SARAH PAXTON**
  (age 64 C of I, housewife):
  53, Windsor Ave. Whitehead*

- *Buried 30.5.1970 **STANLEY PAXTON**
  (age 63, C of I): 53 Windsor Ave.*

X49

- *Buried 13.5.1970
  **HAROLD EDWARD UPTON**
  (age 70, Presbyterian, hotel manager,
  married): 51, Edward Road, Whitehead*

- *Buried 9.9.1988 **Mrs. DORIS UPTON,**
  (age 84, Presbyterian, widow):
  62 Mill Road, Larne*

X50

### McKEE
In loving memory of
A dear husband and father
**DAVID K.**
Died 13th May 1970
Also his loving wife
**MARY W. McKEE**
Who joined him on
29th January 1993
Remembered always by
Their loving family

- *David Kennedy McKee
  (age 59, Presbyterian, lorry driver):
  62 Glenvale Park, Glynn*

- *Mary Woods McKee (age 69, Presbyterian):
  16 Hawthorne Grove, Glynn*

X51

Flower holder
Dear **Mother** died 25.6.1970
Dear **Father** died 16.3.1977

- *Buried 28.6.1970
  **HELEN WATT SMALL LESLIE**
  (age 60, C of I, housewife):
  63, Windsor Ave. Whitehead*

- *Buried 19.3.1977 **ALEXANDER LESLIE**
  (age 80, C of I, widower):
  48 Adelaide Ave. Whitehead*

X52

### CROOKS
In loving memory of
**MINNIE**
Who died 30th October 1970
And her dear husband **JOHN**
Who died 4th May 1977

- *Minnie (age 70, Presbyterian, housewife):
  55 Windsor Ave. Whitehead*

- *John (age 70, Presbyterian):
  6, Alexandra Court, Whitehead*

## X53

Flower holder
In memory of sister **MARY J.C.**

- *Buried 12.10.1971* ***MARY HUNTER*** *(age 66, married, C of I) 18 Premier Drive, Shore Road, Belfast*
- *Buried 15.7.1985* ***ROBERT MUIR HUNTER*** *(age 84, C of I): same address*
- *Buried 4.7.2001* ***Mrs. LAURA WARREN*** *(age 69, C of I): same address*

## X54

**HEDDLES**
In loving memory of
A devoted husband and father
**ROBERT J. HEDDLES**
Who died 23rd September 1970
**RAYMOND McILWAINE HEDDLES**
Beloved husband of Isabel
**ELIZABETH HEDDLES**
Who died 16th November 1992
Beloved wife of Robert J. Heddles

- *Robert John (age 67, Presbyterian, retired sea Captain, married): Breezemount, Islandmagee*
- *Raymond (age 41, Presbyterian, clerk, married): 14 Fairy Knowe Drive, Newtownabbey*
- *Elizabeth (age 88, Presbyterian, widow): 201, Middle Road, Islandmagee*

## X55 unused

## X56

**KERR**
In loving memory of
**ROBERT McCALMONT**
Master Mariner
Died 18th January 1971
Also his dear wife
**EVA**
Died 1st January 1989

- *Robert (age 68, married, Presbyterian, sea Captain): Kilcoan, 155, Low Road, Islandmagee*
- *Eva Maud (age 80, widow, Presbyterian): 51, Islandmagee Road, Whitehead*

## X57

**LYTTLE**
In loving memory of
A devoted wife and mother
**ELIZABETH**
Fell asleep 19th Nov. 1970
Also a devoted husband
And father
**ALEXANDER**
Who joined her 26th Feb. 1972
**ELIZABETH**
Loving daughter
Died 6th Jan. 2002
Severed only till He comes

- *Elizabeth (age 66, Presbyterian) and Alexander T. (age 71, Presbyterian): 1, Mossvale Street, Belfast*
- *Elizabeth Lyttle (age 72, single, Presbyterian): Castleview Nursing Home, Belfast*

## X58

**MACAULEY**
In memory of
**CECIL DAVID**
Died 1st August 1965 aged 4 years
**NORMAN JOHNSTON MACAULEY**
Died 7th March 1993
Dearly loved husband of Julie
And beloved father of James, Cecil,
David and Judith

- *David Cecil (as recorded): Thornfield, Islandmagee Road, Whitehead*
- *Norman (age 77): 150, Islandmagee Road, Whitehead*

## X59

**WILSON**
In loving remembrance
of
**JAMES WILSON** Master Mariner
Died 4th December 1963
His wife **MARY (MAY) WILSON**
Died 28th April 1993

- *James: Remuera, Mullaghboy, Islandmagee*
- *May (age 76): 12, Lunnon Road, Islandmagee*

## X60

**GRAHAM**
In memory of
**JAMES REA** died 5th November 1967
His wife
**ELIZABETH** died 14th April 2001

- *James (age 54, Presbyterian, tailor):*
  *10, Windsor Crescent, Whitehead*
- *Elizabeth Graham (age 87, Presbyterian):*
  *398 Islandmagee Road, Whitehead*

## X61

In fond memory of
**SAMUEL KEALEY**
Loved husband of Ellen
Died 9th April 1970
The above named **ELLEN**
Died 22nd Sept. 1999

- *Samuel*
  *(age 75, Presbyterian, retired signalman):*
  *38, Alexandra Ave. Whitehead*
- *Mrs. Ellen Officer Kealey*
  *(age 94, Presbyterian, widow):*
  *Whitehead Private Nursing Home*

## X62

**RODGERS**
In loving remembrance of
**ERIC RODGERS**
Died 14th April 1971

- *Alfred Eric*
  *(age 61, Presbyterian, commercial artist):*
  *27, Ballystrudder Gardens, Islandmagee*

## X63

**KANE**
In loving remembrance of
**JOHN KANE**
Died 20th September 1967
Also his wife
**JANE TEMPLETON KANE**
Died 29th November 1973

- *John (age 69, Presbyterian, Sea Captain)*
  *and Jane (age 78, housewife):*
  *Riverside, Cloughfin, Islandmagee*

## X64

**KERR**
In loving memory of my dear husband
**JOHN**
Who died 15th March 1971
Also his beloved wife
**ANNIE**
Who died 16th January 1981

- *John (age 68, Presbyterian, retired*
  *businessman) and*
  *Annie (age 74, Presbyterian):*
  *14, Kings Road, Whitehead*

## X65

In fond memory of
**MARGARET**
Loved wife of **David SINCLAIR**
Died 17th April 1971

- *Margaret (age 72, Presbyterian):*
  *Brownsbay, Islandmagee*
- *Buried 14.2.1983*
  ***DAVID AIKEN SINCLAIR** (age 79, C of I,*
  *married): Joymount House, Carrickfergus*

## X66-X67

**McCALMONT**
In loving memory
**JOHN KERR** Master Mariner **M.B.E.**
Died 19th March 1969 aged 88
His wife **LEILEA**
Died 16th November 1974 aged 90
Their elder son
**IVAN JOHN (JACK)** Master Mariner
Died 10th January 1983 aged 61

- *John (Presbyterian) and Elizabeth*
  *(recorded age 91, Presbyterian):*
  *"Anchorage", Dundressan, Islandmagee*
- *Jack (Presbyterian, married,*
  *schoolteacher): 6, Calwell Park, Ballycarry*

X68

Flower holder
**BELL**
In memory of James, Jane and Trevor

- *Buried 6.4.1979 **JANE BELL**
  (age 73, C of I, married):
  1, Ransevyn Court, Whitehead*

- *Buried 16.2.1999 **JAMES BELL** (age 89,
  C of I, widower): 7, Ransevyn Gardens,
  Whitehead*

X69 unused

X70

**JACKETT**
In loving memory of
A devoted husband and father
**WILLIAM FRANCIS JACKETT**
Who died 19th September 1971
Also **MARY HANNAH CANNING**
Died 29th October 1985 aged 89 years
And my dearly loved mother
**HANNAH HELEN JACKETT**
Who died 6th February 1995
The Lord is my Shepherd

- *William
  (age 48, married, C of I, civil engineer),
  Hannah (age 70, C of I) and
  Mrs. Canning (C of I):
  2, York Ave. Whitehead*

X71

**KANE**
In loving memory of
My dear husband
**LAWRENCE**
Who departed this life 1st April 1972
Also his dear wife
**JOAN**
Who departed this life
23rd January 1977
Beloved parents of Joanne
And loving grandparents of Jake
Blessed are the pure in heart

- *Lawrence Heggan Kane (age 43,
  Presbyterian, Merchant Navy officer):
  199 Middle Road, Islandmagee*

- *Elizabeth Joan (age 66, Presbyterian,
  widow): 201 Middle Road, Islandmagee*

X72

**JEFFREY**
In fond remembrance
**WILLIAM JOHN**
Died 22nd August 1968
His wife **EDNA**
Died 19th May 1973

- *William (age 78, retired cashier) and
  Edna (age 80, Presbyterian):
  197, Sandown Road, Knock, Belfast*

X73 unused

X74

- *Buried 20.4.1966
  **MARGARET ELIZABETH CRAWFORD**,
  (age 16): Sunnybank, Ballydown,
  Islandmagee*

- *Buried 6.8.1966 **ROBERT CRAWFORD**
  (age 53, bus driver):
  Sunnybank, Ballydown, Islandmagee*

X75

- *Buried 10.7.1964
  **HUGH GAULT McCORMICK:**
  'Kingslea', 2, Kings Road, Whitehead*

- *Buried 7.10.1979
  **Mrs. MARGARET McCORMICK**
  (age 82): same address*

X76-X77

In loving memory
of
**EDITH BERTRAM KILPATRICK**
Died 3rd Jan. 1969
and her husband
**DAVID STUART**
Died 27th May 1969

- *Edith (age 60, Presbyterian) and
  David (age 67, company director):
  1, Lenamore Drive, Jordanstown*

**X78**

### JAMES A. ARMSTRONG
Whitehead
1896 - 1975
also his dear wife
### MARGARET
Died 8th January 1986
Ever remembered

- *James Arthur*
  *(age 78, Presbyterian, buried 17.9.1975)*
  *and Margaret (age 86, Presbyterian):*
  *52, Cable Road, Whitehead*

**X79**

- *Buried 1.3.1973*
  ***JOHN McMURTRY CAMERON***
  *(age 82, single, Presbyterian):*
  *22, Windsor Crescent, Whitehead*

**X80**

- *Buried 12.6.1975*
  ***ELIZABETH S. SHANKS*** *(age 89, single,*
  *C of I): 26, York Ave. Whitehead*

**X81**

### RANKIN
In loving memory of
### MAURICE RANKIN
Died 24th November 1971

- *Maurice (Presbyterian, docker):*
  *Nirvana, Balfour Ave. Whitehead*

**X82**

### STEWART
### ROBERT
Died 5.4.1972
### MINNIE
Died 8.2.1996
Aged 99 years

- *Robert*
  *(age 75, Presbyterian, retired labourer):*
  *11, Loughview Bungalows, Islandmagee*
- *Mary (Minnie) (widow, Presbyterian):*
  *Inver House, Larne*

**X83**

### JACKSON
In loving memory of
My dear husband
### JAMES
Died 29th May 1972
Also his wife **GLADYS ELIZABETH**
Died 10th September 1983

- *James (age 68, Presbyterian):*
  *Alameda, Islandmagee*
- *Gladys (age 75, Presbyterian):*
  *137, Brownsbay Road, Islandmagee*

**X84**

### FORBES
In loving memory of
My dear husband **JAMES**
who died 5th August 1972
Also his dear wife **NAN**
who died 4th August 1983

- *James (age 77, Presbyterian) and*
  *Annie (Nan, age 86, Presbyterian):*
  *5, Ransevyn Drive, Whitehead*

**X85**

### MONTGOMERY
In loving memory of
A devoted husband and father
### THOMAS WILLIAM ALEXANDER
Died 26th March 1973

- *Thomas*
  *(age 64, farmer, Presbyterian, married):*
  *St. Ronans, Drumgurland, Islandmagee*

**X86**

### GIRVIN
In loving memory of
### LETITIA LUSK (LETA)
Who died 7th February 1973
Beloved wife of William Henry Girvin
At Rest

- *Leta (Presbyterian): 14, Balmoral Ave.*
  *Whitehead*

X87

**WILSON**
In loving memory of
**ROBERT BATES**
Who died 29th November 1978
Dear husband of Esther
Remembered by son Gerald and family

- *Robert (age 78, Presbyterian, painting contractor): 78 Cable Road, Whitehead*
- *Buried 14.3.1993*
  **Mrs. ESTHER ANNIE WILSON** *(age 89, Presbyterian): Chester Private Nursing Home, Whitehead*

X88

**McFARLANE**
In loving memory of
A devoted wife and mother
**MARGARET (MADGE)**
Who died 13th June 1973
And our dear father **WILLIAM**
Who died 22nd May 1975
Worthy of everlasting remembrance

- *Madge (age 74, Presbyterian) and William (age 86, Presbyterian): 12, Marine Parade, Whitehead*

X89

**McKEE**
In loving memory of
Our beloved mother
**DORIS MAY**
Died 17th April 1972
Also our dear father
**JAMES**
Died 6th March 1976

- *Doris (age 70, C of I): 37, Windsor Cres. Whitehead*
- *James (age 82, Congregationalist): 47, Chichester Square, Carrickfergus*

X90 unused

X91

In fond memory of
**WILLIAM**
Loved husband of **Isobella MAIR**
Died 22nd May 1965

- *William (fisherman): 21, Loughview Bungalows, Islandmagee*
- *Buried 14.9.1986* **Mrs. ISABELLA MAIR** *(age 91, home duties) same address*

X92

**GRAY**
In loving memory of my dear husband
**CARSON**
Died 27th February 1972

- *William Carson (age 58, Presbyterian, bank manager): 289, Castlereagh Road, Belfast*

X93

- *Buried 3.12.1967* **WILLIAM JOHN FOY,** *(age 72, married, Methodist): 35, Windsor Cres. Whitehead*
- *Buried 6.5.1985* **HELEN FOY** *(age 78, widow, Methodist): 11, Alexander Court, Whitehead*

X94

Marble Slab
**WILLIAM REID**
3rd Oct.20 - 10th May 73
**SARAH REID**
3rd July 20 – 3rd Jan. 89

- *William (age 53, married, Presbyterian, plumber): Flat 3A Abbotscoole House, Rathcoole, Newtownabbey*
- *Sarah (age 68, widow, Presbyterian): 3, Windsor Walk, Whitehead*

X95

- *Buried 18.8.1973* **WALTER WATSON MAWHINNEY** *(age 68, single, C of I, retired storeman): 23, Loughview Drive, Eden, Carrickfergus*
- *Buried 6.7.2002* **ROBERT JAMES MAWHINNEY** *(age 78, single, Presbyterian): 2, Ford Cottages, Whitehead*

X96-X97

In loving memory of
**THOMAS LYNAGH Surg. Capt. R.N.**
Who died 10th July 1977
aged 76 years
Also his beloved wife
and a dear mother
**MARY (MAY)**
died 1st October 1987 aged 91 years

- *Thomas Bernard (Presbyterian) and*
  *May (Presbyterian):*
  *11, Cable Road, Whitehead*

- *Buried 30.7.2002*
  ***PAMELA MARY LYNAGH*** *(age 65, single,*
  *Presbyterian, bank official):*
  *11, Cable Road*

X98

- *Buried 30.7.1973*
  ***WILLIAM SMYTH HALL***
  *(age 62, married, C of I, docker):*
  *6, Ford Cottage, Whitehead*

- *Buried 13.10.1979* ***ELIZABETH HALL***
  *(age 87, widow, C of I):*
  *101, Ballystrudder Road, Islandmagee*

X99

**ANDERSON**
In loving memory of
A devoted husband and father
**THOMAS JAMES ANDERSON**
Who died 3rd March 1972
Also a dear wife and mother
**MARGARET ELIZABETH ANDERSON**
Who died 17th July 1986
Called to higher service

- *Thomas (age 55, married, Presbyterian,*
  *inspection dept. I.C.I.):*
  *27, Adelaide Ave. Whitehead*

- *Margaret (widow, C of I):*
  *63 Ransevyn Park, Whitehead*

X100

**MAXWELL**
In loving memory of
A devoted husband and father
**THOMAS**
Died 21st March 1971
Also his dear wife **LEONORA**
Died 23rd October 1980

- *Thomas (age 62, C of I, wood machinist):*
  *37, Alexandra Ave. Whitehead*

- *Thomasina Lutton Moore Maxwell*
  *(Leonora) (age 69):*
  *41, Windsor Ave. Whitehead*

X101

Flower holder
In memory of brother **Danny**

- *Buried 1.6.1973* ***DANIEL CLIFFORD***
  *(age 65, widower, Presbyterian,*
  *Sea Captain): Newcastle-on-Tyne*

- *Buried 16.10.1982*
  ***CLIFFORD ROBERT HUNTER*** *(age 52,*
  *C of I): 18, Premier Drive, Belfast*

- *Buried 29.6.2001*
  ***MICHAEL JOHN WARREN*** *(age 72,*
  *C of I): 18, Premier Drive, Belfast*

X102

**GRAY**
**Granny MAUD**
In loving memory of
A devoted wife and mother
Died 19th July 1973
And her loving husband
**JAMES ERNEST GRAY**
died 10th March 1977

- *Martha Jane (Maud)*
  *(age 61, Presbyterian) and*
  *James (age 69, Presbyterian, retired fitter):*
  *39, Serpentine Parade, Newtownabbey*

X103 unused

**X104**

## POAG
In loving memory of
**HARRY**
Beloved husband of Edith
Died 7th October 1971

- *Henry (Harry) (age 64, Presbyterian, farmer): Castletown, Whitehead*
- *Buried 28.2.2001* **Mrs. EDITH POAG** *(age 95, Presbyterian, widow) Cranley Lodge Nursing Home, Bangor*

**X105-X106**

## PITCAITHLEY
In loving memory of
**MARY WINIFRED**
Born 15th December 1894
Died 21st March 1969

**SAMUEL MAGILL**
born 10th April 1908
died 9th October 1966
and his wife
**PHYLLIS MAGGIE**
Born 9th December 1913
Died 12th June 1995

- *Mary (age 76, housewife, C of I): Duncairn Gardens, Belfast*
- *Samuel Pitcaithley (age 58, turf accountant, Methodist): 31 Islandmagee Road, Whitehead*
- *Phyllis Pitcaithley (age 81, housewife, R.C.): 30 Victoria Ave. Whitehead*

**X107**

- *Buried 22.12.1966* **JOHN OAKMAN CHAMBERS** *(age 66, married, C of I, retired commissioner Ulster Transport Authority): 4, Adelaide Ave. Whitehead*
- *Buried 31.3.1972* **MARIAN CHAMBERS** *(age 73, widow, C of I, housewife): same address*

**X108**

## CHAMBERS
In loving memory of
**WILLIAM ANDREW CECIL**
a dear husband and father
Died 29th January 1994

- *William (age 62, married, C of I): 12, Armiston Parade, Belfast*

**X109**

In loving memory of
**CHARLES HENRY ERNEST CROZIER**
who died 1st January 1973

- *Charles (age 72, married, Methodist, retired bank manager): 17, Beach Road, Whitehead*

**X110**

In loving memory of
**WILLIAM**
Beloved husband of Jane Mayberry,
died 11th June 1973
The above named
**JANE MAYBERRY,**
died 1st April 1994

- *William (age 68, Presbyterian, retired labourer): 133 Islandmagee Road, Whitehead*
- *Jane (age 82, Presbyterian): 1, Alexandra Court Whitehead*

**X111**

## MULHOLLAND
In loving memory of
**JOHN**
Died 29th August 1980
Beloved husband of Isabella
Also the above **ISABELLA,**
Died 17th December 1997
"At rest"

- *John (age 71, Presbyterian, retired seaman): 2, Causeway Villas, Ballycarry*
- *Isabella (age 91, Presbyterian): 11, Willowvale Drive, Islandmagee*

X112

**NELSON**
In loving memory of
A dear husband and father
**ANDREW**
whom God called home
8th October 1973
Also **MARY ELIZABETH 'MAISIE'**
Beloved wife and mother
Died 11th January 1979
"In Heavenly Love Abiding"

• *Andrew (age 59, Presbyterian, farmer)*
  *and Maisie (age 51, Presbyterian):*
  *122 Low Road, Islandmagee*

X113

**LAMONT**
In loving memory of
**HUGH J.**
Died 4th October 1994
Aged 77 years

• *Hugh Johnston (Presbyterian):*
  *6, Portmuck Road, Islandmagee*

X114

In fond memory of
**ENA**
Loved wife of John Kerr,
died 7th Sep. 1973
Also her beloved husband
**JOHN KERR**
Died 6th May 1999 in his 101st year.
Beloved Parents and Grandparents

• *Georgina (age 70, Presbyterian) and*
  *John (Presbyterian):*
  *12, Alexandra Ave. Whitehead*

X115

**AIKEN**
In loving memory of
**ROBERT FLOYD**
Who died 30th November 1971
And his wife **ELEANOR MARY**
Who died 29th August 1992

• *Robert (age 82, Presbyterian):*
  *25, Balfour Ave. Whitehead*
• *Eleanor (age 93, widow, Presbyterian,*
  *cremated) Myddleton, Wales*

X116-X117

• *Buried 8.8.1973* ***DAVID CAMPBELL***
  *(age 5, Presbyterian): 45, Middle Road,*
  *Islandmagee*
• *Buried 2.7.1974*
  ***COLIN CHAMBERS CAMPBELL***
  *(age 18, Presbyterian): same address*

X118

**ORR-McAULEY**
In loving memory of
A devoted husband and father
**GEORGE**
Died 12th February 1974
And a beloved wife and mother
**MARGARET**
Died 18th April 19
(Grandmother, may God Bless You
and Keep You)

• *George (age 64, Presbyterian, farmer):*
  *Druids Altar, 91, Ballylumford Road,*
  *Islandmagee*
• *Margaret (age 87, widow, Presbyterian):*
  *3, Ballyliek Lane, Tandragee*

X119

**EDENS**
In loving memory of
**JACK**
Died 31st October 1975
And his wife **MARGARET DOREEN**
Died 15th December 1991

• *John (Jack) (age 77, Congregationalist)*
  *and Margaret (age 74, Congregationalist):*
  *14, Cable Road, Whitehead*

X120

## CLUGSTON
In loving memory of
A devoted husband
and father **THOMAS**
who passed away
29th March 1974
Aged 52 years
Also his only son
**MERVYN**
Who passed away
20th April 1975 aged 14 yrs
**MARY** who joined them on
27th November 2002 aged 80.
What we keep in memory
is ours unchanged forever.

- *Thomas James (age 53, married, C of I,
garage proprietor): 115, Low Road,
Islandmagee*
- *Mervyn Thomas (C of I) and Mary
(age 80, Congregational, widow):
70, Ballystrudder Gardens, Islandmagee*

X121

## MOORHEAD
In loving memory of
Our dear parents
**DAVID MANN**
Died 27th April 1985
**GERTRUDE (PAT)**
Died 20th August 1985)

- *David (age 67, Presbyterian) and
Gertrude Wilma (age 72, Presbyterian):
13, Loughview Bungalows, Islandmagee*

X122

In loving memory of
**ROSE McB. GREGG**
wife of James Gregg
Died 16th September 1974

- *Rose McBirney Gregg (Presbyterian):
89, Cable Road, Whitehead*

X123 unused

X124

## GRAHAM
**JOHN DAVID** Died 1st June 1967
Age 10 months

- *John (Reformed Presbyterian, person in
charge of arrangements J. Leslie Graham):
460, Merville Garden Village,
Newtownabbey*

X125

- *Buried 8.11.1967 **JOHN BOWMAN**
(age 88, widower, Presbyterian,
timekeeper): Sunnyside Cottage,
Ballydown, Islandmagee*
- *Buried 31.10.1970 **COLIN JONES**
(age 1 day, Moyle Hospital).*

X126

- *Buried 10.10.1968 **GEORGE McNEILL**
(age 63, married, Presbyterian, labourer):
Ballydown, Islandmagee*
- *Buried 24.3.1980
**WINIFRED MARY McNEILL**
(age 65, widow): 6, Ballylumford Road,
Islandmagee*

X127

## FERGUSON
In loving memory of
A devoted husband and father
**WILLIAM KANE**
Died 6th May 1973
Also his devoted wife and
my dear mother
**PHYLLIS ELEANOR**
Died 23rd April 1986
"The Lord is my Shepherd"

- *William
(age 67, Presbyterian, retired foreman)
and Phyllis (age 69, Presbyterian):
Meadow View, 50, Middle Road,
Islandmagee*

X128

**BENNETT**
In loving memory
of our darling daughter
**ROSEMARY**
Died 1st August 1974 aged 5 years
Also a devoted wife and mother
**PHYLLIS**
Died 29th April 1988
"In Heavenly Love Abiding"

- *Rosetta Mary (Rosemary) (Presbyterian)
  and Phyllis (age 50, Presbyterian):
  6, Chichester Gardens, Whitehead*

X129

**GRAHAM**
In loving memory of
My dear mother
**ELLEN PATRICIA**
Who died 13th July 1983

- *Ellen (age 76, widow, Presbyterian):
  5, Loughview Bungalows, Islandmagee*

X130

In loving memory of
Our parents
**JAMES DALLAS,** Died 4th Dec. 1974
**KATHLEEN,** Died 2nd Dec. 1977

- *Samuel James (age 66, Congregationalist,
  retired labourer): 48, Adelaide Ave.
  Whitehead*
- *Kathleen (age 73):
  4, Alexandra Court, Whitehead*

X131

In fond memory of
**HARRY BRENNAN**
Loved husband of MARY
Died 29th January 1975

- *Henry (age 55, Presbyterian, farmer):
  25, Gransha Brae, Islandmagee*

X132

**SLOAN**
**Baby**
**LAWRENCE**
Died 16.6.1975

- *Lawrence William Samuel
  (arranged by W. J. Sloan):
  64, Ballystrudder Gardens, Islandmagee*

X133

**McCOY**
**FREDERICK,** Died 8th June 1976
Dear husband of Isobel

- *Frederick (age 77, C of I):
  Orlington, 27, Upper Road, Greenisland*

X134

**MANN**
In loving memory of
**JAMES McALLISTER MANN**
Died 22nd August 1959
Also his beloved wife
**ELLEN**
Died 31st May 1974

- *Ellen (Presbyterian): Isle House, Middle
  Road, Islandmagee*
- *Buried 27.8.2002 **WILLIAM CAMPBELL**
  (age 79, married, Presbyterian):
  45, Middle Road, Islandmagee*

X135

**WILSON**
In memory of
My dearly loved husband
**JAMES J.**
Died 23rd January 1975

- *James Johnston (age 50, Presbyterian,
  Senior Berthing Master):
  15, Ballystrudder Gardens, Islandmagee*

## X136

**McCARTNEY**
In loving memory of
A devoted wife and mother
**MARGARET**
Died 11th July 1976
Also **WILLIAM** her beloved husband
and father of Wilma
Died 22nd January 1997
"The Lord is my Shepherd"

- *Margaret (age 67, Presbyterian):*
  *19, Townlane, Islandmagee*
- *William (age 82, Presbyterian): Joymount*
  *Private Nursing Home, Carrickfergus*

## X137

In loving memory of
**JANE,** dear wife of
**Robtert M. COWAN**
Died 15th October 1975 aged 66 years
Also her beloved husband
**ROBERT M.**
Died 12th November 1982
aged 78 years

- *Jane (Presbyterian) and*
  *Robert Moore Cowan (Presbyterian):*
  *28, Glanworth Gardens, Belfast*

## X138

**HILL**
In loving memory of
A devoted husband and father
**EDWARD S.**
Died 4th March 1976
Also his beloved wife
**ELIZABETH**
A loving mother, gran and friend
Died 13th July 1998

- *Edward Stanley (Eddy) (age 63,*
  *Presbyterian) and*
  *Lily (age 88, Presbyterian):*
  *27A Islandmagee Road, Whitehead*

## X139

Flower holder
In loving memory of
**W.J. DONNAN**

- *Buried 20.6.1980*
  ***WILLIAM JAMES DONNAN** (age 76,*
  *Methodist): 1, Alexandra Court, Whitehead*
- *Buried 4.11.1997 **Mrs. ELLEN DONNAN***
  *(age 99, Methodist, widow):*
  *Chester Park Nursing Home, Whitehead*

## X140

**DICK**
In memory of my husband
**ROBERT**
Died 31st January 1977
and his beloved wife
**MAMIE**
Died 9th July 2000
"The Day Thou Gavest Lord is Ended"

- *Robert (age 69, Methodist):*
  *5, Dunmore Drive, Belfast 15*
- *Mary (age 89, Presbyterian):*
  *56, Lestannon Ave. Whitehead*

## X141

Small granite cross
**HOCKINGS**
**WILLIAM 1967**

- *Buried 17.6.1967*
  ***WILLIAM ERNEST HOCKINGS** (age 54,*
  *Presbyterian, civil servant, married):*
  *6, Malone Ave. Whitehead*

## X142

In loving memory of
**MURIEL LEWIS MAXWELL**
Died 27th January 1971 aged 52 years

- *Muriel (married, C of I):*
  *Cumbrae, Balfour Ave. Whitehead*

## X143 unused

## X144 unused

X145

**CROSSAN**
In loving memory of
A dear husband and father
**BERTIE**
Died 18th May 1992

- *Bertie (age 72, C of I):*
  *96, Windsor Ave. Whitehead*

X146

**DUNCAN**
In memory of our parents
**MARY FRANCES (LATIMER)**
1897 - 1975
Widow of David Cecil Duncan
1898 - 1965 (cremated)
also their son
**Dr. J. C. DUNCAN (JACK)**
1926 - 1986
interred in Canada

- *Mary (buried 10.4.1975, age 77,*
  *Presbyterian, widow): Ferris Bay,*
  *Islandmagee*

X147

**STITT**
In loving memory of
**JAMES STITT** died 21st May 1975
aged 70 years
And his wife **ELIZABETH (DOLLY)**
Died 18th July 1981 aged 78 years

- *James (retired coastguard, C of I)*
  *and Dolly (C of I):*
  *93, Mullaghboy Road, Islandmagee*

X148 unused

X149

In loving memory of
A devoted wife and mother
**MARGARET McBRIDE**
Called home 16th August 1975
Also her husband **ANDREW**
Called home 20th January 1982
Until we meet

- *Margaret (age 69, Congregationalist):*
  *23, Castlemara Drive, Carrickfergus*
- *Andrew (age 84, Church of Nazarene):*
  *18, Prospect Road, Carrickfergus*

X150 unused

X151 unused

X152

In loving memory of
**WILLIAM HEDDLES**
Who died 14th May 1976 aged 77 years
Also his sister
**ANNA MARY HEDDLES**
Who died 25th Oct. 1989 aged 92 years
And their brother
**EDWARD OWENS RENNIE HEDDLES**
Who died 8th June 1992 aged 88 years

- *William (single, Presbyterian) and*
  *Anna (single, Presbyterian):*
  *166, Gobbins Road, Islandmagee*
- *Edward (single, Presbyterian):*
  *1, Millbay Road, Islandmagee*

X153

**SIMMS**
In loving memory of
**DOREEN**
Devoted wife and mother
Died 26th June 1976 aged 40 years
Also her beloved husband **ROBERT**
Died 2nd May 1992 aged 64 years
In Heavenly Love Abiding

- *Doreen (recorded age 41, Presbyterian)*
  *and Robert:*
  *20, Loughview Bungalows, Islandmagee*

X154

**NUTTALL**
In loving memory of
**JEMIMA (MAMIE)**
Died 10th February 1982
At rest

- *Mamie (age 77, Presbyterian, widow):*
  *11, Cable Road, Whitehead*

## X155

**NEILL**
In loving memory of
A devoted wife and mother
**MIRA**
Died 3rd April 1976
Also her husband
**ALBERT**
Died 10th August 1978

- *Mary (Mira) (age 71, Presbyterian):*
  *5, Mullaghboy Bungalows, Islandmagee*
- *Albert (age 79, Presbyterian):*
  *106, Low Road, Islandmagee*

## X156

- *Buried 9.10.1975*
  ***JAMES MOORE CONNOR***
  *(age 75, C of I, retired milk vendor):*
  *4, Railway Houses, Whitehead*
- *Buried 8.6.1983*
  ***Mrs. MARTHA SMYTH CONNOR***
  *(age 78, Jehovah's Witness, widow):*
  *5, Castleview Road, Whitehead*

## X157

**EDENS**
In loving memory of
**MARY**
Died 10th October 1998

- *Mary (age 47, married):*
  *14 Cable Road, Whitehead*

## X158

In remembrance of
**THOMAS STUART PERRY**
Who died 11th August 1976
Also his wife **MAUREEN**
Who died 11th February 1994

- *Thomas (age 66) and Maureen (age 80):*
  *33, Balfour Ave. Whitehead*

## X159-X160-X161

**FORSYTHE**
In loving memory of our dear parents
**SAMUEL** died 10th February 1969
**THOMASINA** died 17th April 1970

**FORSYTHE**
In loving memory of
**JOHN A. (JACKIE)**
A devoted husband, father
and grandfather
Died 20th July 1992
Also his mother-in-law
**MARGARET E. BAXTER**
Died 18th August 1978
In Heavenly Love Abiding

- *Samuel (age 73, Presbyterian, farmer)*
  *and Thomasina (age 60, Presbyterian):*
  *Mullaghboy, Islandmagee*
- *John Alexander (age 64, Presbyterian)*
  *and Margaret Ellen (age 79):*
  *183, Gobbins Road, Islandmagee*
- *Buried 13.1.2000 in X161*
  ***Mrs. GEORGINA CATHCART** (age 84,*
  *Methodist, widow): Edenmore Private*
  *Nursing Home, Whiteabbey*

## X162

In loving memory of
**ERNEST PINK**
Who died 5th March 1975 and his wife
**ETHEL MAY PINK**
Who died 6th May 1975

- *Ernest (age 67, Presbyterian, retired bank*
  *official) and Ethel (age 70, Presbyterian):*
  *24, Ransevyn Drive, Whitehead*

## X163

**GRAHAM**
In loving memory of
A dear husband and father
**SYDNEY**
Died 21st May 1995
Aged 72 years

- *Sydney: 40 Cavehill Road, Belfast*

X164

## NIMICK
In loving memory of
A devoted husband and father
### WILLIAM (BILL)
Died 21st February 1976

- *Bill (age 51, Congregationalist, married, bus driver): 41, Edward Road, Whitehead*

X165

In loving memory of
### ALAN RAYMOND
Darling son of
Charles and Florence **STITT**
Died 2nd October 1977 aged 5 years

- *Alan (C of I): 93, Mullaghboy road, Islandmagee*

X166

- *Buried 4.5.2002 **Mrs. NORAH LESLIE** (age 63, married, Nazarene, housewife): 591 Doagh Road, Newtownabbey*

X167

## HAMILTON
In memory of
**GILBERT YEATES,** Master Mariner
Died 7th January 1976
And his beloved wife
### ELSIE
Died 16th February 1992
Home is the sailor, home from the sea

- *Gilbert (age 70, Presbyterian): 165, Alexander Park Ave. Belfast*

X168

In fond memory of
### ELIZABETH MAY
Loved wife of John **KANE**
Died 28th May 1976

- *Elizabeth (Presbyterian): 30, Ransevyn Drive, Whitehead*

X169 unused

X170

## WALKER
In loving memory of
My dear wife **MARTHA (PAT)**
Who died 20th February 1976
Also her husband **WILLIAM**
Who died 30th June 1977

- *Pat Muir Walker (age 78, Presbyterian): Rockmount, Quarterlands Road, Islandmagee*
- *William: St. Michaels, Islandmagee*

X171

## HOOD
In loving memory of
### JOHN INGLEBY
Died 2nd February 1976 aged 24 years
Dear son of Douglas and Agnes Hood
A dear wife and devoted mother
### AGNES POLLOCK
Died 3rd July 1997 aged 78 years
At rest

- *John (single, ferryman, C of I) and Agnes (C of I): 2, Loughview Bungalows, Islandmagee*

X172 unused

X173 unused

X174

## MANN
In loving memory of
### THOMAS MANN
Who died 18th October 1975
And his beloved wife
### OLIVE MARGARET
Who died 22nd October 1987

- *Thomas (age 71, Presbyterian) and Olive (age 88, Presbyterian): 44, Lestannon Ave. Whitehead*

X175

## CAIRNS
In loving memory of
**ISABELLA**
Died 6th July 1994
**RICHARD**
Died 12th March 1995
Beloved parents
And grandparents
Always in our thoughts

- *Isabella (age 80, C of I):*
  *79, Merville Garden Village, Newtownabbey*
- *Richard (age 87, C of I):*
  *Abbeylands Nursing Home, Whiteabbey*
- *Buried 15.12.1966*
  ***ROBERT JAMES CAIRNS** (age 66, C of I):*
  *Langdale, Ballykeel, Islandmagee*

X176

**SAMUEL T.M. BOYD**
Master Mariner
Born 1910 - died 1974
And his wife
**MARGARET C. BOYD**
Born 1920 - died 1999

- *Samuel (age 63, Congregationalist):*
  *14, Ransevyn Drive, Whitehead*
- *Margaret Crooks (age 79):*
  *10, Donegall Gardens, Whitehead*

X177

- *Buried 5.4.1976 **WILLIAM CORR**
  (age 65, Presbyterian):*
  *8, Kilton Lane, Islandmagee*
- *Buried 29.6.1993*
  ***MARY MULHOLLAND CORR***
  *(age 79, Presbyterian):*
  *same address*

X178

**McILWAINE**
In loving memory of our dear parents
**HUGH**
Who died 13th April 1976
**SARAH**
Who died 14th April 1976

- *Hugh (age 85, Presbyterian) and*
  *Sarah (age 85, Presbyterian):*
  *Blackhead, Whitehead*

X179

**PATTON**
In loving memory of
**HERBERT**
Born 12th June 1908
died 8th October 1976
Also his wife
**MARY LOUISE CHESNEY**
Born 29th April 1910
died 6th February 1980

- *Herbert (age 68, Presbyterian) and*
  *Mary (age 69, Presbyterian):*
  *40, Cable Road, Whitehead*

X180

**MACAULEY**
In loving memory of
**MARY ISABELLA**
died 3rd January 1977
Her husband
**ROBERT CAMBRIDGE,**
Master Mariner
Died 24th July 1980

- *Mabel (Mary, Congregationalist) and*
  *Robert (age 87, Presbyterian):*
  *14, Windsor Ave. Whitehead*

X181

## DORRANS
In loving memory of
A devoted wife and mother
### VALERIE ANN
Died 23rd January 1977
Result of an accident
Grand-daughter
### KARLY VALERIE McMURTRY
Died 10th August 1997
Aged 9 years

- *Valerie (age 30, married, Presbyterian):*
  *60, Ballystrudder Gardens, Islandmagee*
- *Karly (Presbyterian):*
  *57, Ballystrudder Gardens, Islandmagee*

X182

## MONTGOMERY
In loving memory of
### IVAN
Dearly loved husband, father
and grandfather
Died 18th February 1997
The Lord is my Shepherd

- *Ivan (age 70, Presbyterian):*
  *22 Cambourne Park, Belfast*

X183 unused

X184

## BASHFORD
### ROBERT JAMES (JIM)
Loved husband and father
Died 8th October 1976
Also
### MAY (nee Hilditch)
Loved wife and devoted mother
Died 27th February 1984

- *Jim (age 80, Presbyterian) and*
  *Mary (age 72, Presbyterian):*
  *36, Island Road, Ballycarry*

X185

## GOURLEY
In loving memory of
A devoted husband and father
### JAMES MOORE
Died 18th May 1978
Also his beloved wife
### SARAH
Died 4th December 1988

- *James (age 72, C of I) and*
  *Sarah (age 78, C of I):*
  *34, Ballystrudder Gardens, Islandmagee*

X186

## BUCKLE
In loving memory of
Our dear son and brother
### MICHAEL JOHN
Died 10th July 1996
Always in our thoughts

- *Michael*
  *(single, age 26, Presbyterian, engineer):*
  *14, Willowvale Drive, Islandmagee*

X187

## HAMILTON
In loving memory of
A dear husband and father
### JAMES
Died 5th August 1977
The Lord is my Shepherd

- *James*
  *(age 50, Presbyterian, chief engineer):*
  *14 Ballystrudder Road, Islandmagee*

X188

## BUCKLE
In loving memory of
A devoted husband and father
### FRANCIS JACK
Died 10th May 1941
Interred Finchley Cemetery London
Also a beloved wife
### JANE
Died 7th October 1987
At rest

- *Jane (age 83, Presbyterian):*
  *29, Ballystrudder Gardens, Islandmagee*

X189 unused

X190 unused

X191-X192
## SWEETNAM
In
Loving memory of
**SALLY**
Died 23rd April 1977
And **VICTOR DENNIS**
Dearly loved husband and father
Died 22nd December 1996
Also his mother
**ELSIE ROSE DENNIS**
Died 26th August 1979

- *Sarah (married, age 64, C of I) and Victor (age 82, C of I): 30, Brooklands Crescent, Whitehead*
- *Elsie (age 97, C of I, widow): Lis-Garel, Larne*

X193
## DUFF
In loving memory of
**Rev. SAMUEL NOEL DUFF M.A.**
Died 13th September 1967
Minister of
Draperstown Presbyterian Ch.
1950-1967
Also
**EMILY McKINNEY**
Died 16th June 1997

- *Rev. Duff (age 55, married): The Manse, Draperstown*
- *Emily McKinney Duff (age 84, widow, Presbyterian): 22, Reids Road, Islandmagee*

X194
## DAVIDSON
**WILLIAM** died 4th October 1975
Beloved husband of
**PHOEBE ELIZABETH**
Died 11th April 1976

- *William (age 84, Presbyterian) and Phoebe (age 83): 6, Alexandra Ave. Whitehead*

X195
## HEGGAN
In loving memory of
**ARTHUR** died 30th August 1976

- *Arthur (age 61, Presbyterian): 44, Middle Road, Islandmagee*

X196
## REA
In loving memory of
**EDWARD CARSON REA,**
Master Mariner
Devoted husband and dear father
of Norman
Who died 20th November 1976
Also his beloved wife
**AGNES ROBINA (DOT)**
Who died 13th November 1994

- *Edward (age 64, Presbyterian): 15, Alexandra Ave. Whitehead*
- *Dot (age 76, Presbyterian): 37 Old Hill Cottages, Rufford, Lancs.*

X197 unused

X198
## COYLE
Loving memories of
A dear husband and father
**ERNEST VICTOR**
Died 22nd March 1979

- *Ernest (age 73, Methodist): 11, Middle Road, Islandmagee*
- *Buried 17.4.2002 **Mrs. ELSIE COYLE** (age 85, widow, Methodist): 11, Ransevyn Gardens, Whitehead*

X199
## FERRIS
In memory of
**WILLIAM J.** died 22nd July 1977
At rest

- *William Joseph (age 53, married, Presbyterian, fitter): 15, Carnransy Walk, Carrickfergus*

**X200**

## BOSOMWORTH
## HERBERT
Died 24th April 1985
Dear husband of Maureen

- *Herbert George (age 77, Presbyterian):*
  *2, Adelaide Ave. Whitehead*

**X201**

## SERVICE
In loving memory of
## AGNES (NESSIE)
A devoted wife and mother
Died 21st Nov. 1976 aged 45 years

- *Nessie (married, Presbyterian):*
  *20, Asnvale Park, Islandmagee*

**X202**

In fond memory of
## ROBERT JAMES,
loved husband of **Anna KANE**
Died 16th January 1977
Also his beloved wife **ANNA**
Died 21st September 1995

- *Robert (age 67, Presbyterian):*
  *6, Mullaghboy Bungalows, Islandmagee*

- *Anna Mary (age 82, Presbyterian):*
  *Joymount House, Carrickfergus*

**X203**

## WILLIAM JONES KEENAN
Born 24th October 1945
died 27th July 1977
Absent from the body
present with the Lord

- *William (age 31, married, C of I, teacher):*
  *73, Windsor Ave. Whitehead*

**X204**

In loving memory of
## WILLIAM STEVENSON JOHNSTON
Died 27th October 1977

- *William (age 56, married, C of I,*
  *engineer):*
  *75 Low Road, Islandmagee*

**X205**

Captain
## Wm. MARTIN HOUSTON M.B.E.
Master Mariner (M.N.)
Born 14th April 1907
Died 26th November 1977

- *William (age 69, widower, Presbyterian,*
  *retired seaman): 21, Port Road,*
  *Islandmagee*

**X206-X207** unused

**X208**

## DAWSON
In loving memory of our dear son
## WILLIAM
Died 9th January 1978 aged 50 years
Also my dear wife and
our devoted mother
## JENNIE
Died 11th March 1981
Also her beloved husband
And our dear father
## THOMAS
Died 22nd October 1989
At rest

- *William Laverty Dawson (single,*
  *Presbyterian), Jennie (age 78, Presbyterian)*
  *and Thomas Burns Dawson (age 85,*
  *Presbyterian): 16, Adelaide Ave. Whitehead*

**X209**

## MAWHINNEY
In loving memory of
## HAROLD JOSEPH
Died 20th February 1977
Also his wife
## MONA ISOBEL
Died 24th December 1998
Peace perfect peace

- *Harold (age 66, Methodist):*
  *15 Edward Road, Whitehead*

- *Mona (age 78, Methodist):*
  *53 Edward Road, Whitehead*

## X210

- *Buried 5.6.1975*
**FLORENCE EVELINE FOSTER**
*(age 94, Presbyterian, widow, Ednaville):*
*21 Balmoral Ave. Whitehead*

## X211

**JOHNSTON**
In loving memory of
**MAGGIE**
Died 12th August 1974
And her husband
**GEORGE**
Died 9th July 1985
At rest

- *Maggie (age 65, Congregationalist):*
*38 Ballystrudder Road, Islandmagee*

- *George H. (age 78, C.O.I):*
*Abbeydene Old Peoples Home*

## X212

In loving memory of
**TOM McKENZIE**
Beloved husband of Sheelagh
And a devoted father
Died 22nd March 1978
And our dear mother **SHEELAGH**
Beloved wife of Tom
Died 15th September 1981

- *Tom (age 72, C of I) and*
*Sheelagh (nee **Welch**) (age 66, C of I):*
*37, Adelaide Ave. Whitehead*

## X213

**RILEY**
In loving memory of
**RAY**
Dear husband of Jean who died
15 May 1978
Also his wife **JEAN KERR** who died
2nd December 1983
The Lord is my Shepherd

- *Raymond (age 59, Presbyterian)*
*and Jean (Presbyterian):*
*4, Raphael Road, Whitehead*

## X214

**McKAY**
In loving memory of
A devoted wife and mother
**MARTHA JANE**
Died 16th January 1982
And devoted husband
And father
**JOHN**
Died 26th December 1982
The Lord is my Shepherd

- *Martha (age 77, Presbyterian)*
*and John (age 74, Presbyterian):*
*14, Edward Road, Whitehead*

## X215

**McCLURE**
In loving memory of
A dear brother
**JOHN T. THOMPSON R.A.F.**
Died 10th November 1979
aged 64 years
**MARY (MAY) TURNBULL**
Died 2nd February 1996
Dear wife of Bert
Redeemed

- *John Turnbull Thompson*
*(surname, single, Methodist):*
*407, North Queen Street, Belfast*

- *May McClure (age 82, married, Methodist):*
*4, Ransevyn Gardens, Whitehead*

- *Buried 12.12.2001*
**ALBERT JOHN McCLURE**
*(age 89, widower, Methodist):*
*Abbeyfield House Whitehead*

## X216

**MONTGOMERY**
In loving memory of
A devoted wife and mother
**REBECCA**
Who died 20th October 1980
Also
A devoted husband and father
**ISAAC**
Who died 16th January 1982

- *Rebecca (age 74, Presbyterian)*
*and Isaac (age 78, Presbyterian):*
*49, Edward Road, Whitehead*

## X217

In
Loving memory of
A dear wife and mother
**RUBY COYLE**
Died 15th June 1979

- *Ruby (Rebecca) (age 49, married,
  Presbyterian): 75, Islandmagee Road,
  Whitehead*

## X218

**LOGAN**
In loving memory of
Our dear parents
**HUGH**
Died 14th Feb. 1978
**EVA**
Died 25th May 1985
Also their daughter
**MAUREEN**
Died 1st June 1998
The Lord is my Shepherd

- *Hugh (age 80, Presbyterian):
  390, Islandmagee Road, Whitehead*
- *Mrs. Isabel Evelyn Logan (age 85,
  Presbyterian) and Maureen Irvine (age 71,
  Presbyterian):
  45, Ransevyn Drive, Whitehead*

## X219

- *Buried 27.6.1985
  **JOHN BUNTING COOKE**
  (age 78, Presbyterian): 34 Ashvale Park,
  Islandmagee*

## X220

**JOHNSON**
In loving memory of
**MARGARET**
Died 8th September 1978
**WILLIAM**
Died 18th April 1981
In Gods keeping

- *Margaret (age 61, married, Methodist):
  15 Windsor Ave. Whitehead*
- *William Henry (age 68, Methodist):
  4, Balmoral Ave. Whitehead*

## X221

- *Buried 3.6.1978
  **JOHN SAMUEL JOHNSON**
  (age 75, single, Methodist):
  15 Windsor Ave. Whitehead*
- *Buried 28.2.1984
  **JOSEPH CHRISTOPHER JOHNSON**
  (age 78, single, Methodist):
  Abbeydene Old Peoples Home*

## X222

**HERON**
In fond remembrance of
A dear husband and father
**WILLIAM MOORE**
Died 10th January 1978
Peace be thine

- *William (age 72, married, Presbyterian):
  8, Ashvale Park, Mullaghboy*

## X223 unused

## X224

**TYRIE**
In loving memory of
My dear brother **FREDERICK**
Died 28th August 1978 aged 58 years
Also
**MARGARET ROBERTSON TYRIE**
Died 20th September 1989
aged 81 years

- *Frederick
  (single, Presbyterian, Company Director):
  85, Millbay Road, Islandmagee*
- *Margaret (single, Presbyterian):
  85, Fitzroy Ave. Belfast*
- *Buried 11.7.1998
  **Mrs. CATHERINE STUART**
  (age 86, widow, Presbyterian):
  Towell House, Kings Road, Belfast*

## X225

**MAGOWAN**
In loving memory of
My dear wife **MINNIE**
Died 24th January 1979
Also her husband **THOMAS**
Died 12th October 1981
At rest

- *Mary Jane (age 72, Unitarian) and Thomas (age 75, Unitarian): 30, Alexander AV. Whitehead*

## X226

**CAMPBELL**
In loving memory of
**WILLIAM** (Master Mariner)
Beloved husband of Anne Campbell
Died 5th January 1979
Also our dear son **KENNETH**
Died 6th February 1970
And the above named
**ANNE CAMPBELL**
Died 25th August 1987

- *William (age 79, Presbyterian) and Anne (age 85, Presbyterian): 11, Alexandra Ave. Whitehead*

## X227

- *Buried 15.12.1978*
  ***THOMAS EDWARD PHILLIPS***
  *(age 78, married, C of I): 24 Victoria Ave. Whitehead*
- *Buried 14.6.1987*
  ***Mrs. MAUREEN PHILLIPS***
  *(age 96, widow, Congregationalist): 24, Victoria Ave. Whitehead*

## X228

**GREGG**
In loving memory of
**HETTY** and **BERTIE**
**HARRIETT DUNCAN**
11.7.1919 - 24.8.1978
**ROBERT BERTRUDE**
10.4.1920 - 25.11.1993

- *Hetty and Bertie (both Presbyterian): 4, Marine Ave. Whitehead*

## X229

**KANE**
In memory of
A dear husband and father
**WILLIAM** Master Mariner
Died 6th November 1977
Also beloved wife and dear mother
**IRENE** died 25th December 1989
Son **WILLIAM JOHN**
died 22nd November 1986
Beloved husband and father

- *William (age 63, married, Presbyterian, coastguard): 5, Ocean View, Newbiggin, Northumberland*
- *Irene (age 68, Presbyterian): 9, Ballystrudder Gardens, Islandmagee*
- *William (age 40, married, Presbyterian, marine engineer): 26, Brookslands Crescent, Whitehead*

## X230-X231-X232

**WILSON**
In loving memory of
**PATRICIA MURIEL**
A beloved wife and mother
Born 17th March 1925
Died 22nd April 2002

- *Patricia (age 76): 57, Belfast Road, Whitehead*

## X233

In loving memory of
**ROBERT NIXON**
A dear husband and father
died 6th November 1977
And his beloved wife **AILEEN**
died 16th February 1980

- *Robert (age 86, Presbyterian) and Aileen (age 80, Presbyterian): 17, Ransevyn Drive Whitehead*

X234

In loving memory of
**JOHN ROSSBOROUGH**
Who died 2nd January 1978
aged 68 years
Also his beloved wife **AGNES**
Who died 13th January 1991
aged 76 years

- *John (Presbyterian) and*
  *Agnes (Presbyterian):*
  *37, Ferris Bay Road, Islandmagee*

X235

**HALL**
In loving memory of
A devoted husband and father
**ROBERT HUGH**
Died 19th June 1978
Also a dear daughter **META**
died 4th Feb. 1984
And his beloved wife **SARAH**
Died 12th June 1985
In Heavenly love abiding

- *Robert (age 79, Presbyterian) and*
  *Meta (Martha Kennedy Hall) (age 50,*
  *single, Presbyterian, District Nurse):*
  *15, Raw Brae Road, Whitehead*

- *Sarah McFerran Hall*
  *(age 85, widow, Presbyterian):*
  *7, Raw Brae Road, Whitehead*

X236

- *Buried 1.11.1980*
  ***Miss MARTHA GILMOUR***
  *(age 90, Presbyterian):*
  *38, Ballystrudder Gardens, Islandmagee*

- *Buried 25.1.1982* ***Mrs. SARAH CRAIG***
  *(age 80, widow, Presbyterian):*
  *27B Islandmagee Road, Whitehead*

X237 and X238 unused

X239

**FULLERTON**
In loving memory of
**JACK**
Died 19th April 1980

- *John Lawson (Jack) (age 79, Presbyterian):*
  *44, Ferris Bay Road, Islandmagee*

X240-X241

**ROSS**
In loving memory of
**JOHN (ROSSIE)**
Died 31st January 1979 aged 71 yrs.
Also his son **JOHN**
Lost at sea 18th October 1949
Aged 18 yrs.
Also **FRANCES**
wife of the above John Ross
Died 20th September 1994
aged 91 yrs.
**ROBERT**
Elder son of John and Frances
Died 3rd June 2001 aged 73 yrs.

- *John (Presbyterian): 18, Portmuck Road,*
  *Islandmagee*

- *Frances (Presbyterian, widow):*
  *Broadway Nursing Home, Larne*

- *Robert  (married, Presbyterian):*
  *46, Mullaghboy Road, Islandmagee*

X242-X243

**BRENNAN**
In loving memory of
A devoted wife and mother
**ELIZABETH MURRAY (BESSIE)**
Died 15th March 1979
Also her loving husband
And a devoted father **HENRY**
Died 2nd August 1999

- *Bessie (age 69, Presbyterian)*
  *and Henry (age 82):*
  *89, Low Road, Islandmagee*

X244

Flower holder
**CHARLES REYNOLDS**

- *Buried 17.2.1979*
  ***CHARLES THOMPSON REYNOLDS***
  *(age 70, married, C of I):*
  *50A Islandmagee Road, Whitehead*

## X245

In loving memory of
**ELIZABETH ALLEN**
Beloved sister of
James and Sadie
Born 18.1.1920
Died 6.10.1980

- *Elizabeth (age 60, single, Congregationalist): 12, Lumford Ave. Whitehead*
- *Buried 26.7.1983 **MARTHA ALLEN** (age 98, single, Congregationalist): same address*
- *Buried 26.2.1990 **JOHN ALLEN** (age 101, single, Methodist): same address*

## X246-X247

**DEVON**
**ALEXANDER McGREGOR**
1913 – 1977

- *Alexander (buried 13.12.1977, age 64, married, Presbyterian, paint merchant): 38, Cleaver Park, Belfast 9*

## X248

**McKAY**
In loving memory of
**LEWIS**
A devoted husband
father and grandfather
Died 18th January 1995
Also his loving wife
**JOAN**
Died 27th November 1996

- *Lewis (age 76, Presbyterian) and Josephina (age 71, Presbyterian): 79 Old Coach Road, Portstewart*

## X249

**MOWAT**
In memory of
**MARY E.H.S.**
Died 14th July 1972
Beloved wife of
**WILLIAM J.G.**
Died 2nd March 1974

- *Mary (age 86, Presbyterian) and William James Grant (age 91, Presbyterian, retired civil servant): 11, Donegall Ave. Whitehead*

## X250

**WRIGHT**
In loving memory of
A devoted husband and father
**ANDREW**
Died 11th January 1981
Also his beloved wife
**SUSAN MARY ELIZABETH**
Died 4th December 1986

- *Andrew (age 80, Presbyterian): 5, Millbay Road, Islandmagee*
- *Susan (age 78, widow, Presbyterian): 44, Islandmagee Road, Whitehead*

## X251

**JOHNSTON**
In loving memory of
A dear husband and father
**JAMES HOWARD JOHNSTON J.P.**
Died 3rd February 1979

- *James (age 60, C of I, executive engineer post office): 11, Donegal Ave. Whitehead*

## X252 unused

## X253

- *Buried 11.6.1979 **BRIAN TUMELTY** (age 23, married, Protestant, labourer): 38, Adelaide Ave. Whitehead*

X254

### NELSON
In loving memory of
A devoted husband and father
**SAMUEL DOWNEY**
Called home 4th November 1980
Aged 70 years
Also beloved wife and mother
**MARGARET**
Called home 11th August 1998
The Lord is my Shepherd

- *Samuel (farmer, Presbyterian):*
  *1, Gransha Brae, Islandmagee*
- *Margaret (age 78, Presbyterian):*
  *3, Gransha Brae, Islandmagee*

X255

### HIGGINSON

X256-X257

### LAIRD
In loving memory of
**FLORENCE (ANN)**
Died 5th October 1979
beloved wife of James

**MARGARET ANDERSON**
died 17th November 1993

- *Ann (age 53, married, Presbyterian):*
  *196 Middle Road, Islandmagee*
- *Mrs. Margaret Black Anderson (age 90,*
  *widow, Methodist, buried 17.8.1995):*
  *168 Low Road, Islandmagee*

X258

### HUGHES
In loving memory of
My dear husband **ALFRED LESLIE**
Died 4th March 1981
Also his beloved wife
**JENNIE NAPIER**
Died 16th May 1993

- *Alfred (age 82): 9, Brooklands Crescent*
- *Jennie (age 95, widow):*
  *Castlerocklands, Carrickfergus*

X259

### BOYD
In loving memory of
A dear husband and father
**ANDREW KANE**
Died 6th October 1980

- *Andrew (age 48, married, Presbyterian):*
  *83, Mullaghboy Road, Islandmagee*

X260

### KIELTY
In loving memory of
A dear wife
And loving mother
**ELLA**
Died 15th November 1980
Also a devoted husband
And dear father
**JAMES**
Died 20th March 1982

- *Ella (Agnes) (age 66, Presbyterian) and*
  *James (age 82, Presbyterian):*
  *28, Ashvale Park, Islandmagee*

X261

### McMULLAN
In memory of
My dear husband
**FRANK**
Died 2nd July 1980
Aged 81 years
Also his beloved wife
**EMILY**
Died 21st March 1995
Aged 99 years

- *Frank (recorded age 83, Presbyterian):*
  *144, Gobbins Road, Islandmagee*
- *Emily (Presbyterian):*
  *Greenisland House, Carrickfergus*

## X262-X263
In loving memory of
**JANET ISOBEL AGNES ROXALENE
STEELE**
Beloved wife of James
died 14th December 1980
Also the above named
**JAMES STEWART STEELE**
Died 10th February 1990
**STEELE**

- *Janet (age 54, Presbyterian) and
James (age 68, Presbyterian, widower):
84, Low Road, Islandmagee*

## X264
In loving memory of
**VIDA L.W. CROWHURST**
Died 19th Jan. 1980 aged 84 years

- *Vida (C of I, married):
32, Browns Bay Road, Islandmagee*
- *Buried 20.11.1988*
**HENRY CROWHURST**
*(age 89, widower, C of I):
8, Marek Close, Cochan, Lancs. England*

## X265 unused

## X266
**BARCLAY**
In loving memory of
A devoted wife and mother
**MARGARET EVELINE (EVA)**
Who died 9th September 1979
And her beloved husband
**WILLIAM JOHN HOUSTON (BILLY)**
Died 11th November 1986
Also **JANE McLEOD**
Beloved sister of Eva
Died 25th March 1997
Peace perfect peace

- *Eva (age 72, Methodist) and Billy (age 81,
Methodist): 59, Windsor Ave. Whitehead*
- *Jane (age 88, single, Methodist):
Cherry Tree Nursing Home, Carrickfergus*

## X267
**GORDON**
In loving memory of
**EDWIN GRAHAM**
Died 9th July 1996
Aged 91 years
Rest in peace

- *Edwin (married, C of I):
22, Lestannon Ave. Whitehead*

## X268
**BROWN**
In loving memory of
Our dear parents **SARAH NELSON**
died 26th Dec. 1969
**WILLIAM CROTHERS**
died 3rd Jan 1972

- *Sarah (age 61, housewife, Presbyterian):
5, Young Street, Lisburn*
- *William (age 64, widower, Presbyterian,
retired seafaring Chief Engineer):
28, Upper Malone Road, Belfast*

## X269

- *Buried 1.3.1971* **WILLIAM DAVID MANN,**
*(age 59, married, Congregationalist,
Master Mariner): 3, Ardlea Crescent,
Rathcoole Estate, Newtownabbey*
- *Buried 11.5.1983* **Mrs. PHYLLIS MANN,**
*(age 74, Presbyterian): 19, Doagh Road,
Newtownabbey*

## X270 unused

X271

## HARPER
In loving memory of
**ARTHUR**
Died 13th March 1979 aged 79 years
**ELIZABETH**
Died 13th January 1985 aged 89 years
**SUSAN GRANT**
Died 22nd May 1980 aged 72 years
Thy will be done

- *Arthur (age 79, married, Presbyterian)
  and Susan (age 72, single, Presbyterian):
  14 Letannon Ave. Whitehead*

- **Mrs. ELIZABETH HARPER**
  *(widow, Presbyterian): Naprbury Hospital
  London Colony, Hertfordshire*

X272

## BLAKE
In loving memory of
My dear wife
**SALLY**
Died 13th June 1981
Memories keep her ever near

- *Sally (age 57, Presbyterian):
  16, Madigan Park, Carrickfergus*

- *Buried 1.2.2000* **JOHN JAMES BLAKE**
  *(age 86, widower, Presbyterian):
  38, Prospect Park, Carrickfergus*

X273

- *Buried 25.7.1979* **ALBERT DAVIS**
  *(age 59, married, C of I, machinist):
  45A Islandmagee Road, Whitehead*

- *Buried 12.6.2001* **Mrs. JEAN DAVIS**
  *(age 79, widow, C of I):
  Antrim Coast Private Nursing Home*

X274

In loving memory
**LILIAN ANNIE WHITTINGHAM**
Died 24th June 1981 aged 77 years

- *Lilian (age recorded as 76, widow, C of I):
  58, Cobbins Road, Islandmagee*

X275

## HILDITCH
## WILLIAM GEORGE (BILLY)
A loving and much loved
husband and father
3rd February 1938 – 7th March 2001

- *Billy (age 63, married, Presbyterian,
  retired teacher):
  18 McCreas Brae, Whitehead*

X276-X277

## McCALMONT
In loving memory of
**ELIZABETH**
Beloved wife of William
Died 24th November 1980
Also the above **WILLIAM**
Died 8th March 1985

- *Elizabeth (Presbyterian):
  Mervue, Ballydown, Islandmagee*

- *William (age 81, Presbyterian):
  30, Ballylumford Road, Islandmagee*

X278

## HANVEY
In loving memory of
**TOM**
Died 21st March 1981

- *Thomas (age 74, married, C of I):
  19, Edward Road, Whitehead*

X279

- *Buried 9.2.1981*
  **NELLIE BURNS RUTHERFORD** *(age 76,
  widow, C of I): 17, Ransevyn Drive,
  Whitehead*

X280

## PINK
## JOSEPH A. PINK
25th January 1981

- *Joseph Albert (married, Presbyterian):
  51, Ferris Bay Road, Islandmagee*

X281

## LANCASTER
**JAMES SIMON** 1898-1981
Loved father of
Laurence, Mervyn and Helen

- *James (buried 20.8.1981, age 83, married, Presbyterian): 59, Islandmagee Road, Whitehead*

X282

## BOYLES
In loving memory of
**JANE (JEAN)**
Devoted wife and mother
Died 8th February 1980
Also **DAVID**
A dear husband and father
Died 12th March 1987
Till we meet

- *Jane (recorded as Elizabeth, age 67, married, C of I): York Parade, Belfast*

- *David (age 79, widower, Methodist): 8, York Drive, Belfast*

X283-X284

## ROBINSON
In memory of
**THOMAS P.**
Died 21st June 1979
And his sisters
**ANNIE G. CONNOR**
Died 26th January 1982
**GERTRUDE W. ROBINSON**
Died 12th February 1984

- *Thomas Paul (age 86, married, C of I): 3, Edward Road, Whitehead*

- *Annie (age 90, single, C of I): 8, Gloucester Park, Larne*

- *Gertrude Winifred (age 88, C of I): Greenisland Hospital*

- *Buried 31.12.1997*
**Mrs. MARGARET GRAHAM ROBINSON** *(age 90, widow, C of I): 5, Castleview Road, Whitehead*

X285

## SHERIFF
In loving memory of
My dear wife **ANNIE**
Died 29th July 1981

- *Annie (age 71, Presbyterian): 153, Low Road, Islandmagee*

- *Buried 3.1.1990* **JOSEPH SHERIFF** *(age 87, Presbyterian): 153, Low Road*

X286 unused

X287

## WRIGHT
In loving memory of
**SAMUEL JAMES**
Died 29th January 1970
Also his wife **AGNES**
Died 11th July 1974
Also their son
**ROBERT APSLEY WRIGHT**
Master Mariner
Died 4th April 1996

- *Samuel (age 73, Presbyterian): 48, Deerpark Road, Belfast 14*

- *Agnes (age 84, Presbyterian): 47, Norwood Ave. Belfast*

- *Robert (cremated, age 70, married, Presbyterian): 14, Crumlin Road, Glenavy*

X288 unused

X289

## LUCY CLAIRE MOORE
Died 10th Sept. 1981 aged 9 years
Sadly missed

- *Lucy (Methodist): 6, Fairview Drive, Whitehead*

X290

In loving memory of
A devoted wife and mother
**LYDA SAMPSON**
Died 18th September 1981
Also her beloved husband
And our dear father
**GEORGE SAMPSON**
Died 21st March 1986

- *Lyda (age 72, Methodist) and George (age 74, Congregationalist): 32, Lestannon Ave. Whitehead*

X291

- *Buried 2.10.1981*
  **Mrs. SARAH PATTERSON** *(age 71, C of I): 4, Ballystrudder Gardens, Islandmagee*
- *Buried 18.11.1983*
  **WILLIAM JOHN CAMPBELL** *(age 52, Presbyterian): 32, Ashvale Park, Islandmagee*

X292

**McKINSTRY**
In memory of
A devoted husband and father
**ALEXANDER**
Died 18th October 1981

- *Alexander (age 60, married, Presbyterian, labourer): 83, Belfast Road, Carrickfergus*

X293

**BOAL**
**ARCHIBALD (ARTIE)**
A loving husband and father
Died 28th November 1986
Till we meet again

- *Artie (age 65, married, Presbyterian): 2, Ballystrudder Gardens, Islandmagee*

X294

In memory of
**SAMUEL**
Died 5th April 1982
Also his wife
**MINNIE**
Died 25th July 1991
**SURGENOR**

- *Samuel (age 76, Presbyterian): 14, Carneal Close, Carrickfergus*
- *Minnie (age 73): 10A Johns Place, Larne*

X295

**CLARKE**
**LILY MAUDE**
In loving memory of
A beloved wife and devoted mother
Born 4th February 1914
Died 11th April 1982
And **IRWIN**
Dearly loved husband and father
Born 24th January 1908
Died 3rd February 1983
The Lord is my Shepherd

- *Lily (age 68, Presbyterian) and Irwin (age 75, Presbyterian): Flat 12, St. Brigids Fold, Ballyclare Road, Glengormley*

X296-X297

**WILSON**
In loving memory of
A dear husband and father
**ROBERT JOHN (BERTIE)**
Died 13th April 1982 aged 52 years

- *Bertie (married, Presbyterian, fitter): 351, Middle Road, Islandmagee*

## X298

**NOONAN**
In loving memory of
A devoted husband and father
**GEORGE**
Died 18th April 1982 aged 60 years
Also his loving son
**JOHN FREDERICK CHARLES**
With Dad 6th May 1983 aged 22 years
Till we meet

- *George (married, C of I, driver)*
  *and John (single, C of I, waiter):*
  *4, Windsor Park, Whitehead*

## X299

- *Buried 5.7.1991*
  ***Mrs. SARAH REYNOLDS*** *(age 94, widow,*
  *C of I): Inver House, Larne*
- *Buried 23.6.1999*
  ***Baby BETHANY ANN REYNOLDS*** *(C of I):*
  *23 Portland Street, Larne*

## X300

**CAMPBELL**
In loving memory of
A devoted husband
**KEN**
Died 11th June 1982

- *John Kenneth*
  *(age 59, married, Presbyterian):*
  *3, Woodlands, Island Road, Ballycarry*

## X301

**WILSON**
In loving memory of
My dear husband
**WILLIAM**
Died 31st March 1982
Also his beloved wife
**MARY**
Died 14th June 1990

- *William (age 94, married, Presbyterian):*
  *23, Ballystrudder Gardens, Islandmagee*
- *Mary (age 90, Presbyterian):*
  *Chester Park Nursing Home, Whitehead*

## X302

**COOKE**
In loving memory of
A dear wife and devoted mother
**EVELYN MARY**
Called to her rest May 24th 1982
Also **WILLIAM**
Beloved husband and father
God called him home
5th August 1995 aged 79
'Thy will be done'

- *Evelyn (age 57, married, Presbyterian):*
  *3, Reids Road, Islandmagee*
- *William Thomas (Presbyterian, widower):*
  *50, Ballystrudder Gardens, Islandmagee*

## X303

**HANNA**
In loving memory
**SAMUEL**
Died 12th July 1982
And his dear wife
**ISOBEL**
Died 12th June 1994

- *Samuel (age 75, Presbyterian):*
  *1, Lestannon Ave. Whitehead*
- *Isobel (age 85, Presbyterian):*
  *Whitehead Private Nursing Home*

## X304

- *Buried 3.8.1982* ***JAMES BOYD***
  *(age 70, married, Presbyterian)*
  *2, Alexandra Ave. Whitehead*

## X305

**LOWRY**
In loving memory of
A devoted husband
father and grandfather
**JACK**
Died 21st February 1994
Aged 84 yrs.
Precious memories

- *Jack (John) (Presbyterian):*
  *37, Hillside Park, Whitehead*

## X306

In fond memory of
**JAMES GILMORE HANNAH**
Loved husband of Annie
died 26 Novr. 1970

- *James (age 59, C of I, architect):*
  *Granville, 31, Gobbins Road, Islandmagee*
- *Buried 21.1.1994* **Mrs. ANNIE HANNA**
  *(age 76, C of I, housewife):*
  *55, Ballystrudder Gardens, Islandmagee*

## X307

**BROWNLEE**
In loving memory of
**DOROTHY LILIAN**
Died 22nd May 1980
Also her sister
**OLIVE STRONGE**
Died 7th August 1993
Greatly loved

- *Dorothy (age 59, widow, Presbyterian):*
  *Tara, 83, Ballylumford Road, Islandmagee*
- *Olive Stronge (surname) (single, age 85,*
  *Presbyterian): Seymour House, Dunmurry*

## X308

- *Buried 15.4.1989*
  **Mrs. WINIFRED JOAN MONTGOMERY**
  *(age 71, widow, C of I):*
  *52, Jordanstown Road, Newtownabbey*
- *Also two cremation urns – no names*

## X309

**MATEER**
In loving memory of
Our parents
**SAMUEL**
Died 12.3.1982
**GEORGINA**
Died 15.1.1999
So dearly loved, so sadly missed

- *Samuel William*
  *(age 67, married, Methodist, driver):*
  *115, Blythe Street, Belfast*
- *Georgina (burial recorded as 19.1.1998,*
  *age 79, widow, Methodist):*
  *7, Moltke Street, Belfast*

## X310

**ROSS**
In loving memory of
My dear wife and our devoted mother
**MAUREEN**
Who died 31st March 1982
And also our loving father
**JAMES ALEXANDER**
Who died 23rd July 1985

- *Maureen (Mary Ann)*
  *(age 57, married, Presbyterian) and*
  *James (age 65, Presbyterian):*
  *5, De Courcy Ave. Carrickfergus*

## X311

**ISA**
**McCASKEY**
Died 1994

- *Isabella*
  *(buried 2.12.1994, age 79, single, C of I):*
  *Clonlee Private Nursing Home, Antrim*

## X312

**WARWICK**
In loving memory of
**JOHN** died 28th July 1982
Dear husband of Kathleen

- *John (age 79, married, Presbyterian):*
  *28 Wanstead Road, Dundonald*

## X313 unused

## X314

- *Buried 6.11.1982* **JAMES McMASTER**
  *(age 70, married, Presbyterian):*
  *24, Port Road, Islandmagee*
- *Buried 28.8.2002*
  **MARY ELIZABETH ISABELLA McMASTER**
  *(age 78, widow, Presbyterian):*
  *same address*

## X315 unused

**X316**

## ROWE
In loving memory of
A dear husband and father
### FRANK A. B.
Died 10th November 1982

- *Frank (age 71, married, C of I):*
  *344 Merville Garden Village, Whiteabbey*

**X317** unused

**X318**

## WOOD
### MARY A. B. WOOD
Died 16th December 1982

- *Mary Ann Bolton (age 62, Presbyterian):*
  *85 Islandmagee Road, Whitehead*

- *Buried 9.7.1988*
  ***JAMES MORRISON WOOD** (age 81,*
  *Presbyterian): 85 Islandmagee Road*

**X319**

## MONTEITH
In loving memory of
### NEIL
Called to higher service 13th
February 1983
Also his devoted wife
### DOROTHY (DOT)
Reunited 9th August 2001

- *Neil (age 75, married, Presbyterian):*
  *3, Balfour Ave. Whitehead*

- *Sarah Dorothy Monteith*
  *(age 94, widow, Presbyterian):*
  *6, Brooklands Crescent, Whitehead*

**X320**

## NIBLOCK
In loving memory of
My dear husband
### JOHN MAURICE
Died 17th January 1999

- *John (age 79, married, Presbyterian):*
  *4, Gobbins Path, Islandmagee*

**X321**

- *Buried 27.2.1983* **Baby KEITH McCOSH**
  *(age 2 days, Presbyterian):*
  *7, Alexandra Ave. Whitehead*

**X322**

## SIMMS
In loving memory of
### JOHN DAWSON
A devoted husband and father
Died 27th January 1983

- *John (age 49, married, Presbyterian, fitter):*
  *132 Middle Road, Islandmagee*

- *Buried 8.6.2001*
  ***NELLIE ELIZABETH SIMMS***
  *(age 61, widow, Presbyterian):*
  *60 Magee Park, Larne*

**X323**

In loving memory of
A devoted wife and darling mother
### MABEL NEILL
Departed this life August 20th 1983

- *Mabel (age 90, widow, Presbyterian):*
  *12, Brookeborough Ave. Carrickfergus*

**X324**

## HOOD
In loving memory of
### JAMES MARSHALL
Died 22nd December 1980

- *James (age 55, married, Presbyterian):*
  *10, Windsor Ave. Whitehead*

**X325**

## ADAMS
In loving memory of my husband
### ERNEST EDWARD
Died 20th November 1972
Also our dear son
### WILLIAM ERNEST
Died 9th July 1955 aged 3 years

- *Ernest (age 55, C of I, civil engineer):*
  *41, Islandmagee Road, Whitehead*

X326

**FERGUSON**
In loving memory of
**MARION**
Beloved wife of the
**Rev. R. S. Ferguson**
Who died 3rd January 1979
Also the above
**Rev. ROBERT S. FERGUSON**
Who died 29th September 1985

- *Marion (age 59, Presbyterian) and
  Rev. Robert Sylvanus (age 65, Presbyterian):
  The Manse, Low Road, Islandmagee*

X327

**MOORE**
In loving memory of
My dear husband
**SAMUEL ROBERT**
Died 3rd June 1981

- *Samuel (age 68, C of I):
  71, Islandmagee Road, Whitehead*

- *Buried 23.4.2002*
  **Mrs. ELEANOR MOORE** *(age 86, widow,
  C of I): Oakridge Private Nursing Home,
  Ballynahinch, Co. Down*

X328

**GIBSON**
Treasured memories of
A dear husband and devoted father
**JOSEPH (JOE)**
Called home 25th February 1983
aged 60 years
Redeemed

- *Joe (married, Congregationalist, engineer):
  141 Islandmagee Road, Whitehead*

X329

**McFALL**
**THOMAS CAMPBELL WALLACE**
Loving memories of
A dear husband, dad and grandad
Died 3rd March 1983 aged 55 years

- *Thomas (age recorded as 52, married,
  Presbyterian): 31, Edward Road,
  Whitehead*

X330

**BROOKES**
In loving memory of
**CECIL**
A dearly loved husband
Brother and uncle
1921 – 17.4.97
also his dear wife
**KATHLEEN**
Died 21.1.97
Re-united in God's garden

- *Cecil Robert (Presbyterian) and
  Kathleen (age 90, Presbyterian):
  153, Gobbins Road, Islandmagee*

X331

**MARTIN**
In loving memory of
**JOHN**
Died 16th September 1983
Aged 71 years
Also his wife **IVY**
Died 12th June 1988
Aged 70 years

- *John (C of I):
  37, Chester Ave. Whitehead*

- *Ivy (C of I):
  89, Mullaghboy Road, Islandmagee*

X332 unused

X333

**MERCER**
In loving memory of
**GEORGE**
Died 12th October 1983

- *George (age 76, married, Presbyterian):
  53, Ballystrudder Gardens, Islandmagee*

**X334**

**BRIGGS**
In loving memory of
**JESSIE**
Beloved wife of John Briggs
1904 – 1984
**JOHN BRIGGS**
1903 – 1994

- *Jessie (buried 19.1.1984, age 79, C of I)*
  *and John (buried 30.4.1994, age 90, C of*
  *I): 135A Islandmagee Road, Whitehead*

**X335**

**KYLE**
In loving memory of
A devoted husband
And father
**SAMUEL**
Died 31st January 1984
Also his devoted wife
And our dear mother
**JANE**
Died
28th February 1995
The Lord is my Shepherd

- *Samuel (age 89, Presbyterian) and*
  *Jane (age 93, Presbyterian):*
  *55, Edward Road, Whitehead*

**X336**

**JONES**
In memory of
**JAMES JOSEPH**
Master Mariner 1916 – 1984

- *James (buried 14.3.1984, age 68, single,*
  *Presbyterian): 161, Middle Road,*
  *Islandmagee*

**X337-X338**

**COULTER**
In loving memory of
**LAURA**
Died 26th March 1984 aged 4
Loved always

- *Laura (Methodist): 59, Cable Road,*
  *Whitehead*

**X339**

**GARRETT**
**CATHERINE**
Died 19th May 1984
**ELIZABETH**
Died 30th January 1988
**ROBERT BARRY GARRETT**
Died 11th May 1994

- *Catherine Robinson Garrett*
  *(age 70, single, C of I),*
  *Elizabeth Garrett (age 84, single, C of I)*
  *and Robert (age 71, single, C of I):*
  *4, Cable Road, Whitehead*

**X340** unused

**X341** unused

**X342**

**DAVISON**
**ANNIE MARGARET**
1891 – 1984

- *Annie (buried 18.6.1984, age 94, single,*
  *Presbyterian): Inver House, Larne*

**X343** unused

**X344**

**MONTGOMERY**
In loving memory of
**WILLIAM**
Died 29th October 1991
And his beloved wife
**MARY (MAY) ALEXANDRA**
Died 15th May 1992

- *William (age 88, Methodist) and May (age*
  *89, Methodist): Ravenhill Private Nursing*
  *Home, Greenisland*

## X345-X346
### E.A. CRAWFORD
In memory of my dear wife ISA
At rest 9th Jan. 1981
### ERNEST ARTHURS CRAWFORD
21st Feb. 1909 – 30th May 2000

- *Isabella Mather Crawford (Methodist): Ferris Bay Road, Islandmagee*
- *Ernest (Presbyterian): 14, Browns Bay Road, Islandmagee*

## X347
### MONTGOMERY
In loving memory of
My dear wife
### KATHLEEN
Died 7th Dec. 1984
Also her beloved husband
### WILLIAM J.
Died 26th May 1992

- *Kathleen (age77, Presbyterian) and William John (Presbyterian): 45, Mullaghboy Road, Islandmagee*

## X348
### HUNTER
In loving memory of
My dear wife
### MARGARET
Died 13th February 1982
Also her husband **THOMAS A.**
Died 8th July 1989
At rest

- *Margaret (age 59, Presbyterian) and Thomas Alexander (age 62, Baptist): 30 Ashvale Park, Islandmagee*

## X349
### McMAW
In loving memory
Of
### THOMAS HUGH
26th May 1916 – 25th January 1995

- *Thomas (age 79, Presbyterian): 50, Ferris Bay Road, Islandmagee*
- *Buried 17.7.2000* **Mrs. MARY McMAW** *(age 78, Presbyterian): 50 Ferris Bay Road.*

## X350
In
Memory of
### ALBERT D. WOODS
Died 7th August 1983
His wife **EVELYN C. WOODS**
Died 26th April 1991

- *Albert Dodson (age 70, Congregationalist) and Evelyn Catherine (age 72, Presbyterian): 69, Islandmagee Road, Whitehead*

## X351
In
Memory of
### JOHN FRACKELTON
A beloved husband and father
Died 9th July 1991

- *John (age 75, married, Congregationalist): 27, Windsor Ave. Whitehead*

## X352
### McMILLAN
In loving memory of
A devoted husband and father
### JAMES
Died 14th November 1983
Also a dearly loved wife and mother
### ANN JANE
Died 27th June 1994
Always in our thoughts

- *James (age 71, Congregationalist) and Ann (age 81, Congregationalist): 1, Windsor Parade, Whitehead*

## X353
### TIERNEY
In loving memory of
### JOHN ALEXANDER
Died 26th September 1983
Beloved husband of Sadie

- *Buried 8.11.1999* **Mrs. SARAH TIERNEY** *(age 83, widow, Presbyterian): 32, Ballystrudder Gardens, Islandmagee*

**X354**

## DONALD
In loving memory of
Our dear mother
### ELIZABETH
Died 26th August 1984

- *Elizabeth (age 82, widow, Methodist):*
  *54, North Road, Carrickfergus*

**X355**

Treasured
Memories of
My
Dear husband
### GEORGE
### GILBERT
### DRYSDALE
Died Jan. 29 1983
Aged 70 years
In God's own
Time we shall
Meet again

- *George (Presbyterian): 8, Loughview*
  *Bungalows, Islandmagee*

**X356**

### McCLEAN
In loving memory of
My devoted husband
### LOUIS GOTTO
Died 29th March 1987
In life he lived for those he loved
And those he loved remember

- *Louis (age 59, C of I):*
  *20 Brooklands Gardens, Whitehead*

**X357**

### McCULLOUGH
In loving memory of
Devoted parents
**ESTHER** died 1st Oct. 1984
**DAVID** died 14th April 1989

- *Esther (age 71, C of I) and David (age 76,*
  *C of I): 8, Malone Ave. Whitehead*

**X358**

### GRAINGER
In loving memory of
A devoted husband and father
### JAMES McKEEN
Died 3rd April 1987
Also a dearly loved wife and mother
### RACHEL
Died 7th February 1995

- *James (age 72, Presbyterian) and*
  *Rachel (age 74, Presbyterian):*
  *31, Balfour Ave. Whitehead*

**X359**

### IRVINE
In loving memory of
Our beloved mother
### SALLY
Died 9th October 1984
Also our dear father
### BILLY
Died 5th August 1993

- *Sarah Rebecca (Sally) (age 59,*
  *Presbyterian): 11, Ballystrudder Gardens,*
  *Islandmagee*
- *William James (Billy) (age 77,*
  *Presbyterian): 3, Windsor Walk, Whitehead*

**X360**

In
Remembrance of
### BETTY JOHNSON
Who died 10th November 1985
Rest in peace

- *Betty (age 82, widow, Presbyterian):*
  *41, Lestannon Ave. Whitehead*

**X361** unused

X362

**NIBLOCK**
In loving memory of
**JOHN**
A devoted husband and father
Died 18th September 1983
Also a dearly loved wife and mother
**MARGARET**
Died 7th January 2001
In heavenly love abiding

- *John (age 66, Presbyterian) and*
  *Margaret Wilson Niblock*
  *(age 81, Presbyterian, buried 10.6.2001):*
  *77 Low Road, Islandmagee*

X363

**THOMPSON**
In loving memory of
Our dear parents
**MATTHEW** 1899 – 1992
**ELLEN LUSK (EILEEN)** 1904 – 1994
The Lord is my Shepherd

- *Matthew (buried 17.5.1992, age 93,*
  *Unitarian) and Eileen (buried 21.2.1994,*
  *age 90, Unitarian): Cherry Tree Private*
  *Nursing Home, Carrickfergus*

X364  unused

X365

**McDONALD**
In loving memory of
A devoted husband and father
**SAMUEL**
Died 3rd September 1981
Also a devoted wife and mother
**ELIZABETH THOMPSON**
Died 23rd September 1990

- *Samuel (age 73, Presbyterian):*
  *46, Middle Road, Islandmagee*
- *Elizabeth T. McDonald*
  *(age 77, Presbyterian):*
  *7, Gobbins Path, Islandmagee*

X366

**GIBSON**
In loving memory of
A dearly loved son
And brother **MICHAEL**
Died 4th September 1984
Aged 20 years
Peace be thine

- *Michael (single, student, Church of God):*
  *Site 97, Donegall Gardens, Whitehead*

X367  unused

X368

**LOGAN**
In loving memory of
A devoted husband and father
**WALTER**
Died 15th January 1985
Also a beloved wife and mother
**GEORGINA**
Died 10th April 2002
The Lord is my Shepherd
He leadeth me beside the still waters

- *Walter (age 74, married, Presbyterian):*
  *24, Marine Parade, Whitehead*
- *Georgina May (age 91, widow,*
  *Presbyterian): Cherrytree Private Nursing*
  *Home, Carrickfergus*

X369

**McGUIGAN**
Remembering a loving husband
and father
**JOHN H.**
12.1.1909 – 23.2.1988
Thy will be done

X370

## HOUSTON
In loving memory of
**JOHN HAROLD**
Died 15th February 1987 aged 83
And beloved wife
**ELLA**
Died 3rd December 1995 aged 87

- *John (age recorded as 82, Methodist):*
  *1, Donegall Ave. Whitehead*
- *Isabella (Methodist):*
  *Abbeyfield House, Whitehead*

X371

## BRADFORD
In loving memory of
**SAMUEL McCUNE**
Died 11th April 1992
And his loving wife
**LUCY**
Died 29th December 1996
Remembered with love

- *Samuel (age 78, Presbyterian) and*
  *Lucy (age 83, Presbyterian):*
  *61, Wellington Ave. Larne*

X372

## KERBY
In loving memory of
**EDWARD G. W. (TED)**
Died 7th February 1985
And his son **BRIAN EDWARD**
Died 18th June 1953
Aged 2 years 4 months

- *Edward George William*
  *(age 67, married, Presbyterian):*
  *53, Islandmagee Road, Whitehead*

X373

## McLEER
Fondest memories of
A devoted husband and father
**GILBERT**
1908 – 1986
and a dearly loved wife and mother
**CONNIE**
1918 – 1993
Per ardua ad astra

- *Rev. Gilbert Sidney*
  *(buried 9.12.1986, age 78, Methodist):*
  *87, Islandmagee Road, Whitehead*
- *Constance Elizabeth*
  *(buried 2.11.1993, age 75, Methodist):*
  *Castlerocklands, Carrickfergus*

X374 unused

X375 unused

X376

## NOLAN
In loving memory of
A devoted wife and mother
**STELLA**
Died 8th December 1982
Also her son **PHILIP**
Died 8th April 1983

- *Stella Kingsford (age 72, married,*
  *Presbyterian): 3, Caldwell Park, Ballycarry*
- *Philip Joseph Sydney*
  *(age 36, married, Methodist, accountant):*
  *68, Main Street, Ballycarry*
- *Buried 22.4.1986 **JOSEPH NOLAN***
  *(age 75, widower, C of I): Barn Villas*
  *Carrickfergus*

X377

## STITT
In loving memory of
Our dear son and brother
**JOHN CHARLES**
Died 26th April 1985 aged 22 years
At rest

- *John (single, C of I, building labourer):*
  *11, Acreback Road, Whitehead*

X378

## STEWART
## ANNIE ELIZABETH
Beloved wife and mother
Died 12th August 1985
Also beloved husband and father
## WILLIAM
Died 23rd September 1997

- *Annie (age 87, C of I):*
  *141 Castlemara Drive, Carrickfergus*
- *William (age 82, widower C of I):*
  *3, Fergus Court, Carrickfergus*

X379

## BELL
In loving memory of
A dear wife and mother
## MARGARET
Died 30th August 1993
Also a dear husband and father
## WILLIAM JOHN
Died 2nd June 1997
In God's keeping

- *Margaret (age 87, married, C of I):*
  *2, Ranfevyn Gardens, Whitehead*
- *William (age 90, C of I):*
  *Whitehead Private Nursing Home*

X380 unused

X381-X382-X383

## COBURN
In loving memory of
A devoted husband and father
## ALBERT
Drowned at sea 19th December 1982

- *Albert (age 49, married, Presbyterian,*
  *seaman): 16, Millbay Road, Islandmagee*

X384

## O'NEILL
In loving memory of
## ARTHUR STEVE
Died 28th April 1991
Sadly missed by his
Sister Joan and family
You fell asleep with no
Goodbyes but memories
Of you will never die

- *Stephen (age 46, single, Elim):*
  *50A Adelaide Ave. Whitehead*

X385

In memory of
A loving mother and Nan
## ALICE RICHARDSON
Died 9th March 1989

- *Alice Florence*
  *(age 80, widow, Presbyterian):*
  *91, Ballylumford Road, Islandmagee*

X386

## McCREAL
In loving memory of
A devoted husband and father
## ALFRED WILLIAM
died 17th July 1982

- *Alfred (age 73, married, C of I):*
  *16, Victoria Ave. Whitehead*

X387

- *Buried 21.3.1978*
  ***ROWAN HOWARD J. MARTIN***
  *(age 3 months, Presbyterian):*
  *9, Burnthill Crescent, Newtownabbey*
- *Buried 8.1.2002 **JAMES T. RANKIN**
  (age 80, married, Presbyterian):*
  *Whitehead Private Nursing Home,*
  *Whitehead*

X388

In loving memory of
## PATRICK ROBERT ARNOLD
Died 8th February 1983
Aged 22 months

X389

**STAINER**
In loving memory of
**GENEVIEVE**
Died 9th December 1982
And her husband
**THOMAS FREDERICK**
Died 26th September 1986

- *Thomas (age 79, widower, Methodist):*
  *11, Islandmagee Road, Whitehead*

X390

**HARKNESS**
In loving memory of
**WESLEY**
Died 5th May 1989
Also his brother
**JACK**
Died 9th May 1998
Peace perfect peace

- *Wesley (age 65, single, Presbyterian):*
  *28, Ballystrudder Road, Islandmagee*

- *Jack (John, age 83, single, Presbyterian):*
  *84, Middle Road, Islandmagee*

X391

**MATSON**
In loving memory of
**MARGARET ELIZABETH**
Died 8th April 1982
In heavenly love abiding

- *Margaret (age 93, widow, Presbyterian):*
  *54, Ballystrudder Gardens, Islandmagee*

X392

**HANVEY**
In loving memory
of
**HAROLD**
20th August 1928 – 26th August 2000

X393

**JOHNSTON**
In loving memory of
A beloved husband
And Dad
**JAMES FRANCEY**
Died 18th August 1992
Also dearly loved wife
Mum and Nana
**ISABEL**
Died 14th May 1995
At rest

- *James (age 77, C of I) and*
  *Isabella (age 75, C of I):*
  *8, Hillside Park, Whitehead*

X394

In loving memory of
**ROBERT McCULLOUGH ARNOLD**
Died 8th March 1987
Aged 68 years

- *Robert M. (recorded as Macauley, married,*
  *Methodist): 57, Edward Road, Whitehead*

X395

- *Buried 25.6.1995*
  ***Miss. GRACE CROOKS KANE***
  *(age 83, Congregationalist)*
  *4, Shawfield Lane, Whitehead*

X396

**McDOWELL**
Precious memories of
A devoted wife, Mum
Sister and Nanny
**WILHELMINA (WINNIE)**
Died 8th February 1997
Missed for her love
And laughter
Loved always

- *Winnie (age 73, married, Methodist):*
  *83, Islandmagee Road, Whitehead*

- *Buried 11.10.2001*
  ***DAVID LYLE McDOWELL***
  *(age 82, widower, Methodist)*
  *Jordanstown Private Nursing Home*

X397

In
Loving memory of
**PIJUSH KANTI SEN GUPTA
(SEN)**
dearest husband of
Elizabeth Jane
And father of Tusar
Died 20th June 1992 aged 52 years
Till we three meet again

- *Sen (married, shopkeeper):*
  *32, Mullaghboy Road, Islandmagee*

X398

**BURROWS**
In loving memory of
My dear husband
**THOMAS ELLSON**
Died 10th September 2000
In heavenly love abiding

- *Thomas (age 83, married, C of I):*
  *19, Brooklands Crescent, Whitehead*

X399

**LYNN**
Precious memories of
**WILLIAM JOHN**
Beloved husband of Molly
father and grandfather
15-11-1915 - 12-7-1997
**McMURTRY**
Cherished memories of
**ELLEN**
Loving sister of Molly
And Agnes
Died 8th April 1987
Peace perfect peace

- *William (age 81, married, Presbyterian):*
  *33, Bleach Green Ave. Newtownabbey*
- *Elaine McCready McMurtry (Ellen)*
  *(age 80, single, Methodist):*
  *Holywell Hospital, Antrim*

X400 unused

X401

**EVANS**
In loving memory of
A devoted husband
And father
**WILLIAM NORMAN**
Died 29th June 1988
Also a dear wife
And mother
**ELIZABETH**
Died 29th December 1996
Always in our thoughts

- *Norman William*
  *(recorded age 73, Presbyterian):*
  *6, Kings Road, Whitehead*

X402

**HENDERSON
NEIL**
Died 28th July 1989 aged 25 years
Precious memories

- *Laurence Neil (Presbyterian):*
  *37, Mullaghboy Road, Islandmagee*

X403 unused

X404

**RICHARDSON**
In loving memory of
**ROBERT (BOBBY)**
Died 9th Dec. 1989

- *Bobby (age 74, married, Congregationalist):*
  *26 Windsor Ave. Whitehead*

X405

- *Buried 19.10.1965*
  **Mrs. ELEANOR COOK** *(housewife):*
  *Carnspindle, Islandmagee*

X406

- *Buried 29.4.1981*
  **JOHN KENNETH SLATER**
  *(age 69, married, Church of England):*
  *2, Ransevyn Drive, Whitehead*

X407 unused

X408 unused

X409
## STEPHEN RICHARD McALLISTER
Died 15th January 1994
Aged 26 years
Cherished memories

- *Stephen (single, Roman Catholic, labourer): 37 Windsor Ave. Whitehead*

X410 unused

X411 unused

X412 unused

X413
## LYDON
In loving memory of
A beloved husband and father
### MICHAEL
Born Furbo Co. Galway
19 Dec. 1920
Died Whitehead Co. Antrim
16 Nov. 1997
I am going home with thee
Thy child of my love
To the eternal bed
To thy perpetual sleep

- *Michael (age 76, married, Roman Catholic): 36, Brooklands Crescent, Whitehead*

X414
## PAULINE BANNON
nee **LYDON**
Died 27th November 1999
Aged 46 years
Much loved and treasured Mum

- *Pauline Elizabeth (Roman Catholic): 16, Donegall Rise, Whitehead*

X415-X424 unused

X425
## MARGARET FULTON
1898 – 1990
R.I.P.

- *Margaret (buried 1.1.1991, age 92, widow, Roman Catholic): Broadways Nursing Home, Whitehead*

X426
### DEVINE
In loving memory of
### DENNIS
died 21st Dec. 1971 aged 62 years
### BRIAN
died 29th June 1976 aged 6 years
### DANIEL J.
died 14th June 1983 aged 45 years
### ALICE T.
died 7th April 2001 aged 90 years
R.I.P.

- *Denis (recorded age 68, married, Roman Catholic) and Daniel Joseph (single, Roman Catholic): 11, Chichester Park, Whitehead*

- *Brian Joseph (Roman Catholic): 79 Windsor Ave. Whitehead*

- *Mrs. Alice Devine (age 90, Roman Catholic): Chester Park Nursing Home, Whitehead*

X427
### McBRIDE
In loving memory of
A dear wife
### KATHLEEN
Died 8th Feb. 1989
Also her husband
### DANIEL
Died 10th Nov. 1998
R.I.P.

- *Kathleen (age 70, Roman Catholic) and Daniel (age 84, Roman Catholic): 1, Ransevyn Drive, Whitehead*

X428 unused

X429 unused

X430
## MARY ANN WATSON
1911 – 1993
## JAMES WATSON
1912 – 1997
Loving parents
God's will is best
R.I.P.

- *Mary (buried 27.5.1993, age 81, Roman Catholic) and James (buried 4.10.1997, age 85, Baptist, retired joiner): 20, Island Road Lower, Ballycarry*

X431-X436 unused

X437
## BRADY
## MARY THERESA
Born 20-10-38 died 25-6-99
A rose on earth
A star in Heaven
## THOMAS OLIVER
Born 13-7-41 died 26-8-02
Much loved
Two stars in Heaven
Together for ever

- *Mary (age 61, married, Roman Catholic): 35 Ferris Bay Road, Islandmagee*
- *Thomas (age 60, widower, Roman Catholic): 38, Clonmore Green, Rathcoole*

X438 unused

X439 unused

X440
## DONAGHY
In loving memory of
## JOSEPHINE LEONITA
Died 7th May 2000 aged 76 years
Dearly loved wife, mother and
grandmother
Also her dear son
## SEAMUS
Who died in Germany
16th March 2001 aged 49 years
Rest in peace

- *Josephine (married, Roman Catholic): 65, Windsor Ave. Whitehead*

X441-X446 unused

X447
## CLEARY
In loving memory of
A devoted husband & father
## MARTIN E.
Died 24th November 1975

- *Martin (age 57, Roman Catholic, caterer): 55, Cable Road, Whitehead*

X448-X477 unused

X478
In
Loving memory of
## JOHN McAULEY
Died 21st October 1972
Loved husband of Lucinda

- *John Patrick (Roman Catholic, heating engineer): 11, Kings Road, Whitehead*

X479 to X484 unused

## X485-X486
### HAVERON
In loving memory of
### DONARD
27th August 1938 – 5th March 2000

- *Donard (age 61, married, Roman Catholic): 16, Windsor Ave. Whitehead*

## X487-X497 unused

## X498
### CONLON
Precious memories of
Loving parents
And grandparents
### ELLEN (NELLIE)
Died 20th September 1999
### MICHAEL (MICK)
Died 22nd October 1999

- *Ellen Patricia (age 69, Roman Catholic) and Michael Joseph (age 79, Roman Catholic): 35 Windsor Ave. Whitehead*

## X499-X511 unused

## X512

- *Buried 29.6.2002 JOHNNY G. FOX (age 29, single, Roman Catholic, seaman): 87, Ballystrudder Gardens, Islandmagee*

## X513-X522 unused

## X523
### WELSH
In loving memory of
### DAVID
Dearly loved husband
father and friend
Died 25th January 1991

- *David (age 61, married, Presbyterian, self employed): 13, Cooleen Park, Jordanstown*

## X524
### WELSH
In loving memory of
A dear wife and mother
### MAY
Died 28th August 1986
Aged 81 years
Also her daughter
### GLORIA
Died 1st February 1989
Dearly loved wife of
David Bowers

- *May (Mary Ann, widow, Presbyterian): 13, Cooleen Park, Jordanstown*
- *Rosemary Gloria Jean Bowers (age 52, married, Presbyterian): 16, Edward Road, Whitehead*

## X525
### McKINTY
In loving memory of
A devoted husband and father
### CECIL
Died 1st September 1984
Always in our thoughts

- *Cecil (age 64, married, Presbyterian): 5, Islandmagee Road, Whitehead*
- *Buried 6.11.1999 CECIL McKINTY (age 56, single, Congregationalist, seaman): 5, Islandmagee Road*

## X526-X527
### GRAHAM
In loving memory of
### ERNEST
Who died 10th July 2002 aged 87 years

- *Ernest (married, Presbyterian): 1, Portmuck Road, Islandmagee*

X528

## LAWLER
In loving memory of
**PATRICK JAMES**
A dear husband and father
Died 7th April 1989
Aged 72 years
Also his beloved wife
And our dear mother **IRIS**
Died 12-11-00 aged 81 years
Peace perfect peace

- *Patrick (recorded age 73, Presbyterian)*
  *and Ruby Iris (Presbyterian):*
  *5, Ashdale Park, Islandmagee*

X529-X530

## MOORE
In loving memory of
**SYLVIA** (nee **HILL**)
Died 4th November 1985
Beloved wife of William T. Moore
Peace perfect peace

- *Sylvia (age 62, Presbyterian):*
  *6, Ballytober Lane Islandmagee*

X531 unused

X532

## DEMPSTER
In loving memory of
**EDWIN**
Died 21-1-1991
And his wife
**JEAN**
Died 23-1-1991

- *Edwin (age 89, Presbyterian) and*
  *Jean (age 86, Presbyterian):*
  *Old Sea House, Antrim Road, Belfast*

X533

## JONES
In loving memory of
A beloved husband, father
And grandfather
**NELSON**
7th Nov. 1922 – 20th June 1999
In Heavenly love abiding

- *Nelson (age 76, married, Presbyterian,*
  *retired seaman):*
  *28, Carnmoney Road, Newtownabbey*

X534

- *Buried 1.3.1986 **NORMAN MORROW***
  *(age 64, married, C of I):*
  *2, Bentra Road, Whitehead*

X535 unused

X536 unused

X537

## HAWKINS
In loving remembrance of
**OLIVE HAWKINS B.A.**
Died 18th December 1986
Also her husband
**JOHN HAWKINS C.Eng. J.P.**
Died 12th June 1995

- *Violet Olive (age 69, married, Presbyterian)*
  *and John (age 80, Presbyterian):*
  *11, Beach Road, Whitehead*

X538

## HILL
In loving memory of
**WILLIAM JOHN**
Died 28th July 1992

- *William (age 74, married, Presbyterian):*
  *170, Browns Bay Road, Islandmagee*

## X539

**DICK    KERR**
In loving memory of
**JOHN CHARLES DICK**
Died 1st September 1984

- *John (age 71, married, Methodist):*
  *81, Bank Road, Larne*

## X540

**FREIL**
In loving memory of
My dear wife **MARGARET**
Died 26th August 1989
God looked
For an angel to call
He took my love
My life, my all
And her dear husband
**ALEXANDER SAYERS**
Died 3rd October 1996

- *Margaret (age 57, C of I, ancillary worker):*
  *and Alexander (age 84, Presbyterian):*
  *1, Rockview Street, Belfast*

## X541

- *Buried 13.5.1986* **DANIEL McILREAVY**
  *(age 81, married, Presbyterian):*
  *31, Ethel Street, Belfast*

- *Buried 12.12.2001*
  **ELIZABETH McILREAVY** *(age 94, widow,*
  *Methodist): Lisburn Road, Belfast*

## X542

**ATKINSON**
In loving memory of
**HELEN**
Beloved daughter and sister
Died 13th February 1996
Till we meet

- *Helen Lusk Atkinson (born 11.12.1938,*
  *single, C of I, civil servant):*
  *68, Ballystrudder Road, Islandmagee*

## X543 unused

## X544

- *Buried 12.1.1992*
  **Mrs. ANNIE McMASTER**
  *(age 76, married, Presbyterian):*
  *21A Port Road, Islandmagee*

- *Buried 30.12.1997*
  **THOMAS SAMUEL McMASTER** *(age 84,*
  *widower, Presbyterian): same address*

## X545

**CRAMPTON**
In loving memory of
**ELIZABETH VIOLET**
Dearly loved wife of Edward
Died 26th February 1992

- *Elizabeth (age 87, C of I):*
  *89, Cable Road, Whitehead*

## X546 unused

## X547

**HIGGINSON**
In loving memory of
Infant son **ALEXANDER**
Died 21st June 1997
Safe in God's keeping

- *Alexander (Presbyterian):*
  *9, Willowvale Crescent, Islandmagee*

## X548

- *Buried 28.9.1992*
  **Baby JAMES SKELTON**
  *(Congregationalist):*
  *11, Chester Ave. Whitehead*

## X549

**THOMAS SKELTON**
Writer
1911 – 1993

- *Thomas (buried 24.4.1993, age 81,*
  *Congregationalist):*
  *93, Ballylumford Road, Islandmagee*

- *Buried 5.9.1999*
  **Mrs. CHRISTINE M. SKELTON**
  *(age 79, widow, Presbyterian):*
  *2 Ferris Bay Road, Islandmagee*

## X550 unused

X551
## HIGGINSON
In loving memory of
A dear husband and Grandpa
### GEORGE
Died 21st May 1992

- *George Alexander
(age 68, married, Presbyterian):
22, Willowvale Drive, Islandmagee*

X552 unused

X553 unused

X554
## McKINTY
In memory of
A loving husband
And father
### WILLIAM
Died 14th August 1988

- *William (age 74, Presbyterian):
49, Ballystrudder Gardens, Islandmagee*

X555
## NIBLOCK
In loving memory of
A devoted husband and father
### BARCLAY
8th Nov. 1916 – 2nd Feb. 1987

- *Samuel Barclay Murray Niblock
(age 70, married, Presbyterian):
6, Gobbins Path, Islandmagee*

X556
## McKINTY
Precious memories of
A much loved husband
And father
### IVAN
Died 27th February 1997
Loved always

- *Ivan Hubert
(age 63, married, Congregationalist):
12, Ransevyn Court, Whitehead*

X557
## ARMSTRONG
In loving memory of
My devoted husband and
our dear father
### BRIAN
Died 2nd August 1993
Always in our thoughts

- *Arthur Brian
(age 60, married, Presbyterian):
1, Islandmagee Road, Whitehead*

X558
## CUNNINGHAM
In loving memory of
### JAMES WILLIAM
Died 12th June 1997
Aged 81
### ANNIE EVELINE
Died 8th March 2001
Aged 89

- *James William McC. Cunningham
(recorded age 84, Presbyterian):
236 Merville Garden Village,
Newtownabbey*

- *Annie (recorded age 85, Presbyterian):
Chester Park Nursing Home, Whitehead*

X559 unused

X560 unused

X561
## FORD
Treasured memories of
Our beloved son
Brother and Grandson
### JAMES NORMAN
Died 3rd May 1997 aged 16
The ones we love don't go away
They live inside us every day

- *James (Presbyterian):
22, Loughview Bungalows, Islandmagee*

X562-X567 unused

## X568-X569
### ARMOUR
In loving memory of
My beloved husband
### JOHNNIE
Died 3rd March 1993 aged 66 years
The Lord is my Shepherd

- *John
(recorded age 65, married, Presbyterian):
147, Gobbins Road, Islandmagee*

## X570
### McILROY
In memory of
A dearly loved
husband and father
### MALCOLM
Died 29th December 1991
Also his beloved wife
And our dear mother
### RACHAEL LOUISA
Died 23rd October 1996
Loving Grandparents

- *Malcolm
(recorded as 1992, age 81, Presbyterian)
and Rachael (age 78, Presbyterian):
36, Islandmagee Road, Whitehead*

## X571
### BROWN
In loving memory of
### DAVID HOLMES BROWN
Died 20th April 1998
And his dear wife **EVELYN MAY**
Died 6th August 2000

- *David (age 80, Presbyterian) and
Evelyn (age 75, Presbyterian):
1, Donegall Walk North, Whitehead*

## X572-X574 unused

## X575
### HAMILTON
In precious memory of
A loving sister
### MOLLY
Died 20th February 1992
Also sister
### JEAN
Died 15th December 1997
Our hearts still ache with sadness
And silent tears do flow
What it meant to lose you
No one will ever know

- *Molly (Mary Wilhelmina, age 70, single,
Presbyterian): 15 Alexandra Ave.
Whitehead*
- *Jeannie Kane Hamilton (single):
49, Edward Road, Whitehead*

## X576
- *Buried 20.6.1993
**Miss MARY JANE BOLES** (age 87, C of I):
161, Low Road, Islandmagee*

## X577
### BURNS
In loving memory of
### NORMAN
Died 24th May 1984
I know that my Redeemer liveth

- *Norman (age 61, married, Presbyterian):
62, Main Street, Ballycarry*

## X578 unused

## X579
### McDOWELL
### ELLEN
Beloved wife and mother
Died 24th June 1995
### ROBERT WILLIAM
Devoted husband, father
grandfather and
Great grandfather
Died 5th Aug. 2001

- *Ellen (age 79, C of I):
15, Ransevyn Court, Whitehead*
- *Robert (age 87, C of I): same address*

X580

### FOSTER
In loving memory of
A devoted wife
mother and grandmother
### FLORA McINTYRE
25th Aug. 1920 – 16th Nov. 1997

- *Flora (age 77, married, C of I):*
  *6, Victoria Court, Whitehead*

X581

### WELLS
In loving memory of
### ROBERT (BOBBY)
A devoted husband, father
And grandfather
Died 16th April 2000
Aged 80 years
Also daughter
### CHRISTINE
Died 27th September 2002
Aged 51 years
The Lord is my Shepherd

- *Bobby (age recorded as 81, Presbyterian):*
  *2, Mullaghboy Bungalows, Islandmagee*
- *Christina J. (cremated, single):*
  *2, Mullaghboy Bungalows, Islandmagee*

X582

### SLOSS
### ROBERT JOHN
27.6.1932 – 2.7.1995
In loving memory of a
Devoted husband and father
Forever in our thoughts

- *Robert (age 63, married, C of I):*
  *6, Cloughfin View, Islandmagee*

X583 unused

X584

### McDOWELL
In loving memory of
A dear husband,
father and grandfather
### EDWARD HUNTER
Died 2nd December 1992 aged 72 years

- *Edward (married, Presbyterian):*
  *40, Mullaghboy Road, Islandmagee*
- *Buried 5.4.2002*
  ***Mrs. ELSIE McDOWELL** (age 81, widow,*
  *Presbyterian): 40 Mullaghboy Road*

X585 unused

X586

### WILSON
In loving memory of
A devoted husband and father
### STANLEY
Died 28th November 1992
Always in out thoughts

- *Stanley Ed. R.*
  *(age 54, married, Presbyterian, decorator):*
  *16, Lunnon Road, Islandmagee*

X587-X589 unused

X590

### MONTGOMERY
In loving memory of
### ISABELLA HANNAH
March 31st 1892 – Dec. 12th 1987
Also her loving sisters
### ANNIE
March 20th 1898 – Nov. 5th 1989
### THOMASINA RODGERS
27th Dec. 1900 – 27th Dec. 1993

- *Isabella (age 95, single, Presbyterian) and*
  *Annie (age 91, single, Presbyterian):*
  *355 Middle Road, Islandmagee*
- *Thomasina Rodgers*
  *(surname, age 93, widow, Presbyterian):*
  *Greenville Manor Clinic, Belfast*

X591

### DEANE
In loving memory of
**JOHN DOUGLAS**
Died 29th May 1985
Also his wife
**MARGARET JANE**
Died 16th July 1993

- *John (age 83, Methodist):*
  *1, Donegall Drive, Whitehead*
- *Margaret (age 81, Methodist):*
  *1, Grange Road, Coleraine*

X592-X595 unused

X596

### HUGHES
In loving memory of
**ELIZABETH** died 10th April 1994
**BRIDGET** died 8th March 1996
At home with the Lord

- *Elizabeth (age 90, single, C of I) and*
  *Bridget (age 97, single, C of I):*
  *17, Adelaide Ave. Whitehead*

X597-X598-X599

### HALL
Precious memories of
A devoted husband and dear father
**GEORGE**
Passed away 20th February 1996
Always in our thoughts

- *George (age 76, married, Presbyterian):*
  *27, Brookslands Gardens, Whitehead*

X600

### REID
Precious memories of
A loving husband
father and grandfather
**JOSEPH (JOE)**
Died 4th August 1993
Safe in the arms of Jesus

- *Joe (age 85, Methodist):*
  *9, Windsor Walk, Whitehead*
- *Buried 19.1.2001* **Mrs. JEANNIE REID**
  *(age 90, widow, Methodist):*
  *Whitehead Private Nursing Home*

X601-X606 unused

X607

### HOUSTON
Fondest memories of
A devoted husband and father
**JAMES**
Died 12th June 1985
Also his beloved wife and
our dear mother
**MARGARET ELIZABETH**
Died 10th October 1999
The Lord is my Shepherd

- *James McLernon (age 65, Presbyterian):*
  *2, Sunningdale, Islandmagee*
- *Margaret (age 81, Presbyterian):*
  *37 Arching Fold, Glengormley*

X608

### McMAW
In loving memory of
**WILLIAM JOHN**
Devoted husband, father and
grandfather
Died 7th September 1999

- *William (age 80, married, Presbyterian):*
  *58, Ferris Bay Road, Islandmagee*

X609

### GILROY
Precious memories of
A much loved husband
father and grandfather
**BRYAN DUDLEY ALEXANDER**
Died 26th November 2001 aged 71
In Heavenly love abiding
Those we love don't go away
They live within us every day

- *Bryan (married, C of I, Irish international*
  *hockey player 1951 – 1953):*
  *53, Glenkeen Drive, Greenisland*

X610

- *Buried 16.5.1991* **ROBERT CRAIG**
  *(age 73, widower, Presbyterian):*
  *Cherrytree Nursing Home, Carrickfergus*

X611 unused

X612

**GILBERT**
In memory of
A much loved husband
father and grandfather
**LOUIS**
Died 7th March 1996
Peacefully sleeping

- *Charles Louis*
  *(age 83, married, Presbyterian):*
  *81, Ballystrudder Gardens, Islandmagee*

X613 unused

X614 unused

X615

**WILSON**
In loving memory of
A devoted husband and father
**WILLIAM**
Died 30th October 1992

- *William (age 74, married, Presbyterian):*
  *3, Upper Road, Greenisland*

X616 unused

X617

**HOUSTON**
In loving memory of
**ALEXANDER**
Died 25th March 1997
Devoted husband of Isobel
The Lord is my Shepherd

- *Alexander McAllister (age 88, married,*
  *Presbyterian): 27, Port Road, Islandmagee*

X618

- *Buried 15.12.1997* **EDWARD PRENTER**
  *(age 60, married, C of I):*
  *23, Ransevyn Park, Whitehead*
- *Buried 21.12.2002*
  **ROSS ARAN JOHN PRENTER**
  *(age 23, single, Bank Manager, C of I):*
  *same address*

X619

**CLELAND**
In loving memory of
Our dear parents
**JAMES** died 28th April 1994
**MARGARET** died 14th February 1993
At rest

- *James (age 65, widower, C of I:*
  *11, Loughview Bungalows, Islandmagee*

X620

**MacDONALD**
In loving memory of
**WILLIAM THOMAS,** Master Mariner
Died 10th April 1995
Dear husband, father and grandfather

- *William (age 83, Presbyterian):*
  *16, Acreback Road, Whitehead*
- *Buried 17.8.1998*
  **Mrs. ELIZABETH MacDONALD**
  *(age 79, Presbyterian): 16, Acreback Road*

X621 unused

X622 unused

X623

**ATKINSON**
**DOROTHY WRIGHT**
Died 22nd June 1992
Dearly loved mother
Of Sylvia and Kenneth

- *Dorothy (recorded as surname Wright,*
  *age 90, widow, C of I):*
  *Castlerocklands, Carrickfergus*

X624

## JOAN BROWN
Died June 18 1988
Aged74
Loved by all her family
And friends
### JAMES ANDERSON BROWN
Died April 2nd 1991
Aged 81
Morning has broken
With her Lord

- *Joan (age recorded as 73, Baptist)
  and James (Baptist):
  46, Ferris Bay Road, Islandmagee*

X625

## YOUNG
In loving memory of
A devoted husband and father
### JAMES
Died 5th November 1996 aged 85

- *James (married, Presbyterian):
  22, Chaine Memorial Road, Larne*

X626

## ROSS
In loving memory of
Our infant daughter
Died 23rd December 1988

### REBECCA JANE BEATTIE
Died 5th February 1989 aged 89
Suffer little children to come unto me

- *Baby Ross: Moyle Hospital, Larne*
- *Rebecca (widow, Roman Catholic):
  7, Windsor Walk, Whitehead*

X627

## KERR
In loving memory of
**Captain SAMUEL JAMES**
Died 31st October 1972
Interred Ballynure
Dear husband of
Mary Ann (Minnie)
Also her cousin
### NANCY HEDDLES
Died 8th August 1991

- *Maureen Agnes Campbell (Nancy)
  (age 78, single, Presbyterian):
  31, Claremont Street, Belfast*

X628-X629 unused

X630

## ROSS
In loving memory of
My devoted husband
### SAMUEL THOMAS (TOM)
Master Mariner
Beloved father and grandfather
Died 4th February 1994 aged 74 yrs
The Lord is my Shepherd

- *Tom
  (recorded age 80, married, Presbyterian):
  2A Balmoral Ave. Whitehead*

X631

- *Buried 4.12.1990
  **Mrs. ELEANOR HUGHES MEEK**
  (age 67, married, C of I):
  54 Ferris Bay Road Islandmagee*

**X632**

## BONAR
In loving memory of
A devoted wife and mother
**EDITH**
Died 22nd October 1990
Also a beloved husband and father
**ROBERT KNOWLES**
Died 26th August 1992
The Lord is my Shepherd

- *Edith (age 78, Presbyterian):*
  *81, Islandmagee Road, Whitehead*

- *Robert Bonar (age 80, Presbyterian):*
  *Chester Park Nursing Home, Whitehead*

**X633**

- *Buried 17.12.1990*
  ***Mrs. EMILY WHITALL***
  *(age 85, widow, Methodist):*
  *Chester Park Nursing Home, Whitehead*

- *Buried 31.1.1999*
  ***Mrs. IRENE ANNA WHITALL***
  *(age 72, married, Methodist):*
  *60, Ballystrudder Gardens, Whitehead*

- *Buried 8.4.2001*
  ***FREDERICK GEORGE WHITALL***
  *(age 75, widower, Methodist):*
  *Whitehead Private Nursing Home*

**X634-X635-X636**

## FOSTER
**ALEXANDER** 20.3.21 – 9.10.87
In loving memory

- *Alexander (married, farmer, C of I):*
  *60, Rawbrae Road, Whitehead*

**X637**

In loving memory of
**WILLIAM BRIAN DICK**
1912 – 1994
One of nature's gentlemen

- *William (buried 4.11.94, age 82, single,*
  *Presbyterian):*
  *79 Portmuck Road, Islandmagee*

**X638**

## WHITE
## WILLIAM THOMAS
In loving memory
Of a devoted husband
And father
May 7 1922 – April 23 1994

- *Thomas (age 71, Methodist):*
  *21 Ballytober Lane, Islandmagee*

**X639**  unused

**X640**

## ORR
In loving remembrance of
**WILLIAM**
Died 21st March 1988 aged 80 years
Devoted husband of
**JENNY KAIN (AINZIE)**
**AINZIE**
Died 21st December 1997 aged 89 years

- *William (Presbyterian) and Ainzie*
  *(Presbyterian): 74, Rawbrae Road,*
  *Whitehead*

**X641**  unused

**X642**

## PICKEN
In loving memory of
**ISOBEL**
Died 12th May 1988 aged 3 weeks

- *Baby Isobel: 20, Ormiston Crescent, Belfast*

X643
## PICKEN
In loving memory of
A dear wife, mother and grandmother
**GRACE CATHERINE**
Died 11th July 2000
Aged 78 years
A beloved husband, father and
grandfather
**JAMES** Master Mariner
Died 2nd December 2000
Aged 79 years

- *Grace (recorded age 79, Presbyterian)*
  *and James (C of I):*
  *3, Jordanstown Road, Whiteabbey*

X644
## Baby W. K. FORD
20-7-90 – 19-11-90
"When he cried he broke his heart
when he smiled he broke mine"
Time goes by so slowly
And time can do so much
Follow me and I will make you
fishers of men
**"SPIKEY"**
"Once loved, never forgotten"

- *Baby William Kenneth (Salvationist):*
  *36, Edward Road, Whitehead*

X645 unused

X646
## DRILLINGCOURT
In loving remembrance
Of a dear wife and mother
**SANDRA ELIZABETH**
Died 21st March 1989 aged 38 years
Perfectly restored in Thee

- *Sandra (married, C of I):*
  *11, Mullaghboy Road, Islandmagee*

X647 unused

X648 unused

X649
## HENDERSON
Precious memories of
Our dearly loved son
**EDWARD JAMES**
Died 16th March 1989 aged 7½ years
Loving memories of our
brother Edward

- *Edward (Presbyterian):*
  *48A Mullaghboy Road, Islandmagee*

X650
## TELFORD
In loving memory of
**JAMES HERBERT ERNEST**
Died 8th December 1990
The Lord is my Shepherd

- *James (age 62, married, C of I):*
  *3, Coast Road, Larne*

X651
## BAILLIO
## JEAN CHRISTINA
## PASQUALI
26th October 1988
"Love is the one means that
ensureth true felicity
both in this world
and the next"
Bahai writings

- *Jean (age 54, married, Bahai):*
  *624 Shore Road, Jordanstown*

X652
## McKNIGHT
Treasured
Memories of
**GEORGE REDVERS**
**MINTER**
Died 16th January 1992
Peacefully at home
With his wife and family
The Lord is my Shepherd

- *George*
  *(age 63, married, carpenter, Presbyterian):*
  *40, Drumboy Drive, Carrickfergus*

X653

**McGOOKIN**
In loving memory of
A devoted husband, father
and grandfather
**SAMUEL**
Called home 6th May 1994
I know that my Redeemer liveth

• *Samuel (age 70, married, Presbyterian):*
*1, Hilview Ave. Carrickfergus*

X654

**MARTIN**
Treasured memories of
**ALFRED GILBERT**
A beloved husband and father
Died 1st June 2001

• *Alfred (age 86, married, Presbyterian):*
*51, Cable Road, Whitehead*

X655

**ROSSBOROUGH**
In loving memory of
A devoted husband and father
**HENRY ALEXANDER (HARRY)**
Died 24th December 1993 aged 82
Abide with me

• *Harry (married, Presbyterian):*
*153, Ballysnod Road, Larne*

X656 unused

X657

**FORSYTHE**
Cherished memories of
A devoted husband, father
and grandfather
**ALEXANDER**
Died 18th November 1988
Also his beloved wife
And a dear mother and grandmother
**ELLEN HUNTER (NELLIE)**
Died 28th December 2000

• *Alexander (age 69, Presbyterian) and*
*Nellie (age 77, Presbyterian):*
*7, Loughview Bungalows, Islandmagee*

X658

**FORD**
Treasured memories of
Our devoted parents
**FRANCIS CHARLES (FRANK)**
Died 7th April 1993
**AGNES McCREA**
died 28th October 1993
Peacefully sleeping

• *Frank (age 62, married, C of E):*
*214 Wrexham Road, Brynteg, Wrexham,*
*Clwyd, North Wales*

• *Agnes Ford (age 63, C of E);*
*25, Joymount, Carrickfergus*

X659 unused

X660

**BONAR**
In loving memory of
**STANLEY**
Died 17th January 1991

• *Stanley (age 82, single, Presbyterian):*
*81, Islandmagee Road, Whitehead*

X661

**BONAR**
In loving memory of
A devoted husband and father
**KENNETH**
Died 6th April 1995
Aged 47 years

• *Kenneth (age recorded as 48, married,*
*Presbyterian): 18, Broadacres,*
*Templepatrick*

X662 unused

X663

**PICKEN**
In loving memory of
**ROBINA**
Died 8th November 1991
At rest

• *Robina (age 85, widow, Presbyterian):*
*19, Ballytober Lane, Islandmagee*

## X664-X665
### BONAR
In loving memory of
### RAYMOND
9th October 1945-20th November 2000
Beloved husband of Rosemary
and loving father of
Karl, Andrew, Ingrid and Jordan

- *Raymond Alexander (age 55,*
  *Presbyterian): 47, Low Road, Islandmagee*

## X666
### DAVEY
In loving memory of
A dear wife, mother and grandmother
### SARAH ELIZABETH (SALLY)
Died 21st March 1991
The Lord is my Shepherd

Flower holder
**Sally** from Jack and Lottie

- *Sally (age 70, married, Presbyterian):*
  *8, Seahill Road, Seacourt, Larne*

## X667
### RIDDLE
Precious memories of
A dear husband, father and Pa-Pa
### KENNETH LEONARD FRANCIS (KEN)
Passed away 12th August 1995
His beloved wife
### AUDREY
Loving mother and Granny
Passed away 21st December 1997
Re-united

- *Ken (age 71, C of I) and*
  *Audrey (age 67, C of I):*
  *3, Brookborough Ave. Carrickfergus*

## X668
- *Buried 29.11.1991* ***GEORGE TAGGART***
  *(age 64, married, Presbyterian):*
  *51, Edward Road, Whitehead*

## X669
### FLACK
In memory of
### WILBUR
Dearly loved husband of Isobel
And devoted father of Derek and John
Died 14 March 2002 aged 88 years

- *Harry Wilbur*
  *(age 88, married, Protestant):*
  *7, Moss Road, Ballynahinch, Co. Down*

## X670
- *Buried 9.9.1988*
  ***Mrs. MILDRED SCHOLEY***
  *(age 65, married, Methodist):*
  *407 North Queen Street, Belfast*

## X671-X672
### McCALMONT
In loving memory of
My dear wife
### AGNES ELSPETH
Died 17th October 1985
And her beloved husband
### Capt. ANDREW McCALMONT
Marine pilot
Died 23rd October 1989
Loving parents and grandparents

- *Agnes (age 72, Methodist):*
  *105, Dunlambert Drive, Belfast*
- *Andrew (age 83, Presbyterian);*
  *63, Mullaghboy Road, Islandmagee*

## X672
### DICK
Treasured memories of
A devoted husband, father
and grandfather
### HUGH TEMPLETON
Died 16th June 1994 aged 59 years

- *Hugh (Presbyterian):*
  *107, Low Road, Islandmagee*

## X673 unused

X674

## RENWICK
In loving memory of
**GEORGE** died 2nd August 1986

- *George (age 75, married Presbyterian): 27, Middle Road, Islandmagee*

X675-X679 unused

X680

## WARING
In loving memory of
**LILIAN LOUISE WARING**
Died 18th June 1990

- *Lilian (age 69, married, C of I): 9, Middle Road, Islandmagee*
- *Buried 29.10.1996 **JOSEPH WARING** (age 76, C of I): 9, Middle Road*

X681 unused

X682 unused

X683

## SLOAN
In
Loving memory of
A devoted wife
mother and grandmother
**ELIZABETH**
Died 19th February 1992

- *Elizabeth Douglas Sloan (age 55, married, Presbyterian): 39, Ballystrudder Gardens, Islandmagee*

X684

## STEPHENS
## JOAN
Died 3rd December 1999
Beloved wife and mother
A love that wilt not let me go

- *Joanna Rosemary (age 75, married, Presbyterian): 7A Brooklands Drive, Whitehead*

X685-X686

## McMAW
In loving memory of
A devoted husband and father
**ROBERT**
Died 26th January 1987
Always in our thoughts

- *Robert (age 73, married, Presbyterian): 28, Portmuck Road, Islandmagee*

X687

## LORIMER
In loving memory of
Our dear parents
**MARGARET**
Died 12th August 1986
**ALEXANDER**
Died 20th May 1989
Also their dear son
A beloved husband
And father
**DAVID MICHAEL**
Died 29th August 1998

- *Margaret Jane (age 67, Congregationalist): 4, Ransevyn Gardens, Whitehead*
- *Alexander Woods (age 87, widower, Congregationalist) and David (age 52, married, master butcher, Congregationalist): 8, Ransevyn Park, Whitehead*

X688

## TEMPLETON
In loving memory of
A devoted husband and father
**JOHN DAVIS TEMPLETON F.C.A., J.P.**
Died 27th March 1998 aged 90 years
Also a beloved wife and mother
**ANNIE TEMPLETON**
Died 5th August 1999 aged 88 years
Much loved and loving parents
of Meriel
The Lord is my Shepherd

- *John (Presbyterian) and Annie (Presbyterian): 381, Middle Road, Islandmagee*

X689 unused

X690

**ROSS**
In loving remembrance of
**ROBERT THOMAS SMYTH**
Master Mariner
Died 6th August 1986
Also his beloved wife
**ELLEN ELIZABETH (ELSIE)**
Died 16th August 1995
And **THOMAS HILL**
Brother of Elsie
Died 1st October 1994

- *Robert (age 76, Presbyterian) and Elsie (age 81, Presbyterian): 29, Gobbins Path, Islandmagee*

- *Thomas Hill (age 78, single, Presbyterian): 61, Low Road, Islandmagee*

X691

**M.N.**
**POLLIN**
In loving memory of
**NATHANIEL JAMES (NAT)**
A dearly loved husband
father and grandfather
Died 3rd April 1992
Loved and always remembered

- *Nat (age 58, married, Presbyterian): 1, Loughview Bungalows, Islandmagee*

X692 unused

X693 unused

X694

**ROSS**
In loving memory of
A devoted husband, father
and grandfather
**JAMES**
1st October 1913 – 10th July 1991

- *James (age 77, Congregationalist): 15, Islandmagee Road, Whitehead*

X695 unused

X696

**McNEICE**
In loving memory of
A beloved husband
father and grandfather
**TOM**
Died 3rd June 1997
Also a devoted wife, mother
and grandmother
**DORIS EILEEN**
1-4-1914 – 22-3-1999

- *Thomas (age 83, Presbyterian) and Doris (age 84, Presbyterian): 14, Somerton Close, Belfast*

X697-X698

**KILEY**
**CHARLES RICHARD (CHARLIE)**
26 Nov. 1954 – 29 May 1997
Much loved husband and friend
Life is eternal, love is immortal
Sadly missed by his family and friends
**ALBERT RICHARD**
12 Apr. 1908 – 21 May 1996
till we meet

Flower holder
To **Dad**
from Nicky, Denise and Alison

- *Charlie (age 42, Congregationalist): 97, Islandmagee Road, Whitehead*

- *Albert (age 88, married, Presbyterian): 47, Windsor Ave. Whitehead*

X699 unused

X700

**CARSON**
In loving memory of
**MINA**
Died 4th May 1992
And **ROBERT**
Died 8th September 1995

- *Wilhelmina Alice (age 73, Methodist) and Robert Nelson Carson (Methodist): 24, Ballystrudder Road, Islandmagee*

X701 unused

X702 unused

X703

**CALWELL**
In loving memory of
Our parents
**MARGARET E. M.** nee **EARLS**
1906 – 1986
**HUGH GAULT**
1901 – 1986
**WILLIAM HUGH**
1941 – 1989

- *Margaret Elizabeth May*
  *(buried 11.7.1986, age 82, widow, C of I):*
  *9, Marine Parade, Whitehead*
- *William Hugh Hamilton Calwell*
  *(buried 2.12.1989, age 47, married, doctor):*
  *4, Priory Road, Easton, Bristol*

X704

In
Loving memory of
**STELLA LECKIE**
Died 16th August 1987
I am trusting Thee Lord Jesus

- *Stella (age 65, married, Brethern):*
  *31, Victoria Ave. Whitehead*

X705 unused

X706 unused

X707

**RAMSEY**
In loving memory of
A devoted wife and mother
**LARAINE**
Died 30th September 1989

- *Laraine (age 48, married, Methodist):*
  *44, Castledona Park, Belfast*

X708-X709

**BELL**
In loving memory of
**DAVID KERR**
Died 4th March 1998

- *David*
  *(age 63, married, Congregationalist):*
  *1, Fairview Park, Whitehead*

X710 unused

X711

**SMITH**
**JOHN ADAIR**
In loving memory
20.4.1989

- *John (age 72, married, Presbyterian):*
  *67, Brownsbay Road, Islandmagee*

X712 unused

X713

Precious memories of
**JOAN REID**
A devoted wife, mother
And grandmother
Died 21st December 1997
Till we meet again

- *Josephine (age 54, married, C of I):*
  *12, Windsor Walk, Whitehead*

X714-X716 unused

## X717-X718
**GRAHAM**
In loving memory of
A dear husband, father
and grandfather
**HENRY (HARRY)**
Born 5th March 1906
died 18th January 1997
And his devoted wife
**ANNIE** nee **Logan**
Born 27th March 1908
died 6th November 2001

- *Harry (age 90, married, Presbyterian):*
  *42, Alexandra Ave. Whitehead*
- *Annie McVicker Graham*
  *(age 94, widow, Presbyterian):*
  *Whitehead Private Nursing Home*

## X719 unused

## X720

- *Buried 7.4.1988*
  ***Mrs. MARGARET POLLOCK***
  *(age 78, Presbyterian):*
  *14, Gobbins Road, Islandmagee*

## X721

- *Buried 23.3.1995*
  ***Mrs. MARGARET VIOLET WILSON***
  *(age 87, widow, C of D):*
  *Chester Park Nursing Home, Whitehead*

## X722

**HOWLIN**
In loving memory of
A dearly loved sister and Aunt
**JEANNIE K.**
Died 7th June 1989
Aged 85 years
At home with the Lord

- *Jeannie*
  *(recorded as Howling, widow, Brethern):*
  *Chester Park Nursing Home, Whitehead*

## X723

- *Buried 27.8.1990* ***Mrs. AGNES LAING***
  *(age 81, married, Presbyterian):*
  *25, Middle Road, Islandmagee*

## X724

- *Buried 20.4.2001*
  ***FRANCIS JAMES McCONNELL***
  *(age 75, married, Roman Catholic):*
  *33, Belfast Road, Whitehead*

## X725

In loving memory of
**JOSEPH ROBIN WILSON**
Died 29th Sept. 1990 aged 54 years
Life shall be Thy service Lord
And death the gate of Heaven
**WILSON**

- *Joseph (married, postman, C of D):*
  *73, Donegall Ave. Whitehead*

## X726-X727

**REDFORD**
In loving memory of
**GEORGE**
A devoted husband, father
and grandad
Died 14th August 1993 aged 74 yrs.

- *George Arthur (recorded age 73, married,*
  *Methodist): 2, Windsor Parade, Whitehead*

## X728

Loving
Memories of
**STANLEY CECIL**
Died 10th
August 1993
His beloved wife
**MAY**
Died 28th
December 1997
**KNOX**

- *Stanley (age 89, Presbyterian):*
  *Clanrye Nursing Home, Larne*
- *May (age 89, widow, Presbyterian):*
  *Seapark Nursing Home, Whiteabbey*

X729 unused

X730

**CLARKE**
In loving memory of
A devoted husband
And father
**JOHN RODNEY**
1944 – 1994

- *John*
  *(age 49, married, architect, Presbyterian):*
  *16, Caple Road, Whitehead*

X731

**McGOWAN**
In loving memory of
**WILLIAM**
A dearly loved husband
father, grandfather and
Great grandfather
Died 18th October 2000

- *William (age 80, married, Methodist):*
  *101 Islandmagee Road, Whitehead*

X732-X735 unused

X736

**GILLILAND**
In loving memory of
My dear sister
**SADIE**
Who died 16th January 1988
Also **AGNES BENNETT**
Devoted sister of Sadie and beloved
mother of Jos
Who died 25th November 1997
Until we meet again

- *Sarah (age 80, single, Presbyterian) and*
  *Agnes (age 84, married, Presbyterian):*
  *58, Larne Road, Ballycarry*

X737-X738

**GRAHAM**
In loving memory of
**JIM** died 14th September 1989
**PATRICIA McHUGH** nee **BELL**
14.12.1933 – 14.11.1998
At peace

- *James (age 63, Presbyterian):*
  *24, Hillside Park, Whitehead*
- *Patricia (age 64, widow, Presbyterian):*
  *9, Ransevyn Gardens, Whitehead*

X739

**CHRISTINE HEATHER**
**GRACEY**
31.8.1991
much loved and
sadly missed daughter
of Winn and Martin
The Lord gave
and the lord has
taken away
may the name of the
Lord be praised
Job 1 v.21
and He took the
children in his arms
put His hands on them
and blessed them
Mark 10 v.16

- *Baby Christine: Belfast City Hospital*

X740-X742 unused

X743-X744

**JONES**
In loving memory of
A dear husband and father
**LESLIE**
Died 17th February 1997

- *Leslie (age 80, Presbyterian):*
  *38, Mullaghboy Road, Islandmagee*

X745 unused

X746

**BAIRD**
Precious memories of
A loving husband and father
**TERENCE VIVIAN**
Died 16th January 1995
The Lord is my Shepherd

- *Terry (age 41, married, shop keeper,*
  *Methodist): 9, Millbay Road, Islandmagee*

X747 unused

X748

**BAIRD**
In loving memory of
A dear wife and devoted mother
**ISABELLA BOYD**
Died 20th January 1990 aged 39 years

- *Isabel (married, Methodist):*
  *139, Brownsbay Road, Islandmagee*

X749 unused

X750 unused

X751

**MOODY**
In memory of
My beloved husband
**JAMES**
Died 26th December 1986
aged 73 years
Also his beloved wife
**MARIE HELENE**
Died 23rd September 1999
aged 79 years

- *James (Presbyterian) and*
  *Marie (Presbyterian):*
  *5, Ransevyn Gardens, Whitehead*

X752

**FINLAY**
In loving memory of
A dear wife and mother
**ELIZABETH (LILY)**
Died 18th March 1991
Also **WILLIAM (BILLY)**
Died 17th April 1997
a devoted husband and father
The Lord is my Shepherd

- *Lily (age 67, married, Presbyterian):*
  *3, Ballystrudder Gardens, Islandmagee*
- *Billy (age 79, widower, Presbyterian):*
  *48, Ballystrudder Gardens, Islandmagee*

X753

**KANE**
In loving memory of
**FREDERICK WILLIAM (FRED)**
Died 18th September 2001
aged 84 years
What a friend we have in Jesus

- *Fred (age 84, married, Presbyterian):*
  *4, Mullaghboy Bungalows, Islandmagee*

X754

- *Flower holder* ***AGNES WELSH***
  *17-4-1904 – 7-2-1994*
  *Widow, Presbyterian:*
  *27 St. Judes Parade, Belfast*

X755

In memory of
**WILLIAM HALLIDAY RYAN**
15-9-1917 – 13-4-1995
a loving husband and father
who gave 61 years
of faithful service in the Boys Brigade
Sure and Stedfast

- *William (age 77, married, C of I):*
  *134, Station Road, Greenisland*

X756-X757
**McCAMMON**
In loving memory of
A dear wife and mother
**MARY ALEXANDER**
Died 4th July 2000 aged 78 years
Also her dear husband
**THEO**
Died 17th Nov. 2002 aged 86 years
- *Mary (married) and Theophilus (age 86): 18, Hillside Park, Whitehead*

X758
**LUCAS**
Precious memories of
A devoted husband and father
**COLIN LESLIE**
Died 30th March 1998
Always in our thoughts
- *Colin (age 47, married, sales director, Congregationalist): 34B, Balfour Ave. Whitehead*

X759 unused

X760 unused

X761
**NIBLOCK**
Cherished memories of
**ANNA**
Dearly loved wife and mother
Who passed away 17th May 1995
- *Charlotte Anna Burns (age 62, married): 11, Lumford Ave. Whitehead*

X762
**McWILLIAM**
In loving memory of
**THOMAS (TOMMY)**
Dear husband and father
Died 12th May 1995
In Gods keeping
Erected by son Stephen
- *Tommy (age 69, married, garage owner): 37 Island Road, Ballycarry*

X763 unused

X764
**ADAMS**
Cherished memories
Of a much loved husband
father and grandfather
**WILLIAM McBRIDE**
Died 11th March 1995
- *William (age 75, married C of I): 40, Ballystrudder Road, Islandmagee*

X765
**LYLE**
In loving memory of
A dear husband, father
and grandfather
**ARTHUR JAMES PICKEN**
1907 – 1994
- *Arthur (buried 19.6.1994, age 86, married, Presbyterian): 14, Brooklands Gardens, Whitehead*

X766 unused

X767
**LAPPIN**
In loving memory of
My dear wife
**ISABELLA**
Died 19th September 1987
- *Isabella (age 65, married, Presbyterian): 21, Town Lane, Islandmagee*
- *Buried 29.8.2002 **THOMAS LAPPIN** (age 79, widower, Presbyterian) 21, Town Lane*

X768 unused

X769
In
Loving memory of
**MABEL COWELL** (nee **DOUGLAS**)
Died 22nd June 1990
Aged 83 years
- *Mabel (widow, C of I): Lisgarel Home, Larne*

X770 unused

X771-X772

**KEATLEY**
In loving and abiding memory of
**WILLIAM McBURNEY**
died 26th April 1996
A deeply devoted and most loving
husband and father
Perfectly restored in Thee

- *William*
  *(age 62, married, Master Mariner, C of I):*
  *2, Donegall Close, Whitehead*

X773 unused

X774

**TOMASSO**
In loving memory of
**MARCUS JOHN**
Died 13th February 1997
Dear husband of Mabel Robina

- *Marcus*
  *(age 77, married, Congregationalist):*
  *18, Chester Ave. Whitehead*

X775

**MILLAR**
In loving memory of
A dear wife and mother
**OLIVE SCOTT**
Died 16th September 1995
Forever in our thoughts

- *Olive (age 74, married, C of I):*
  *15, Princes Park, Whitehead*

X776-X777

**ABBOTT**
In loving memory of
**GEORGE NORMAN**
1920 – 1997
Beyond death – life

- *George (buried 1.6.1997, age 76,*
  *married, Methodist):*
  *78, Cable Road, Whitehead*

X778-X782 unused

X783

**TOPPING**
Cherished memories of
A loving husband
father and grandfather
**JOHN GARDNER**
Died 10th September 1989
Always in our thoughts

- *John*
  *(age 58, married, farmer, Presbyterian):*
  *23, Ballylumford Road, Islandmagee*

X784 unused

X785 unused

X786

**MANN**
In loving memory of
**SARAH ELIZABETH
(BET)**
Died 18th Aug. 1998
**ROBERT JOHN**
lost at sea
28th April 1972

- *Bet (age 82, Presbyterian):*
  *1, Ballytober Road, Islandmagee*

X787 unused

X788

**CHAMBERS**
In fondest memory of
**RHONA MAGGIE**
9th October 1995
beloved and loving wife,
mother, Gran and friend
You live in
Our hearts forever

- *Rhona Margaret (age 71, married, C of I):*
  *70, Cable Road, Whitehead*

X789 unused

X790 unused

X791-X792-X793
### ARTHURS
Erected by David in memory
of his wife
### EVA (nee GILLESPIE)
22 Dec. 1922 – 4 June 2000
Safe on the Heavenly shore
Where life's storms are past
for ever more

- *Eva (age 77, married, Presbyterian):*
  *81, Ballylumford Road, Islandmagee*

X794
### MacKENZIE
In loving memory of
A dear husband and father
### DONALD (DON)
Died 14th October 1996
Age 49 years
The day Thou gavest Lord is ended

- *Don (married, Presbyterian):*
  *12 Willowvale Grove, Islandmagee*

X795-X797 unused

X798

- *Buried 20.8.2002*
  ***SARAH AUGUSTA McDEVITTE***
  *(age 85, married, Methodist):*
  *12 Colinview, Ballyclare*

X799

- *Buried 30.10.2001*
  ***Mrs. META CAMPBELL ADAMS***
  *(age 74, married, Presbyterian):*
  *3, Brownsbay Drive, Islandmagee*

X800
### MACAULAY
Erected by
James Macaulay
In memory of his wife
### JANE MONTGOMERY (JANIE) DOUTHER,
who died 31st March 1985 aged 77
The above named
### JAMES MACAULAY
Who died 15th December 1991
aged 82 years

- *Janie Macaulay (Presbyterian) and*
  *James (age recorded as 81, Presbyterian):*
  *18, Reids Road, Islandmagee*

X801

- *Buried 9.9. 1996*
  ***WILLIAM WILSON McCLUNG***
  *(age 84, married, Pentecostal):*
  *Victoria Nursing Home, Belfast*

X802

- *Buried 3.4.1990*
  ***Miss. ROBERTA STEWART*** *(age 75, C of*
  *D): 175, Low Road, Islandmagee*

X803

- *Buried 8.10.1995*
  ***Miss EMILY CAMPBELL*** *(age 85,*
  *Methodist): 2, Ashvale Park, Islandmagee*

X804
### HAMILTON
In loving memory of
### BRIAN JAMES
Died 23rd May 1998

- *Brian (age 53, married, Presbyterian):*
  *13, Donegall Rise, Whitehead*

X805-X808 unused

**X809**

Ubique
Quo fas et gloria ducunt
**RIDES**
Precious memories of
A devoted husband, father
and grandfather
**WILLIAM**
Died 31st October 1996
Till we meet and never part

- *William (age 75, married, Presbyterian):*
  *23, Lunnan Road, Islandmagee*

**X810** unused

**X811-X812-X813**

**LONG**
Treasured memories of
A devoted husband, father and
dearly loved son
**MARK WILLIAM**
Died 3rd February 2000 aged 36 years
The Lord is my Shepherd

- *Mark (married, Policeman, Presbyterian):*
  *32, Island Village, Islandmagee*

**X814**

**McALLISTER**
Precious memories of
A loving husband, dad and grandad
**WILLIAM JOHN**
Died 5th August 2001
Forever one

- *William (age 60, married, Baptist):*
  *26, Ballystrudder Road, Islandmagee*

**X815** unused

**X816**

**McSPADDEN**
In loving memory of
A dear husband and father
**ROBERT JAMES (BOBBIE)**
Died 31st May 1990
Mizpah

- *Bobbie (age 65, married, C of I,*
  *member of LOL 1297):*
  *10, Ballystrudder Road, Islandmagee*

**X817** unused

**X818-X819**

**GLASS**
In loving memory of
A devoted husband and father
**WILLIAM JOHN (BILLY)**
Died 4th March 1996
Aged 90 years
Safe in God's keeping

- *William John Andrew (married, C of I):*
  *31, Alexandra Ave. Whitehead*

**X820**

- *Buried 14.3.1997,*
  ***Mrs. MARY AGNES BOYLE***
  *(age 91, widow, Methodist):*
  *Riverside Residential Home, Antrim*

**X821-X824** unused

**X825**

**LINTON**
In loving memory of
**HAZEL FLLOYD**
4-8-1919 – 4-5-2000

- *Hazel (age 80, married, Presbyterian):*
  *34, Marine Parade, Whitehead*

**X826**

- *Died 9.9.2002 **Mrs. MYRTLE DOBBIN**
  (age 59, Presbyterian):*
  *37 Brooklands Park, Whitehead*

X827

## HOUSTON
Precious memories of
A loving husband
### JOHN ALEXANDER
Called home 5th April 2001
Redeemed

- *John (age 67, married, Presbyterian):*
  *8, Brookslands Gardens, Whitehead*

X828-X831 unused

X832

- *Buried 7.11.2002*
  ***SAMUEL DAVID BLAIR FORSYTHE***
  *(age 38, farmer, single, Presbyterian):*
  *32 Askvale Park, Islandmagee*

X833 unused

X834

In memory of
### CRAWFORD WAVELL CAMPBELL
Kilcoan, Islandmagee
Who died on 13th April 1990
Aged 49 years

- *Crawford*
  *(single landscape gardener, Presbyterian):*
  *Millbay Road, Islandmagee*

X835

## HAWKINS
Cherished memories of
### WILLIAM (BILLY)
Died 18th December 1995
Devoted husband of Molly
And much loved father
And grandfather
The Lord is my Shepherd

- *Billy (age 68, married, Baptist):*
  *2, Sunningdale Crescent, Carrickfergus*

X836-X839 unused

X840-X841-X842-X843
## WOODSIDE
In loving memory of
### THOMAS WILSON
died 30th December 1996

- *Thomas (age 73, married, Brethren):*
  *139, Gobbins Road, Islandmagee*

X844 unused

X845-X846

- *Buried 30.11.2000*
  ***ROBERT STEVENSON BUSBY***
  *(age 84, married, C of I):*
  *59, Gobbins Road, Islandmagee*

X847-X850 unused

X851

## WILSON
In loving memory of
Our devoted parents
### JOSEPH
Died 28th May 1991
### THOMASENA
Died 12th April 1994
Also their grand-daughter
### AMANDA McNEILL
Died 22nd May 1989

- *Joseph (age 83, Presbyterian):*
  *Sandown Private Nursing Home, Belfast*

- *Thomasena (age 83, widow, Presbyterian):*
  *Church Road, Killinchy*

- *Amanda Joanne McNeill*
  *(age 24, single, Presbyterian):*
  *35, McCreas Brae, Whitehead*

X852
## HAWKINS
Treasured and loving memories of
### NEIL
Beloved special son of
June and Raymond
And much loved brother of Jane
Died 14th April 2001
So dearly loved so sadly missed

- *Neil (age 40, single, Presbyterian):*
  *12, Princes Park, Whitehead*

X853
### BETTY GIBSON
Loving mother of Noreen
Died 7th July 1995
Also **JOHN BEGGS**
Family friend
Died 5th October 1996
At rest

- *Elizabeth (age 79, widow, Methodist) and*
  *John (age 90, single, Methodist):*
  *Chester Park Nursing Home, Whitehead*

X854 unused

X855 unused

X856

- *Buried 3.2.1998*
  ***EDWARD GEORGE HIGGINSON***
  *(age 78, married, Methodist):*
  *Chester Park Nursing Home, Whitehead*
- *Buried 14.8.2002* ***ANNA HIGGINSON***
  *(age 81, widow, Methodist):*
  *Tamlaght Nursing Home, Carrickfergus*

X857 unused

X858
### McKEOWN
In loving memory of
### OLIVE
A devoted wife, mother
and grandmother
10th March 1941 – 24th January 2001
Safe in the arms of Jesus

- *Catherine Olive (age 59, married, C of I):*
  *6, Ransevyn Park, Whitehead*

X859 unused

X860
### NEWBOLD
### FRANCIS WILLIAM
26th March 2002
dearly loved husband
father and grandfather
The Lord is my shepherd

- *Francis (age 84, married, Presbyterian):*
  *50, Alexandra Ave. Whitehead*

X861 unused

X862-X863
### HANNA
Precious memories of
A loving husband and devoted father
### WILLIAM JOHN
Called home 8th December 1998
Also a beloved wife and mother
### EMILY JANE
Called home 21st February 2001
Redeemed

- *William (age 81, Congregationalist):*
  *10 Hillside Rise, Whitehead*
- *Emily (age 82):*
  *Chester Park Nursing Home, Whitehead*

X864

- *Buried 17.3.2002*
  ***Mrs. MARY ELIZABETH GILMOUR***
  *(age 98, widow, Presbyterian):*
  *Whitehead Private Nursing Home*

X865-X867 unused

X868

### BROWN
Treasured memories of
A devoted husband, father
and grandfather
**WILLIAM DAVID MANN**
1st December 1931 – 13th April 1993
He lived for those he loved
And those he loved remember

- *William (age 63, married, company*
  *director, Presbyterian):*
  *28, Upper Malone Road, Belfast*

X869-X873 unused

X874-X875

### CALWELL
(Plantin Head)
In loving memory of
**NANCY**
A wonderful lady
1913 – 2000

- *Nancy (buried 15.8.2001, age 87, married,*
  *Presbyterian): 29, Acreback Road,*
  *Ballycarry*

X876

### BOYLES
In loving memory of
**SANDRA EVELINE**
A dear wife and Mum
Died 5th May 1993
God bless

- *Sandra (age 51, married, C of I):*
  *2, Ranzevyn Court, Whitehead*

X877 unused

X878

- *Buried 5.2.2002*
  **DOROTHY MAY GILMORE**
  *(age 7_, single, Methodist):*
  *11A cable Road, Whitehead*

X879

- *Buried 9.4.1999* **Mrs. ELLEN SMYTH**
  *(age 75, widow, Baptist): 1, Lurganboy,*
  *Manorhamilton, Co. leitrum*

X880-X884 unused

X885

### HEGGEN
In loving memory of
A devoted husband and father
**ROBERT S.**
Died 10th December 1989

- *Samuel Robert*
  *(age 77, married, Presbyterian):*
  *15, Low Road, Islandmagee*

X886 unused

X887

Wooden cross
**YVONNE**
22nd May 1996 age 24

- *Buried 25.5.1996*
  **YVONNE MARGARET ANNE McCUNE**
  *(single, Congregationalist):*
  *2, Windsor Crescent, Whitehead*

X888 unused

X889 unused

X890-X891

- *Buried 21.4.2000*
  **Mrs. MAUREEN VIOLET McFARLANE**
  *(age 73, married, Pentecostal):*
  *21, Adelaide Ave. Whitehead*

X892-X894 unused

X895

### WILSON
In loving memory of
A dear husband, father
And grandfather
**CECIL FREDRICK**
Died 19th Sept. 1998

- *Cecil (age 82, married, Methodist):*
  *29, Mountcollyer Ave. Belfast*

X896 unused

X897 unused

X898

### CRAIG
In loving memory of
### LILY
A dear wife and mother
Died 27th March 2001

- *Elizabeth (age 63, married, Presbyterian):*
  *4, Chichester Park, Whitehead*

X899-X901 unused

X902-X903

In
Loving memory of
### ANNA DOROTHEA BLACKWOOD
### MARTIN
14th July 1905 – 4th January 1993
### JOHN WYLIE MARTIN
22nd April 1905 – 13th July 2001

- *Anna (age 87, Presbyterian) and*
  *John (age 96, Presbyterian):*
  *16, Carrington Court, Belfast*

X904

### ALEXANDER
In memory of
A loving husband
father and grandfather
### JOHN NOEL WALKER
27-12-1927 – 30-9-1995
Return unto Thy quiet rest,
O my soul

- *John (age 67, married, Presbyterian):*
  *10, Kilton Lane, Islandmagee*

- *Buried 5.3.2002*
  ***MARY KANE NIBLOCK ALEXANDER***
  *(age 71, widow, Presbyterian):*
  *10, Kilton Lane*

X905-X909 unused

X910

### ELLIOTT
### THOMAS
22nd August 1931 – 6th April 2001
In loving memory of
A devoted husband, father
and grandfather

- *Thomas (age 69, married, Presbyterian):*
  *42, Ballystrudder Gardens, Islandmagee*

X911-X927 unused

X928

### BLACK
In loving memory of
A dear husband and father
And grandfather
### JIM
Called home 8th December 2000
At home with the Lord

- *Jim (age 77, married, Congregationalist):*
  *89, Ballystrudder Gardens, Islandmagee*

X929-X935 unused

X936

### McCORMICK
In loving memory of
A devoted wife
And mother
### ROSE
Died 20th August 1990
At rest

- *Anna Rose (age 70, C of I):*
  *1, Hillside Park, Whitehead*

- *Buried 24.3.1995* ***ROBERT McCORMICK***
  *(age 79, C of I): same address*

X937

### HOPE
In loving memory of
### JAMES ROWLAND (RONNIE)
Died 4th July 2000
Much loved husband of Helen

- *Ronnie (age 76, Congregationalist):*
  *13, Victoria Ave. Whitehead*

X938 unused

X939

### DONALD
Treasured memories of
A devoted husband, father
And grandfather
**ROBERT JOHN (BOBBY)**
Called home 13th September 1998
Always in our thoughts

* *Bobby (age 66, married, Presbyterian):*
  *26, Islandmagee Road, Whitehead*

X940

### WOLFE
In loving memory of
**GEORGE ERNEST**
A dearly loved husband, father
And grandfather
1-4-1910 – 4-4-2001

* *George (age 91, married, C of I):*
  *88, Ransevyn Park, Whitehead*

X941 unused

X942

### RUNNING
In loving memory of
**JIMMY**
Devoted husband and father
Died 27th November 1999
In Heavenly love abiding

* *James (age 79, married, Methodist):*
  *8, Chichester Park, Whitehead*

X943-X953 unused

X954

### HEYBURN
In loving memory of
**WILLIAM GEORGE HEYBURN**
**A.R.I.B.A.**
16th June 1928 – 4th December 2001

* *William (age 73, married, C of I):*
  *30 Brownsbay Road Islandmagee*

X955-X969 unused

X970

### DITTY
In loving memory of
**WILLIAM JOHN (BILLY)**
Died 10th October 2000
Devoted husband, father
and grandfather
The Lord is my Shepherd

* *Billy (age 80, Married, Presbyterian):*
  *11, Kilton Lane, Islandmagee*

X971

### REYNOLDS
In loving memory of
A dear husband, father
and grandfather
**WILLIAM** died 4th May 1997

* *William (age 68, married, Presbyterian):*
  *19, Brooklands Park, Whitehead*

X972

Treasured
Memories
**ANN LOUISE
GRAY**
Born
24th August 1985
died
9th December 1999
14 years
in Heavenly
love abiding

Not till the loom is silent
and the shuttles cease to fly
shall God unroll the pattern
and explain the reason why
The dark threads are as needful
in the weavers skilful hand
as the threads of gold and silver
in the pattern He has planned

- *Ann (Presbyterian):*
  *22, Ballylumford Road, Islandmagee*

X973 unused

X974

**LOWRY**
In loving memory of
**MERVYN DAVID**
A dearly loved husband, father
And grandfather
Died 25th April 2000 aged 64 years
At rest with the Lord

- *Mervyn (married, school principal):*
  *20, Alexander Park, Carrickfergus*

X975-X977 unused

X978

**McLAUGHLIN
ROBERT GEORGE McLAUGHLIN
M.B.E.**
Assistant Chief Constable RUC
In loving memory of
**ROBIN**
A devoted husband, father
and grandfather
Died 17th July 1995 aged 56 years

- *Robin (married, C of I):*
  *19, Lower Woodlands, Ballycarry*

X979-X986 unused

X987-X988

- *Buried 4.1.2001*
  ***RICHARD HUGH BRUNT***
  *(age 78, married, C of I):*
  *18, Loughview Bungalows, Islandmagee*

X989-X1003 unused

X1004-X1005
In loving memory of
A devoted husband and father
**ARCHIBALD URQUART**
2.1.1908 – 14.3.1993
"My heart's in the Highlands"

- *Archibald (age 72, married, Presbyterian):*
  *23, Notting Hill, Malone Road, Belfast*

X1006

**SMYTH**
In loving memory of
**HERBERT WILLIAM (HERBIE)**
Died 29th January 2000
Aged 68 years
Forever in our thoughts

- *Herbie (Presbyterian):*
  *1, Windsor Ave. Whitehead*

X1007-X1024 unused

X1025

## LEITCH
In loving memory of
My dear husband
**ALBERT HENRY**
Died 30th April 2000
At rest

- *Albert (age 69, married, Presbyterian):*
  *46, Lestannon Ave. Whitehead*

X1026–X1031 unused

X1032

## BOYD
In loving memory of
A dear wife, mother
And grandmother
**RAE**
22.8.1919 – 3.4.2001
Forever in out Thoughts

- *Rachael (cremated, age 81, married,*
  *Presbyterian): 38, Ransevyn Drive,*
  *Whitehead*

X1033–X1037 unused

X1038

Marble Cross
Cover anted to eternal life through
the blood of Jesus
**ANDREA MARY McKECHNIE**
24th May 1999

- *Andrea*
  *(age 56, married, Inter Church, manager):*
  *1, Loughview Bungalows, Islandmagee*

X1039–X1054 unused

X1055

## NEILL
## JOHN
Died 29th Dec. 1999
Aged 73 years
At rest

- *John (buried 2.6.2000, age 73,*
  *single, Presbyterian):*
  *5, Mullaghboy Bungalows, Islandmagee*

X1056

## WELLS
## JAMES (JIM)
Died 11th May 2001
Aged 66 years
Dearly loved son of
Robert and Elizabeth Wells
The Lord is my shepherd

- *Jim (age 74, single, Presbyterian):*
  *22, Ashvale Park, Islandmagee*

X1072–X1073–X1074
## MONTGOMERY – WATSON
In memory of
Our beloved twins
**JACOB ANDREW**
And **SOPHIE MARY**
18th December 1999

- *Twins (Presbyterian):*
  *377, Middle Road, Islandmagee*

X1075–X1076 unused

X1077

## NESBITT
In loving memory of
A dear husband and father
**Wm. THOMAS**
Died 25th March 2000 aged 90 years
Awaiting the return of the Lord

- *Thomas (married, Seventh day Adventist):*
  *30, Balfour AV. Whitehead*

X1078–X1102 unused

X1103

In loving memory of
**PATRICIA**
**MAGUIRE**
Died 3rd February 1996
Much loved wife
mother and friend

- *Patricia (age 50, married, C of I):*
  *New Mills, Island Road, Ballycarry*

X1104 unused

# SEAFARING

# SECTION

~~~~~

The seafaring lore of Islandmagee is well known. It is admired and respected. It is an honoured tradition. Islandmagee seamen sailed to the furthest corners of the world, faced danger, bore hardship with fortitude, faced trial with courage and established the tradition that is admired and respected. In at least one major harbour abroad, the Harbour Master was an "Island Man" and a seaman from Islandmagee, irrespective of rank, would be assured of a visit from the main man of the port for a chat about home.

Today, seamen are entitled to and, indeed, deserve comfort especially when they are at sea. In days gone by, particularly in the days of sail, the situation was different. A £40 Surety for apprenticeship was required to be paid when the Articles of Agreement were signed. The Articles included a pledge not to frequent taverns or alehouses, to keep the Master's secrets and not to do him any damage. The Articles bound the youngster for four years without pay as it was considered that he was receiving the benefit of training for seamanship.

His initiation on the deck would be a torrent of bewildering and, to him, incomprehensible commands – "stand by the halliards"; "haul round the foreyards"; "set the headsails". Apprenticeship was harsh and there was the ever-prevalent danger of risk to life and limb. Navigation was an exacting and often dangerous calling. Over a hundred years ago, the *Colorada* was lost without trace on her voyage from Ayr to Demerara – many of her crew were from Islandmagee.

The introduction of steam and other advanced methods of propulsion often brought little or no improvement in comfort or safety to the seaman. Many still perished at sea, and warfare brought new, terrifying dangers to be faced. In the quiet peace of the graveyard, memorials of a few lines, belie epic tales of bravery, suffering and danger.

Samuel Caldwell, 2nd Officer on *S.S. Teelin Head,* died in 1918 when his ship, on passage from Belfast to France, was sunk by a mine or torpedo in the English Channel.

His son, Samuel John Caldwell, perished in 1941 when the *MV Atheltemplar* was bombed.

William English was on *H.M.S. Daring* in February 1940 when she was one of four destroyers escorting a convoy from Norway to Britain 30 nautical miles from Duncansby Head, Northern Scotland, torpedoes fired from a U-Boat under the command of Captain Ober-Lt. Otto Kretschmer sank this destroyer.

Hill Kane was on *MV Elmbank* in September 1940, in Convoy HX 72, when it was savagely attacked by U-Boats. The following extract is taken from the log of the same U-Boat Captain, Otto Kretschmer: "03.47: Single torpedo at the largest freighter from 1,000 metres. Direct hit amidships. Ship veers away and stops with heavy list to starboard. She transmits her name and position. She is the *Elmbank*, 5,156 tons."

The ship did not sink immediately. Another U-Boat Captain was unsuccessful in his attempt to complete the sinking with gunfire and Kretschmer was forced to use his last two torpedoes to finally sink the ship.

These examples of wartime incidents show but a small part of the proud tradition of Islandmagee seafaring.

"They that go down to the sea in ships" should be admired and remembered.

J. Ian Duffin

# JOHN KERR – A WARTIME SURVIVOR

Although the fate of so many mariners, especially in wartime, was to be 'lost at sea', there were some who survived and ended their days on land.

One such survivor was Chief Engineer Officer John Kerr, late of Islandmagee and Whitehead, who passed away shortly after he attained his one-hundredth birthday, the occasion of which had been marked by a great gathering of his friends and many former seafaring colleagues at a venue close to the 'Island'.

John Kerr was on one of his numerous North Atlantic voyages when he was involved in an incident, which although tragic in that lives were lost, was to play a significant part in the eventual success in the 'battle of the Atlantic'. In May 1941, the Ulster Steamship Company's SS. *Bengore Head* was one of the leading ships in a convoy of about forty vessels sailing for North America when it was attacked and sunk by torpedoes from a German submarine, U-110. Another ship in the convoy, the *Athenia,* was also torpedoed and sunk. John Kerr, along with other survivors, was rescued by the trawler *St. Apollo* and it was from her deck that he witnessed the dramatic events that followed.

The escorts to the convoy launched a series of depth charges and forced U-110 to the surface. While on the surface she was rammed by one of the escorts and her German crew was forced to abandon her. In the ensuing panic, the wireless operator and radio petty officers failed to destroy the German signalling system, Enigma M-3, together with its operating signal logs, ciphers, codes and setting tables. This capture of the secrets of the German U-boat code system enabled the Royal Navy to decipher later signals, resulting in the re-routing of subsequent convoys around the U-boat packs and in large measure contributed to the final elimination of the U-boat menace in the Atlantic.

At a subsequent investiture, the award of the DSO to the leader of the boarding party on the U-110, King George VI described the event as "the most important single action of the war at sea".

*John Kerr, second left, front row, celebrating his 99th birthday with seafaring colleagues.*

# SEAFARERS INDEX

# SEAFARERS INDEX

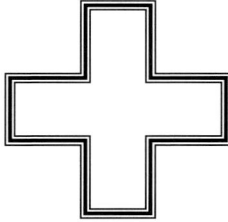

# WAR GRAVES

# DEDICATIONS

The publishers are grateful for the permission of
The Commonwealth War Graves Commission
to use the Memorial Dedications
from the Debt of Honour Register.

The contents of this Register are copyright
The Commonwealth War Graves Commission.

# DEBT OF HONOUR REGISTER

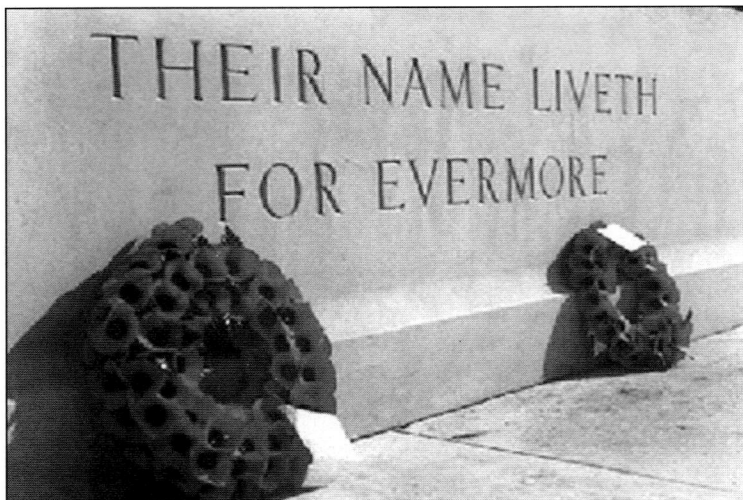

*"We can truly say that the whole circuit of the earth is girdled with the graves of our dead . . . and, in the course of my pilgrimage, I have many times asked myself whether there can be more potent advocates of peace upon earth through the years to come, than this massed multitude of silent witnesses to the desolation of war."*

*King George V, Flanders, 1922*

*The Commemorations in this section are dedicated
to members of the Royal Navy and of the Merchant Navy*

DAVID HENSHAW

JAMES NIBLOCK

JAMES RANKIN

JAMES ROSS

WILLIAM THOMAS CLARKE ADAIR

WILLIAM BOYD

SAMUEL JOHN CALDWELL

JOHN LEONARD CRESSWELL

WILLIAM FERGUSON

WILLIAM JAMES HAY

HILL KANE

SAMUEL KANE

JOSEPH MANN

JAMES MAWHINNEY

THOMAS HAMILTON McCOSH

ANDREW McKAY

WILLIAM McMASTER

JOSEPH CHANDLER

S.(AMUEL) CALDWELL

WILLIAM ENGLISH

JOHN NICOL, MBE

JOHN MOLSEED SCOTT

ANDREW McNEILLY WRIGHT

# DEBT OF HONOUR REGISTER

Cemetery: **ISLANDMAGEE (BALLYHARRY) CEMETERY
Co. Antrim, United Kingdom**

In Memory of

**DESMOND HENSHAW**

Leading Airman
FX85331
H.M.S. Daedalus, Royal Navy
who died age 19
on Monday 15 December 1941.

Airman HENSHAW,
Son of Joseph McKeown Henshaw
and Lillian Henshaw, Whitehead.

Remembered with honour

Grave Reference Number: Sec. D. Grave 49.

~~~~~

In Memory of

**JAMES NIBLOCK**

Master
S.S. Stramore (Belfast), Merchant Navy
who died age 41
on Thursday 18 October 1945.

Master NIBLOCK,
Son of James and Mary Niblock;
husband of Mary Frances Niblock, Island Magee

Remembered with honour

Grave Reference Number: Sec. B. Grave 16-17.

~~~~~

# DEBT OF HONOUR REGISTER

**ISLANDMAGEE (BALLYHARRY) CEMETERY**
**Co. Antrim, United Kingdom**

In Memory of

## JAMES RANKIN

Steward
S.S. Duke of Rothesay (Lancaster),
Merchant Navy
who died age 61
on Thursday 7 December 1944 .

Steward RANKIN,
Son of Thomas and Mary Rankin;
husband of Mary Agnes Rankin, of Whitehead.

Remembered with honour

Grave Reference Number: Sec. B. Grave 158.

~~~~~

In Memory of

## JAMES ROSS

Chief Officer
S.S. Orlock Head (Belfast), Merchant Navy
who died age 49
on Sunday 28 July 1940.

Chief Officer ROSS,
Son of Thomas and Annie Ross;
husband of Agnes Isobel Ross, of Whitehead.

Remembered with honour

Grave Reference Number: Sec. B. Grave 43.

~~~~~

Historical Information: There are 5 Commonwealth burials of the 1939 - 1945 war here.

# DEBT OF HONOUR REGISTER

**TOWER HILL MEMORIAL,**
             **LONDON, UNITED KINGDOM**

Historical Information:
The Tower Hill Memorial commemorates men of the Merchant Navy and Fishing  Fleets who died in both world wars and who have no known grave. It stands on the south side of the garden of Trinity Square, London, close to the Tower of London.

In the First World War, the civilian navy's duty was to be the supply service of the Royal Navy, to transport troops and supplies to the armies, to transport raw materials to overseas munitions factories and munitions from those factories, to maintain, on a reduced scale, the ordinary import and export trade, to supply food to the home country and - in spite of greatly enlarged risks and responsibilities - to provide both personnel and ships to supplement the existing resources of the Royal Navy. Losses of men and vessels were high from the outset, but had peaked in 1917 when in January the German government announced the adoption of "unrestricted submarine warfare".

The subsequent preventative measures introduced by the Ministry of Shipping - including the setting up of the convoy system where warships were used to escort merchant vessels - led to a decrease in losses but by the end of the war, 3,305 merchant ships had been lost with a total of 17,000 lives.

In the Second World War, losses were again considerable in the early years, reaching a peak in 1942. The heaviest losses were suffered in the Atlantic, but convoys making their way to Russia around the North Cape, and those supplying Malta in the Mediterranean were also particularly vulnerable to attack.. In all, 4,786 merchant ships were lost during the war with a total of 32,000 lives. More than one quarter of this total were lost in home waters.

The First World War section of the Tower Hill Memorial commemorates almost 12, 000 seamen who have no grave but the sea. The memorial was designed by Sir Edwin Lutyens with sculpture by Sir William Reid-Dick.

The Second World War extension, designed by Sir Edward Maufe, with sculpture by Charles Wheeler, bears almost 24,000 names.

# DEBT OF HONOUR REGISTER

In Memory of

Chief Officer **WILLIAM THOMAS CLARKE ADAIR**

S.S. Tia Juana (London), Merchant Navy
who died age 30
on Monday 16 February 1942.

Chief Officer ADAIR,
Son of Robert and Mary Adair;
husband of Margaret Isobel Adair,
of Larne, Co. Antrim, Northern Ireland.

Remembered with honour

**TOWER HILL MEMORIAL**

Reference Panel Number:  Panel 108.

~~~~~

In Memory of

Master **WILLIAM BOYD**

S.S. Castlehill (Belfast), Merchant Navy
who died age 56
on Sunday 2 March 1941.

Master BOYD,
Husband of Margaret Boyd,
of Portmuck, Island-Magee, Co. Antrim,
Northern Ireland.

Remembered with honour

**TOWER HILL MEMORIAL**

~~~~~

# DEBT OF HONOUR REGISTER

In Memory of

Third Officer **SAMUEL JOHN CALDWELL**

M.V. Atheltemplar (Liverpool), Merchant Navy
who died age 22
on Saturday 1 March 1941.

Third Officer CALDWELL,
Son of Samuel John and Mary Elizabeth Caldwell.

Remembered with honour

**TOWER HILL MEMORIAL**
Reference Panel Number:  Panel 12.

~~~~~

In Memory of

Chief Engineer **JOHN LEONARD CRESSWELL**

S.S. "Huntsmoor" (London), Mercantile Marine
who died age 34
on Wednesday 20 February 1918.

Chief Engineer CRESSWELL,
Son of Eliza Jane Cresswell (nee Thompson),
of "Craigmore," Kirkliston Drive, Belfast,
and the late William James Cresswell.
Born at St. John's Place, Larne.

Remembered with honour

**TOWER HILL MEMORIAL**

~~~~~

# DEBT OF HONOUR REGISTER

In Memory of

**WILLIAM FERGUSON**

Able Seaman
S.S. Castlehill (Belfast), Merchant Navy
who died age 19
on  Sunday 2 March 1941.

Seaman FERGUSON,
Son of James and Martha Ferguson,
of Belfast, Northern Ireland.

Remembered with honour

**TOWER HILL MEMORIAL**
Reference Panel Number:  Panel 24.

~~~~~

In Memory of

**WILLIAM JAMES HAY**

Sailor
S.S. "Garron Head" (Belfast), Mercantile Marine
who died age 19
on Friday 16 November 1917 .

Seaman HAY,
Son of John and Helena Hay,
of Balfour Avenue, Whitehead, Co. Antrim.

Remembered with honour

**TOWER HILL MEMORIAL**

~~~~~

# DEBT OF HONOUR REGISTER

In Memory of

Master **HILL KANE**

M.V. Elmbank (Glasgow), Merchant Navy
who died age 39
on Monday 12 February 1940.

Master KANE,
Husband of Agnes Kane,
of Island Magee, Co. Antrim, Northern Ireland.

Remembered with honour

**TOWER HILL MEMORIAL**
Reference Panel Number: Panel 37.

~~~~~

In Memory of

Chief Officer **SAMUEL KANE**

S.S. San Nicolas (London), Merchant Navy
who died age 28
on Monday 16 February 1942.

Chief Officer KANE,
Son of George and Cis Kane;
husband of Isabel Kane,
of Greenisland, Co. Antrim, Northern Ireland.

Remembered with honour

**TOWER HILL MEMORIAL**
Reference Panel Number: Panel 92.

~~~~~

# DEBT OF HONOUR REGISTER

In Memory of

Master **JOSEPH MANN**

who died age 45
on Wednesday 3 February 1943.

Master MANN,
Husband of Elizabeth Mann,
of Island Magee, Co. Antrim, Northern Ireland.

Remembered with honour

**TOWER HILL MEMORIAL**

~~~~~

In Memory of

Mate **JAMES MAWHINNEY**

S.S. Corbet (Belfast), Merchant Navy
who died age 36
on Saturday 3 May 1941.

Mate MAWHINNEY,
Son of William and Abby Mawhinney,
of Island Magee, Co. Antrim, Northern Ireland;
husband of Esther Jemima Mawhinney,
of Belfast, Northern Ireland.
Master Mariner, Merchant Navy.

Remembered with honour

**TOWER HILL MEMORIAL**

~~~~~

# DEBT OF HONOUR REGISTER

In Memory of

## THOMAS HAMILTON McCOSH

Able Seaman
S.S. Inver (Belfast), Merchant Navy
who died age 26
on Tuesday 17 December 1940.

Seaman McCOSH,
Son of Alexander McCosh and
of Margaret McCosh (nee Purdy).

Remembered with honour

## TOWER HILL MEMORIAL

Reference Panel Number: Panel 58.

~~~~~

In Memory of

## ANDREW McKAY

Second Officer
S.S. Sheaf Mead (Newcastle-on-Tyne), Merchant Navy
who died age 61
on Monday 27 May 1940.

Second Officer McKAY,
Son of Andrew and Eliza McKay;
husband of Mary McKay,
of Gransha, Island Magee, Co. Antrim, Northern Ireland.

Remembered with honour

## TOWER HILL MEMORIAL

Reference Panel Number: Panel 95.

~~~~~

# DEBT OF HONOUR REGISTER

In Memory of

## WILLIAM McMASTER

Master
S.S. Punta Gorda (London), Merchant Navy
who died age 44
on Monday 18 September 1944.

Master McMASTER,
Son of William and Jane McMaster;
husband of Annie A. McMaster,
of Island Magee, Co. Antrim, Northern Ireland.

Remembered with honour

## TOWER HILL MEMORIAL

Reference Panel Number: Panel 85.

~~~~~

# DEBT OF HONOUR REGISTER

In Memory of

**JOSEPH CHANDLER**

Chief Officer
H.M. Coastguard
who died on
Saturday 5 February 1916 .

Chief Officer CHANDLER, Son of Mrs. Chandler,
of 4, Windsor Terrace, Whitehead, Co. Antrim.

Remembered with honour

Cemetery: **OMEY (CHRIST CHURCH)**
**CHURCH OF IRELAND CHURCHYARD**
**County Galway, Republic of Ireland**

Grave Reference Number: Near South-West boundary.

Historical Information:
There is 1 Commonwealth burial of the 1914-1918 war here.

~~~~~

# DEBT OF HONOUR REGISTER

In Memory of

## S. CALDWELL

Second Mate
S.S. "Teelin Head", Mercantile Marine
who died on
Monday 21 January 1918.

Remembered with honour

Cemetery: **PORTSMOUTH (KINGSTON) CEMETERY
Hampshire, United Kingdom**

Reference Panel Number: Benjamin's. 13. 5.

Historical Information:
This cemetery is about 1.5 kilometres from the Guildhall, in St. Mary's Road, Kingston, a locality in Portsmouth County Borough. It covers 32 hectares, and is the largest of three cemeteries owned by the Corporation. Opened in 1856, and taken over by the Corporation in 1895, it contains service war graves of both World Wars.

The 1914-1918 burials are in many different parts of this large burial ground After the war a Cross of Sacrifice was erected on an island site facing the main entrance, in honour of all the servicemen buried in the cemetery.

The 1939-1945 War graves, too, are widely distributed, but there is a group of 20 graves about 200 metres north-east of the chapel. Of the 1939-1945 burials, many were the result of enemy air raids on Portsmouth.

# DEBT OF HONOUR REGISTER

In Memory of

**WILLIAM ENGLISH**

Cook (S), C/MX 52431
H.M.S. Daring, Royal Navy
who died age 22
on Sunday 18 February 1940.  .

Cook ENGLISH, Son of Thomas and Elizabeth English of Belfast.

Remembered with honour

Cemetery:  **CHATHAM NAVAL MEMORIAL
Kent, United Kingdom**

Reference Panel Number: 39, 2.

Location:
The Memorial overlooks the town of Chatham and is approached by a steep path from the Town Hall Gardens.

Visiting Information:
As a result of constant vandalism at the Memorial, the Commonwealth War Graves Commission has had to arrange for it to be regularly patrolled and public access limited to the period from 08.30 to 17.00. Should for any reason the Memorial be closed during the stated hours, please telephone the Guard Room at Brompton Barracks on 01634 822442 who will arrange for the gates to be opened. Any inconvenience to visitors is greatly regretted. A copy of the Memorial Register is kept in the Naval Chapel of Brompton Garrison Church and may be consulted there.

Historical  Information:
After the First World War, an appropriate way had to be found of commemorating those members of the Royal Navy who had no known grave, the majority of deaths having occurred at sea where no permanent memorial could be provided. An Admiralty committee recommended that the three manning ports in Great Britain - Chatham, Plymouth and Portsmouth - should each have an identical memorial of unmistakable naval form, an obelisk, which would serve as a leading mark for shipping. The memorials were designed by Sir Robert Lorimer, who had already carried out a considerable amount of work for the Commission, with sculpture by Henry Poole.
After the Second World War it was decided that the naval memorials should be extended to provide space for commemorating the naval dead without graves of that war, but since the three sites were dissimilar, a different architectural treatment was required for each. The architect for the Second World War extension at Chatham was Sir Edward Maufe (who also designed the Air Forces memorial at Runnymede) and the additional sculpture was by Charles Wheeler and William McMillan. Chatham Naval Memorial commemorates more than 8,500 sailors of the First World War and over 10,000 from the Second World War.

~~~~~

215

# DEBT OF HONOUR REGISTER

In Memory of

## JOHN NICOL  MBE

Chief Engineer
S.S. Glendalough (Belfast), Merchant Navy
who died age 58
on Friday 19 March 1943.  .

Chief NICOL, Son of John and Agnes Nicol;
husband of Hilda Nicol, of Swansea.

Remembered with honour

Cemetery:  **GRIMSBY (SCARTHO ROAD) CEMETERY
Lincolnshire, United Kingdom**

Grave Number:  Sec. 116. Row E. Grave 10.

## Historical Information:

During the two world wars, the United Kingdom became an island fortress used for training troops and launching land, sea and air operations around the globe. There are more than 170,000 Commonwealth war graves in the United Kingdom, many being those of servicemen and women killed on active service, or who later succumbed to wounds. Others died in training accidents, or because of sickness or disease. The graves, many of them privately owned and marked by private memorials, will be found in more than 12,000 cemeteries and churchyards.

Grimsby ( Scartho Road ) Cemetery contains 281 scattered burials of the First World War, many of them seamen who served with the Auxiliary Patrol which operated out of Grimsby. Included in the total are special memorials to three casualties buried in Grimsby Old Cemetery where their graves could no longer be maintained.

During the Second World War, boats of the Grimsby fishing fleet were attacked at sea, and the town and port were bombed many times, incurring casualties among servicemen as well as civilians. The cemetery contains 257 Second World War burials, almost 200 of them forming a war graves plot.  There are also 17 war burials of other nationalities, many of them German prisoners of war from the camp at nearby Weelsby.

~~~~~

# DEBT OF HONOUR REGISTER

In Memory of

Lieutenant **JOHN MOLSEED SCOTT**

H.M. Trawler Ellesmere,
Royal Naval Volunteer Reserve
who died age 36
on Saturday 24 February 1945.

Lieutenant SCOTT,
Son of Joseph and Louisa Scott.

Remembered with honour

Cemetery: **LOWESTOFT NAVAL MEMORIAL**
**Suffolk, United Kingdom**

Reference Panel Number: Panel 16, Column 2.

Location:
The Naval Memorial is located to the north of the town alongside the A12 Yarmouth Road, approximately one mile north of the harbour. The memorial is in a prominent position within a local authority gardens, known as Bellevue Park. The park is on the top of the cliffs and the memorial itself is on the edge of the cliff so providing an unobscured view of the foreshore and sea. Commemorating almost 2,400 men of the Royal Naval Patrol Services who have no grave but the sea, the memorial consists of a fluted column rising from a circular base 12 metres in diameter surmounted by a bronze ship device (Lymphad), the uppermost point of which is over 15 metres from the ground level. Around the circular base are arranged bronze panels that bear the names. The panels are set in recesses and protected from the weather by a cornice. A Portland stone panel at the front of the Memorial, flanked on either side by the Naval Crown with wreath and foul anchor, faces towards the sea.

~~~~~

# DEBT OF HONOUR REGISTER

In Memory of

## ANDREW McNEILLY WRIGHT

Master
S.S. Eskwood (Goole), Merchant Navy
who died age 43
on Thursday 8 March 1945.

Master WRIGHT,
Son of James Wright, and of Margaret Wright,
of Island Magee, Co. Antrim, Northern Ireland.

Remembered with honour

Cemetery:     **BAYEUX WAR CEMETERY,**
**Calvados, France**

Location:
The town of Bayeux, in Normandy, lies 24 kilometres northwest of Caen.
Bayeux War Cemetery is situated in the south-western outskirts of the town
on the by-pass, which is named Rue de Sir Fabian Ware. On the opposite
side of the road stands the Bayeux Memorial.

Historical Information:
The Allied offensive in north-western Europe began with the Normandy
landings of 6 June 1944. There was little actual fighting in Bayeux although
it was the first French town of importance to be liberated. Bayeux War
Cemetery is the largest Commonwealth cemetery of the Second World War in
France and contains burials brought in from the surrounding districts and
from hospitals that were located nearby. BAYEUX WAR CEMETERY contains
4,144 Commonwealth burials of the Second World War, 338 of them
unidentified. There are also 505 war graves of other nationalities, the majority
German. The BAYEUX MEMORIAL stands opposite the cemetery and bears
the names of more than 1,800 men of the Commonwealth land forces who
died in the early stages of the campaign and have no known grave. They died
during the landings in Normandy, during the intense fighting in Normandy
itself, and during the advance to the River Seine in August.

~~~~~

*The Commemorations in the next section are dedicated
to personnel who served in other branches
of the Armed Forces and in the Civilian Services*

**THOMAS NICOL**

**ANDREW MAWHINNEY**

**JOHN McADAM**

**ALEXANDER WILSON MacLAUGHLIN**

**WILLIAM JOHN GRAY GORDON**

**FRANCIS JACK BUCKLE**

# DEBT OF HONOUR REGISTER

In Memory of

## THOMAS NICOL

Private 7367
2nd Bn., Highland Light Infantry
who died on
Tuesday 18 May 1915.

Remembered with honour

Cemetery:

## LE TOURET MEMORIAL
### Pas de Calais, France
Reference Panel Number: Panel 37 and 38

### Location:

Le Touret Memorial is located at the east end of Le Touret Military Cemetery, on the south side of the Bethune-Armentieres main road. From Bethune follow the signs for Armentieres until you are on the D171. Continue on this road through Essars and Le Touret village. Approximately 1 kilometre after Le Touret village and about 5 kilometres before you reach the intersection with the D947, Estaires to La Bassee road, the Cemetery lies on the right hand side of the road. The Memorial takes the form of a loggia surrounding an open rectangular court. The court is enclosed by three solid walls and on the eastern side by a colonnade. East of the colonnade is a wall and the colonnade and wall are prolonged northwards (to the road) and southwards, forming a long gallery. Small pavilions mark the ends of the gallery and the western corners of the court.

The names of those commemorated are listed on panels set into the walls of the court and the gallery, arranged by Regiment, Rank and alphabetically by surname within the rank. Over 13,000 names are listed on the memorial of men who fell in this area before 25 September 1915 and who have no known grave.

### Visiting Information:

The Panel Numbers quoted at the end of each entry relate to the panels dedicated to the Regiment served with. In some instances where a casualty is recorded as attached to another Regiment, his name may alternatively appear within their Regimental Panels. Please refer to the on-site Memorial Register Introduction to determine the alternative panel numbers if you do not find the name within the quoted Panels.

### Historical Information:

The Memorial in Le Touret Military Cemetery, Richebourg-l'Avoue, is one of those erected by the Commonwealth War Graves Commission to record the names of the officers and men who fell in the Great War and whose graves are not known. It serves the area enclosed on the North by the river Lys and a line drawn from Estaires to Fournes, and on the South by the old Southern boundary of the First Army about Grenay; and it covers the period from the arrival of the II Corps in Flanders in 1914 to the eve of the Battle of Loos. It does not include the names of officers and men of Canadian or Indian regiments; they are found on the Memorials at Vimy and Neuve-Chapelle.

~~~~~

# DEBT OF HONOUR REGISTER

Cemetery:     **YPRES (MENIN GATE) MEMORIAL**
              **Ieper, West-Vlaanderen, Belgium**

## Location:

Ypres (now Ieper) is a town in the Province of West Flanders. The Memorial is situated at the eastern side of the town on the road to Menin (Menen) and Courtrai (Kortrijk). Each night at 8 pm the traffic is stopped at the Menin Gate while members of the local Fire Brigade sound the Last Post in the roadway under the Memorial's arches.

## Visiting Information:

The Panel Numbers quoted at the end of each entry relate to the panels dedicated to the Regiment served with. In some instances where a casualty is recorded as attached to another Regiment, his name may alternatively appear within their Regimental Panels. Please refer to the on-site Memorial Register Introduction to determine the alternative panel numbers if you do not find the name within the quoted Panels.

## Historical Information:

The Menin Gate is one of four memorials to the missing in Belgian Flanders which cover the area known as the Ypres Salient. Broadly speaking, the Salient stretched from Langemarck in the north to the northern edge in Ploegsteert Wood in the south, but it varied in area and shape throughout the war. The Salient was formed during the First Battle of Ypres in October and November 1914, when a small British Expeditionary Force succeeded in securing the town before the onset of winter, pushing the German forces back to the Passchendaele Ridge. The Second Battle of Ypres began in April 1915 when the Germans released poison gas into the Allied lines north of Ypres. This was the first time gas had been used by either side and the violence of the attack forced an Allied withdrawal and a shortening of the line of defence. There was little more significant activity on this front until 1917, when in the Third Battle of Ypres an offensive was mounted by Commonwealth forces to divert German attention from a weakened French front further south. The initial attempt in June to dislodge the Germans from the Messines Ridge was a complete success, but the main assault north-eastward, which began at the end of July, quickly became a dogged struggle against determined opposition and the rapidly deteriorating weather. The campaign finally came to a close in November with the capture of Passchendaele. The German offensive of March 1918 met with some initial success, but was eventually checked and repulsed in a combined effort by the Allies in September. The battles of the Ypres Salient claimed many lives on both sides and it quickly became clear that the commemoration of members of the Commonwealth forces with no known grave would have to be divided between several different sites. The site of the Menin Gate was chosen because of the hundreds of thousands of men who passed through it on their way to the battlefields. It commemorates those of all Commonwealth nations except New Zealand who died in the Salient before 16 August 1917. Those United Kingdom and New Zealand servicemen who died after that date are named on the memorial at Tyne Cot, a site which marks the furthest point reached by Commonwealth forces in Belgium until nearly the end of the war. Other New Zealand casualties are commemorated on memorials at Buttes New British Cemetery and Messines Ridge British Cemetery. The YPRES (MENIN GATE) MEMORIAL now bears the names of more than 54,000 officers and men whose graves are not known. The memorial, designed by Sir Reginald Blomfield with sculpture by Sir William Reid-Dick, was unveiled by Lord Plumer in July 1927.

# DEBT OF HONOUR REGISTER

In Memory of

Lance Corporal **ANDREW MAWHINNEY**

8841
2nd Bn., Irish Guards
who died age 18
on Tuesday 31 July 1917.

Lance Corporal MAWHINNEY,
Son of William and Abby Mawhinney,
of Carnspindle, Islandmagee, Co. Antrim.

Remembered with honour

Cemetery:       **YPRES (MENIN GATE) MEMORIAL**

~~~~~

# DEBT OF HONOUR REGISTER

In Memory of

Lieutenant **ALEXANDER WILSON MacLAUGHLIN**

1st Sqdn., Royal Flying Corps
who died age 23
on Monday 29 October 1917.

Lieutenant MacLAUGHLIN,
Son of the Rev. David MacLaughlin, Ph.D.,
and Annie MacLaughlin, of Druminnis Manse, Armagh.

Remembered with honour

Cemetery: **ARRAS FLYING SERVICES MEMORIAL**
**Pas de Calais, France**

## Location:

The Arras Flying Services Memorial will be found in the Faubourg-d'Amiens Cemetery, which is in the Boulevard du General de Gaulle in the western part of the town of Arras. The cemetery is near the Citadel, approximately 2 kilometres due west of the railway station.

## Historical Information:

The French handed over Arras to Commonwealth forces in the spring of 1916 and the system of tunnels upon which the town is built were used and developed in preparation for the major offensive planned for April 1917. The Commonwealth section of the FAUBOURG D'AMIENS CEMETERY was begun in March 1916, behind the French military cemetery established earlier. It continued to be used by field ambulances and fighting units until November 1918. The cemetery was enlarged after the Armistice when graves were brought in from the battlefields and from two smaller cemeteries in the vicinity.

The cemetery contains 2,651 Commonwealth burials of the First World War. In addition, there are 30 war graves of other nationalities, most of them German. The graves in the French military cemetery were removed after the war to other burial grounds and the land they had occupied was used for the construction of the Arras Memorial and Arras Flying Services Memorial. The ARRAS MEMORIAL commemorates almost 35,000 servicemen from the United Kingdom, South Africa and New Zealand who died in the Arras sector between the spring of 1916 and 7 August 1918, the eve of the Advance to Victory, and have no known grave. The most conspicuous events of this period were the Arras offensive of April-May 1917, and the German attack in the spring of 1918. Canadian and Australian servicemen killed in these operations are commemorated by memorials at Vimy and Villers-Bertonneux. A separate memorial remembers those killed in the Battle of Cambrai in 1917. The ARRAS FLYING SERVICES MEMORIAL commemorates more than 1,000 airmen of the Royal Naval Air Service, the Royal Flying Corps, and the Royal Air Force, either by attachment from other arms of the forces of the Commonwealth or by original enlistment, who were killed on the whole Western Front and who have no known grave. The British Air Services originated in the use of balloons for purposes of reconnaissance. The balloon gave way to power-driven air machines and in 1911 an Air Battalion of the Royal Engineers was formed. In 1912 the Air Battalion was absorbed into the Royal Flying Corps which consisted of a Naval Wing and a Military Wing and a Central Flying School. These two wings developed during the course of the war, both sections expanding greatly until they combined and the Royal Air Force came into being on the 1 April 1918. During the Second World War, Arras was occupied by United Kingdom forces headquarters until the town was evacuated on 23 May 1940. Arras then remained in German hands until re-taken by Commonwealth and Free French forces on 1 September 1944. The cemetery contains seven Commonwealth burials of the Second World War. Both cemetery and memorial were designed by Sir Edwin Lutyens, with sculpture by Sir William Reid Dick.

# DEBT OF HONOUR REGISTER

In Memory of

## WILLIAM JOHN GRAY GORDON

Aircraftman 1st Class
616725
802 Sqdn., Royal Air Force
who died age 24
on Sunday 9 June 1940.

Aircraftman 1st Class GORDON,
Son of Joseph P. and Jamesina Gordon,
of Island Magee, Co. Antrim.

Remembered with honour

Cemetery: **RUNNYMEDE MEMORIAL**
Surrey, United Kingdom

Reference Panel Number: Panel 25.

Cemetery:
This Memorial overlooks the River Thames on Cooper's Hill at Englefield Green
between Windsor and Egham on the A308, 4 miles from Windsor.

Historical Information:
The Air Forces Memorial at Runnymede commemorates by name over 20,000
airmen who were lost in the Second World War during operations from bases in
the United Kingdom and North and Western Europe, and who have no known
graves. They served in Bomber, Fighter, Coastal, Transport, Flying Training and
Maintenance Commands, and came from all parts of the Commonwealth. Some
were from countries in continental Europe which had been overrun but whose
airmen continued to fight in the ranks of the Royal Air Force.

The memorial was designed by Sir Edward Maufe with sculpture by Vernon Hill.
The engraved glass and painted ceilings were designed by John Hutton and the
poem engraved on the gallery window was written by Paul H Scott.

~~~~~

# DEBT OF HONOUR REGISTER

In Memory of

Sergeant **JOHN McADAM**

748076
Pilot
41 Sqdn., Royal Air Force Volunteer Reserve
who died
on Thursday 20 February 1941.

Remembered with honour

Cemetery: **ISLANDMAGEE (BALLYHARRY) CEMETERY,
Co. Antrim, United Kingdom**

Grave Reference Number: Sec. D. Grave 48.

~~~~~

# DEBT OF HONOUR REGISTER

In Memory of

**FRANCIS JACK BUCKLE**

Fire Fighter

of 40 Tavistock Terrace, Upper Holloway.
Husband of Jane Buckle.
Age 40

Who died as a result of enemy action
on Sunday 11 May 1941
at Old Compton Street.

Commemorated in the

**CITY OF WESTMINSTER**

**Section of the Civilian War Dead Register**

~~~~~

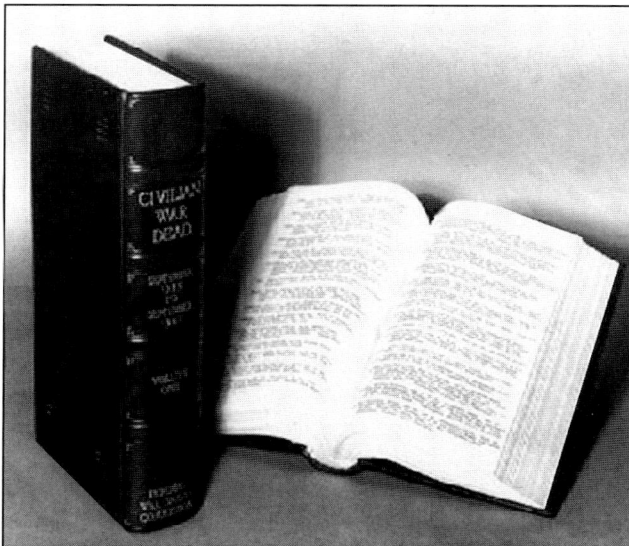

*Commemorated in perpetuity by*
*the Commonwealth War Graves Commission*